TAKE A SHOT AT HAPPINESS

HOW TO WRITE, DIRECT & PRODUCE THE LIFE YOU WANT

MARIA BALTAZZI, PhD, MFA

EMMY AWARD-WINNING PRODUCER

Post Hill
PRESS

T0035203

A POST HILL PRESS BOOK
ISBN: 978-1-63758-860-4
ISBN (eBook): 978-1-63758-861-1

Post Hill Press
New York • Nashville
posthillpress.com

Published in the United States of America
1 2 3 4 5 6 7 8 9 10

To Big G upstairs and my parents, Dr. Evan and Nellie Baltazzi.
They are my alpha and omega.

Contents

PREFACE

On a steamy jungle island in the middle of the South China Sea, a small remote television stage is lit by tiki torches illuminating a show host, a jury of seven contestants sitting on tree stumps, and the final two runners-up for a million dollars, a male and a female. Sitting not far away, I could sense projecting from the stage the type of anger that only comes from a person feeling so betrayed as I watched one of the jurors take the stand before an open fire pit. They first addressed the male contestant sitting on the other side of the pit. No love was shared, though there was a shred of respect for how they played the game. Then, with eyes stone-cold and unflinching, they addressed the female, "If I were ever to pass you along in life again and you were lying there dying of thirst, I would not give you a drink of water. I would let the vultures take you and do whatever they would want with ya, with no ill regrets." Our production team drew a collectively shocked gasp so loud the contestants could hear us as we sat in the nearby television control room made of plywood and nails.

Oh, my God. Did Sue Hawk just say those now-infamous words to Kelly Wiglesworth at the first *Survivor* Tribal Council that drew 51.7 million viewers? It was only the first season of CBS's competition show, *Survivor.* I would observe much about one's motivation, ability to forgive, to show gratitude, and to form cautious bonds during my time on one of the longest-running unscripted television series. I was one of the original supervising producers. My five years on that show and, more so, other television projects eventually became the catalyst to an inner journey toward happiness that I am still and will always be on.

Those *Survivor* contestants, especially in the earliest seasons, were stripped of everything except one luxury item, a small ration of rice, and water, leaving them with their wits and each other to survive on a beach while trying to win a million dollars. It always struck me that only then did they see their true selves and the potential of others, good or bad. So, taking a page from that experience, I realized I could only see my true self if I took the time to strip off the negativity, poke at my beliefs, pay closer attention to my actions, and ask some tough questions about who and what I am. What did I want? Why am I here? And how did I want to get to where I was going? This book gathers the lessons I learned about being happy from my time in the entertainment industry, observing people and events, and traveling around the world. I hope to inspire and engage you to creatively go on your own happiness journey with me through photo and journal assignments I share in each chapter.

However, first things first.

AS WE BEGIN

"Life is like a film camera.
Focus on what is important, capture the good times,
develop from the negatives, and if things do not work out,
take another shot."

My Not So Still Life

Trust me. I have taken many shots in life, and kind of like 35mm film, I have developed from loads of negatives. However, thankfully, my life's image bank is filled with even more good times, precious times, and thoughtful times.

When I look back on my journey, it makes sense that I became a television producer and director. I have always seen life as a series of images. It is the way I process information, thoughts, and events. Even as an elementary school girl reading my first book, I saw the story instead of just hearing the narrative in my head. As I grew older, there were also defining moments where I consciously saw how the power of imagery impacted the way I saw the world.

The first time was working as a television director on *Great Drives* for PBS. Each episode featured one of our country's hallmark journeys, hence the name. I was assigned to follow A1A along the East Coast of Florida. My job was to produce and direct our show on location with a camera crew. The production company also gave me a second video camera to shoot additional footage—except for one thing. I had never personally used a video camera and was incredibly nervous, thinking, "Please, God! I just have to get a few good shots we can use in the show." I was mortified about failing. With fear as a great kick-my-ass motivator, I was glued to the viewfinder, looking for precisely the picture information I wanted in each frame. My fear of failure became one of my best image composition teachers and, oddly, life teachers. It helped me discover that I disliked unmotivated camera moves. I was not fond of pans that seemed aimless or did not reveal anything compelling. I later realized this reflects how useless I feel when life seems aimless. I did not like the feel of zooms to or from a subject. I thought it took the viewer out of the moment, reflecting my eventual learned desire to be mindful of the present moment.

This experience was the first time I remember coming back to the production office and showing a colleague a bit of the video, and the reaction being, "Wow, you've got an eye!" Little did my colleague know it had nothing to do with my eye and everything to do with my desire not to embarrass myself with my lack of skill—this became my first conscious lesson in developing from a negative.

Another impactful moment happened after being in television production for a couple of years and deciding to go to graduate film school. As I was getting my MFA at the ArtCenter College of Design in California, I had writing, directing, and cinematography classes every term. When I did my cinematography assignments, my instructor asked that our class shoot stills using motion picture stock to understand how film translates to the final product. I found myself, once again, absorbed in what was inside my picture frame. Because it was a cinematography class, I was paying even closer attention to my composition as I learned about the quality of light and color. During this class, I also started to look for design patterns that help create the mood of an image that tells a story in one frame.

After film school, I continued working as a television producer and director, thinking it would be exciting to work on bigger and more adventurous shows, including *Survivor*, only to discover that production is very demanding and often dominated by extreme personalities. Being part of a television series that got Super Bowl numbers during its early years, then later working on shows that had me in the middle of the African bush filming wildlife one month and the next on a boat within several feet of a skyscraper-tall glacier in Antarctica was exhilarating; however, the magic of why I fell in love with producing and directing was overshadowed by political infighting and toxic personalities. Before I knew it, other people's stuff was becoming my stuff and increasingly emotionally unhealthy for me. So, I opted to check out of my career for a long time. Without realizing or naming it at the time, I basically semi-retired from producing and directing to save myself. I took time to heal my mind, body, and, most of all, my spirit. I started studying the science of happiness and wellbeing, positive and spiritual psychology, mindfulness, and meditation. Eventually, I got a PhD in Conscious-Centered Living.

While rescuing myself, I consciously did something every day that made me feel good and used my phone camera to capture these moments. When I paused and allowed myself to sink into that intentional moment of taking a picture, everything that stressed me out or any negative emotion that was present in my life melted away. Taking photographs in such a thoughtful way became meditative. Especially after studying mindfulness, I saw the gift of focusing my attention and allowing everything else to go out of focus. Over time, I could let go of the chatter, the judgment, and the useless stories. I discovered that when life rose to a boil for me, I could allow those annoying and often insignificant details to fade when I set my viewfinder on a single rose, statue, doorknob, or whatever captured my curiosity. This practice of regularly, deliberately, and delightfully taking photographs became part of my daily routine for five years and is now essential to my emotional and spiritual toolbox. It inspired me to write this book and show others how the practice of pausing to capture their world one frame at a time could transform their entire lives.

Why This Book Now

If there was ever a time this world needed to embrace happiness and to do so through the power of thought and shifting the mental pictures in our minds, it is now. So many people feel disconnected, isolated, scared, disquieted, uneasy, and are at a loss for what to do about it. Individually and collectively, the world needs to keep raising its consciousness level, or we will not survive climate change, social injustice, conservation issues, or ourselves without deliberate thought to reframe how we see the world. The bottom line is that every human matters. If we matter, then our happiness and wellbeing most certainly matter.

I think it is safe to say we all want to be happy with our lives. We want our relationships, things, and accomplishments to be meaningful, yet we do not always know how to get there. We go to school to learn to be accountants, historians, engineers, doctors, filmmakers, and so on. However, we are not taught how to create an overall sense of happiness and wellbeing. Nor how to be conscious of our happiness, joy, and contentment. Most of us have not made enough time to think about how we emotionally, mentally, and spiritually can take care of ourselves, others around us, and our world. The world we see and feel is the product of our thoughts. Our thoughts motivate our behavior and, ultimately, our destiny. The solution to moving through our perceived obstacles is to reframe how we think about developing a joyfully fulfilling life by pursuing and finding everyday practices that will move us toward a more consistent state of happiness and wellbeing. More specifically, *Wholebeing*, where you are engaged three-dimensionally in mind, body, and spirit.

My book takes a creative approach to developing the eight core values, the essential virtues and qualities, I believe universally support consciously living a purposeful, good life. Virtues being your personal or moral standards: Faith, Love, Gratitude, Forgiveness, Peace. Qualities being the attributes or characteristics you value: Health, Detachment, Abundance. And I think some can be viewed as both a virtue and quality. I view these eight essentials, what I call Happiness Essentials, similarly to how you would set up a camera to shoot pictures on a tripod:

Life's details become sharper when you focus on *Faith*. Your thoughts and actions become more evident.

Love filtered through the lens of the heart fixes, comforts, and enriches anything you can name.

Health is the tripod of life, what stabilizes you. Your optimal state of health serves as the leg of the mind, the leg of the body, and the leg of the spirit.

If there is a lens of choice, let it be *Gratitude*. The only prayer you ever need to say is "thank you."

Opening your heart's aperture to allow in the light of *Forgiveness* enables life again. For-giving is for-living.

Peace is the available inner light that radiates from within you, reflecting outwardly to the people you touch.

Detachment is like setting your intention on auto. You intend a desire, then allow the universe to choose the correct shutter speed. There is your timing and perfect timing.

Abundance is the picture frame of all possibilities. If you can see it in your viewfinder, you can capture it.

Everything within these pages comes from walking my talk, intensive studies, and the belief that there is a way forward that better serves me and those I touch. I draw from the secular and non-secular worlds and piece things together in ways that make an impactful difference when the ideas in this book are put into action. These are effective ways to reframe negative thinking into constructive thinking—a more reflective view of positive thinking.

Finally, the use of the number eight throughout this book is intentional. In chemistry, the number eight is the atomic number of the oxygen we all need to live. Same for needing happiness to *really* live. In astronomy, eight planets orbit the sun, which gives us light. Happiness is our inner-wellbeing sun. In Chinese culture, eight is an auspicious number because it sounds similar to their word for prosperity or wealth—something we would all like to have and is part of what creates Happiness.

How to Use This Book

Take a Shot at Happiness helps those beginning their journey or wanting a fresh perspective on making the conscious choice to be happy each day, then taking consistent, intentional action to reframe one's thinking from negative to positive. I encourage you to be open to putting recently discovered and established wellbeing concepts into action to create a more qualitative version of your Wholebeing.

As the chapters unfold, I share in detail each Happiness Essential. You will find that several concepts and methods apply to more than one Happiness Essential and why they are intertwined. Throughout my writing, I draw from my life and the 24/7 demands of being an Emmy-winning television producer, international traveler, and Greek American. I share quotes, insights, observations, and stories about people around me, drawing from books, films, television shows, and the news media that support the points I believe impact one's thoughts and behavior. So, please do not expect a book solely about my experiences on *Survivor*. There is some of that. However, it is about so much more.

This book is meant to be experienced slowly and thoughtfully. You may even choose to spend months going through it. Shifts in ways of seeing, thinking, and behaving take time. Give yourself this grace and savor the journey. You and your wellbeing are worth it. These pages are designed as an interactive experience to help you realize and become aware of the effects of your thoughts and behavior, to see how your mindset plays out in your understanding of everyday things while offering the following benefits:

- Proven methods to develop Happiness and Wholebeing habits from leading experts and researchers that support living consciously.
- Activities to help reframe long-held negative perspectives that are often unconscious, and inspire new ways of being.
- Photographic assignments, Photo Ops, intended to help you break through mental and emotional blocks.
- Reflective questions that are Action Opportunities to develop and grow around each Happiness and Wholebeing concept.
- Centering Thoughts, Affirmations, and Meditation Prayers to reflect and meditate upon to help embody each chapter's concepts. They are all written by me with you lovingly in mind—the same for the Photo Ops and Action Opportunities.

  o Centering Thoughts are short statements, almost like a mantra, used to focus and settle turbulent thoughts.
  o Affirmations are longer declarative statements used to reframe or create positive thoughts, habits, speech, or actions.

o Meditation Prayers thoughtfully quiet the mind and body so you can petition your greater source for guidance.

• A supportive community available to you as you go through the book's conscious-living activities.

You will be guided in three ways: photography, journaling, and community.

The Power of Photography. I invite you to use photography to mindfully absorb each chapter's teachings and explore your world with openness, curiosity, sensitivity, and humor. The concepts presented in this book can be abstract and trying to understand them visually can anchor and make them more meaningfully relevant to you. There is no right or wrong way to do the assignments, only your way. So, allow your creativity to flourish and flow. A phone camera is all you need to do these Photo Ops. Previous photography experience is not required.

The Photo Ops are opportunities to widen your lens of self-knowledge and awareness to improve your state of being and how you interact with others, including, and most importantly, yourself. It can bring aspects of life experiences into positive focus, enhancing your self-worth and esteem. I found the act of taking pictures made me appreciate things more profoundly, which motivated me to engage even more in the present moment. Afterward, you can look at your photos and notice the emotions they evoke, the details you did not see when you took the image, and possibly the new thoughts that arise. Ultimately, taking pictures deepens your insights, *ah-has*, and communicates them in meaningful ways that words cannot.

Our thoughts form pictures in our minds. Yet, so often, they are repetitive negative images of the several thousand thoughts we have during an average day that we desperately want to change and make constructive to be more loving toward ourselves and others. Photographs enhance the ability to process the world, connecting you to the environment and culture in a visceral way in how you perceive them, intellectually and emotionally, by being present and immersed in the moment. Using imagery creates a direct, sensory connection between you and your subject, opening new ways of seeing the world and understanding yourself. This can help reframe unproductive thoughts to ones that will uplift your mood and worldview. It is also a way to process difficult emotions by creating space for awareness, reflection, and acceptance of a situation.

The Power of Journaling. Writing is an effective way to temper, integrate, and transform thoughts and emotions, especially complicated ones. Research shows that writing through emotional upsets enables lasting increases in mood, health, and relationships, *ergo*, your Happiness and Wholebeing. Committing to prose develops the ability to observe and turn the barrage of unproductive, negative thinking into more profound, richer epiphanies. Writing helps you access who you were and who you are now, which informs your future. It can unlock what lies in the subconscious, one's unconscious self, to learn new things about yourself, tap into your creativity, and awaken your spiritual awareness.

The Action Opportunities ask you to use words to express thoughts and feelings to help connect your mind to your body's experiences and make positive shifts by working through them. I am a testimonial to this. Writing through my upsets, disappointments, and eventual epiphanies became the building blocks for this book.

The Power of Community. You are encouraged to share photos and reflections with others in our *Take a Shot at Happiness* social media group and on our companion app. When you share your images and talk about them, it increases your Happiness. Why? Being in a group makes learning more enjoyable. It also gives you accountability and exposure to different perspectives, adding greater depth, breadth, and inspiration than just going through your journey alone.

By the time you complete this book, if you fully participate, you will have a useful foundation for creating and sustaining a healthier state of Happiness and Wholebeing, even when life turns upside down, along with a community that can continue supporting you long afterward.

Take a Shot at Happiness is more than a book. It is more than a shift in perspective. It is a consciously chosen way of life. So, take a shot at living the life you want!

PICTURING HAPPINESS

Picturing
/ˈpik(t)SHər/iNG/

verb
: represent (someone or something) in a photograph or picture
: form a mental image of

Happiness
/ˈhapēnəs/

noun
: a state of being happy

Wellbeing
/ˈˌwel’ˌbēiNG/

noun
: the state of being comfortable, healthy, or happy

Wholebeing
/hōl/ˌbēiNG/

noun
: the state of being comfortable, healthy, or happy as an
assemblage in mind, body, and spirit

♥ ♥ ♥

*"Happiness is a joyful conscious choice
you can make in every moment of your life."*
—Maria Baltazzi, PhD, MFA

SNAPSHOT OF PICTURING HAPPINESS

In My Viewfinder

The *Survivor* contestants were well into the game in an environment that was bone-dry and furnace-hot. I do not recall what day it was, though I remember taking closer note of Tina Wesson, who would eventually win the *Australian Outback* season. She was cast as our soccer mom and was a worthy competitor at the challenges. The thing separating Tina from the rest was that she seemed to be a constant bright light despite hunger, uncomfortable sleep, and harsh living conditions. She was not consumed with talking about game strategy. Instead, she spent most of her time getting to know the others and learning about their families. I did enough interviews with her to see that she was genuinely interested in her tribemates, and I believe that is what won her the million dollars. Tina seemed to be at peace and connected to her priorities: God, herself, and family and friends, in that order. Because of this, of all the contestants that season she radiated an inner happiness that I most clearly saw in her and gave rise to two words I started to think about more and more.

Be happy!

Well, for many, perhaps including you, being happy is something you would want to be yet put off for another time when you are less busy, less overwhelmed, less stressed. You will do it when you have the luxury of extra time.

Newsflash.

Your overall happiness and wellbeing are not luxuries. They are necessities. It makes this realm, our planet, a better place, along with you and your relationships in it. Being Happy (big H), like most things in life, is a matter of choice. You can choose to wallow in the overwhelming, in the stress of day-to-day life, the pain of the past, the worry about the future, or pick the alternative: Happiness. Then, actively do something about improving the quality of your life, reframing your thoughts and developing habits that support your wellbeing holistically in mind, body, and spirit, *ergo*, your *Wholebeing*.

Philosophers, mystics, sages, and spiritualists over the millennia and into contemporary times all talk about the power of choice. Science backs this up more and more. Our conscious awareness informs our thoughts and actions. In My Viewfinder of the world, your level of awareness plus conscious choice equals your Happiness and Wholebeing (big W too). You can be the conscious creator of being Happier.

When I speak about Happiness, it is not in the context of looking at life through rose-colored glasses, nor always having a song in your heart. It is not that you no longer feel life's hurts and disappointments, or that anger and frustration cease to exist. Instead, Happiness means that, on balance, you feel aligned with your choices and living your purpose on purpose. What do you value most, the virtues and qualities in harmony with how you are present in the world, your decisions, and what you ultimately aim for in life? You also have emotional and mental tools to help navigate challenging times. Happiness is resilience wrapped in hopeful packaging.

We talk a lot about our wellbeing, Happiness, or lack thereof, because we all want this. We talk about the "Pursuit of Happiness." It is even seeded in our country's Declaration of Independence as an inalienable right endowed by our Creator. To me, Happiness is not a pursuit, like it is a commodity. It is not something you check off your list as being done. It is never done because it is something you continually create and develop throughout your life, changing and evolving as you do. The repeated, thoughtful, purposeful development of one's virtues and qualities will improve the quality of life. These values define how you see, react, and move through the world, acting as a Happiness reservoir from which you can always draw, enabling you to productively meet the joys of life, and its challenges, as they rise and fall.

So.

Ask yourself one critical question: Do you want to be Happy? The choice is yours to make; indeed, it is. Because whether you realize it or not, you have conditioned, accepted, or unknowingly limited your state of Happiness. How? By the influences of your outer sphere of family, friends, and community, which directly impact your belief system. Your belief system sets the governor on your level of Happiness, therefore, the condition of your life. All of which can change if you are willing to put in the effort.

Happiness should be an unconditional choice, not one based on other people or circumstances that will inevitably happen. Your plane will get delayed. Someone will show up at a party in the same outfit. The stock market will have its bear days. Nevertheless, you consistently choose to be Happy without any what-ifs, ands, or buts—no qualifiers. When you choose to be Happy for now and always, you put yourself on a path to enlightenment. Change your thoughts, change your life. It is that simple, which brings us to the other point to keep in mind as you read this book, one that already exists inside of you. It is your Happiness Set Point, which is influenced by several factors.

According to leading Happiness researcher Professor Sonja Lyubomirsky at the University of California Riverside, 50 percent of your Happiness is determined by a genetic set point passed on from one or both of your biological parents. It is a potential state of being baseline that you return to no matter how good or bad it gets. Your life circumstance defines 10 percent. Forty percent is determined by how you think, actions resulting from your thoughts, and intentional activities. The key is the remaining 40 percent that is within your control. So, if you want to be Happy, develop Happy people's habits, virtues, and qualities. That means you are taking control of your thoughts and emotions. You are going out into the world, making things happen, and achieving something. You are not just sitting around depressed, accepting an unfulfilled life as your lot. Really take in that your thoughts and actions profoundly impact your level of Happiness. More so than your Happiness Set Point or life circumstance. This point is hugely significant to everything else that follows within these pages.

The other notable part about one's Happiness Set Point is that your genes determine 50 percent. However—*this is a critical however*—your brain's hardwiring is dramatically influenced by your behavior and experiences and how you perceive them, which are not defined by your genes. For your genes to fully express themselves as a low or high Happiness Set Point, they must be in the right environment to turn on. So, in fact, you can do a great deal to improve your level of Happiness by way of conscious, intentional, purposeful activities—and this is the crux of *Take a Shot at Happiness*.

Happiness Essentials

Faith, Love, Health, Gratitude, Forgiveness, Peace, Detachment, and Abundance are the virtues and qualities I have operated with for over a decade. They guide how I move through the world every moment of the day. Consciously developing these eight core values shifted the quality of my life from unhappy and discontented to Happy and contented. Each began as a thought that eventually found its way into my heart and transformed my state of Wholebeing.

Admittedly, living into these Happiness Essentials is not always easy. Sometimes I do not feel grateful or forgiving towards someone disturbing my peace. Sometimes, I must work hard to settle back into a quiet mind or a loving heart. For all the inner work I have done, I still have emotional triggers. Just ask my family. However, now I catch my temper flares, let go of them sooner, and am far less stubborn about my point of view when a situation upsets me. I like the saying that "we are both masterpieces and works-in-progress." That is me for sure: still a work-in-progress.

Happiness and Wholebeing Survey

Before you further read, consider how you rank the eight Happiness Essentials on a scale of one to eight, with one being the highest priority. It could determine how you use this book, whether you go section by section as written or in the order of how you want to develop these Happiness Essentials. Know this inner work is not always, although it is transformative in ways you may not have ever considered.

_____ Faith. Read Happiness Essential One: Picturing Faith (p. 27).

_____ Love. Read Happiness Essential Two: Picturing Love (p. 59).

_____ Health. Read Happiness Essential Three: Picturing Health (p. 91).

_____ Gratitude. Read Happiness Essential Four: Picturing Gratitude (p. 127).

_____ Forgiveness. Read Happiness Essential Five: Picturing Forgiveness (p. 155).

_____ Peace. Read Happiness Essential Six: Picturing Peace (p. 181).

_____ Detachment. Read Happiness Essential Seven: Picturing Detachment (p. 213).

_____ Abundance. Read Happiness Essential Eight: Picturing Abundance (p. 245).

_____ Using the same scale, rate your overall level of Happiness and Wholebeing.

After going through the book, retake this survey to see what has shifted. Consider which other Happiness Essentials you would like to continue improving. Then, go back to that chapter and spend more time doing the Photo Ops and Action Opportunities. *Take a Shot at Happiness* is a book you can return to time and again. Allow it to become a life-enriching companion you can always carry around with you.

♥ ♥ ♥

*"To enjoy good health, to bring true happiness to one's family,
to bring peace to all, one must first discipline and
control one's own mind. If a man can control his mind
he finds the way to Enlightenment,
and all wisdom and virtue will naturally come to him."*

—BUDDHA

HAPPINESS ESSENTIAL ONE

PICTURING FAITH

Faith

\ˈfāth\

noun

: strong belief or trust in someone or something

: belief in the existence of God

: strong feelings or beliefs

: fidelity to one's promises

: sincerity of intentions

: firm belief in something for which there is no proof

: complete trust

: something that is believed especially with strong conviction

♥ ♥ ♥

"Postulates are based on assumption and adhered to by faith.
Nothing in the universe can shake them."

—Isaac Asimov
Award-winning Author, Foundation

SNAPSHOT OF FAITH

In My Viewfinder

Six twenty-three a.m., the chatter of birds outside my window, the whooshing sound of cars passing my street corner, early light seeping between my upper and lower eyelids stirs me awake.

"God, thank you for this day I am about to begin. Please guide me in your ways. Help me not to do something stupid or mean today. With all my heart, your path is mine, always. Amen."

I throw off my bedcovers. Left foot, right foot onto the floor. Time to motivate, get this show going—this is the way I start every morning. Nothing happens without first checking in with Big G upstairs. Faith is the foundation for everything; that is how I see it.

Faith comes in all forms and is not just connected to religion or spirituality. While for many, there is Faith in a guiding force more significant than themselves, there is also the unexplained Faith that things in life will somehow work out. Faith that your best friend will be there for you when you fall. A belief that you will get up in the morning to begin a new day. Trust that you will get on a plane in Los Angeles and safely land in New York. So, whether you believe in God or not, you have some kind of Faith.

It is Faith that keeps us moving forward. When we feel stalled out, we have Faith that "this too shall pass," 2 Corinthians 4:17–18 (KJV), and we will get to the other side of things; things will become brighter one day. Spiritual Faith is my bedrock. When I do not pay enough attention to it is when things go upside down. Those who have spent time studying

Happiness know that having a spiritual dimension to your life is essential to one's overall Happiness. Spirituality can be infused into anything by the meaning you give it. It does not have to be a specific religious doctrine. It can be as simple as communing with nature. Yet, the concept of any kind of spiritual Faith escapes many.

I have a friend who is a non-practicing Roman Catholic who loves being on a surfboard in the ocean. When his parents were around, they were very involved in the church, though, somehow, the practice eluded him. More than once, he told me that he wished for my kind of Faith, wanted his parents' Faith, which always mystified me, thinking, "Well, you can." You can, if you make the intention to seek, learn, and put into practice what it is to have spiritual Faith, Catholic or otherwise. It is like going to the gym to get that hot abdominal six-pack, the same with spirituality. You go to the spiritual gym. Be it in the mountains, on the water, in a church, and do sit-ups in the form of prayer, meditation, and communion. "Seek, and you will find."—Matthew 7:7. God is not hiding. He is there, all around you, if you pay attention. If you engage Him, He will captivate you. For my defunct Roman Catholic friend, perhaps his spiritual Faith is found riding waves and calls God by another name. Spiritual Faith will be where he finds meaning in an experience that fulfills and enlightens him. Same for you.

Snapshots on Developing Unwavering Faith

Faith Snapshot No. 1:
Believe in Something Beyond Yourself

"Oh my God, turn on the news!" popped up in my computer chat as I was engrossed in working on a script. I ran into the living room to turn on the television. Breaking news headlined every channel. American Airlines Flight 11 had just crashed into the North Tower of the World Trade Center in Lower Manhattan. Seventeen minutes later, United Airlines Flight 175 took out the South Tower. The country was stunned in disbelief. It was surreal to accept the crash replays and hear the cries of the first-hand accounts. *What? Why?* Not since World War II have our country's shores been hit by foreign invaders.

The first Sunday after 9/11 happened, I went to church. Parishioners filled the pews and lined the walls like it was Easter. We had liturgy as we did every Sunday. In the end, the priest gave a sermon. I do not remember what he said. It does not matter because what happened afterward remains etched in my mind and heart. After the homily, we all sang "God Bless America." The entire church, everyone, wept for the state of our country. Up until that point, going to church had been just to talk to Big G, hear the choir and the week's sermon with the other churchgoers as ambiance. This day was the first time I felt moved by the importance of being part of a Faith community during times of grief. That is when I realized that spirituality as a concept, whether a religious doctrine you follow or not, is a vessel for hope and comfort. Everyone in that church wanted the same thing: solace and hope. It was palpable, drawing me in like a big comforting hug, bringing me closer to my Faith, opening an inner aperture that has allowed my Faith to become stronger with each passing day and year. It is what gets me through the day, the tough times, my darkest hours, and leads me to the light once again. Maybe it is true: "There are no atheists in foxholes."

Now, I am not pushing for a particular spiritual practice or religion. That is a highly personal path. However, whether it is Christianity, Buddhism, Hinduism, Islam, or calling on a Divine entity, the Creator, the Greater Universe, the Quantum Field, the Source, or nothing-at-all, I feel it is soothing to believe in a nurturing, energetic force you can turn to in times of need, in times of question, and in times of gratitude. Having this in my life is powerful beyond all measure. It is my vessel for hope, solace, direction, clarity, peace, love, gratitude, and forgiveness and is a place to put the unexplainable. Faith in a greater force helps you feel that you are not alone. Recent research at Stanford University points to prayer being beneficially similar to mindfulness and cognitive behavior therapy. It allows you to process something upsetting or frightening and shift your focus to something more constructive and comforting. That is why our congregation filled the church and prayed that Sunday as our worlds were in shock and mourning. For me, I felt the reassurance that God was paying attention.

Centering Thought. Believe.

Affirmation. The Creator of all things is the supportive guiding force in all I do.

Faith Snapshot No. 2:
Choose to Live in a Friendly Universe

"The most important decision we make is whether we believe we live in a friendly or hostile universe."

This decision point that Einstein supposedly suggested we each make, consciously or unconsciously, determines how we perceive the world and whether our state of being is positive and used as a force for good. It will determine how you feel supported, guided, or not, and whether you accept the possibility of alternative realms in the form of God, universal energy, life force, the quantum field, or whatever name serves you. I call it God, the intelligent, friendly universe that runs the show.

From a broadly simplified metaphysical interpretation, quantum physics describes an invisible energetic field of all possibilities beyond space-time as we know it. It contains everything and nothing all at once. Here particles made of matter dance about the universe as energy waves. Each particle is a unique possibility that, once you observe, becomes your reality. Seeing one of these particles within the waves causes it to collapse, from the infinite to the specific, to become what you now experience, known as the "Observer Effect." So, your conscious awareness of something is the energetic picture you hold in your mind, your view of a friendly or hostile world, how you think and feel. The good news is that you can affect your worldview by your choice to be Happy. See the old reality that is not working and choose to see a new one. The level of your conscious awareness is the reality that informs your thoughts, beliefs, and how and where you put your Faith.

We often ask the universe for help and guidance, then do not take it because it is not what we want to do or hear—forgetting the friendliness of the universe and its infinite possibilities. If you wish for great financial abundance, there is a reality where this exists. If you want to be healed, there is a reality where this exists. If you desire a loving relationship, there is a reality where this exists too. If you are asking for direction, the invitation is to be open to seeing the suggestions coming back to you and consider observing a new reality. How? By taking steps toward the reality you want to happen. Collapse the waves that create your bestseller, go on your dream safari in Botswana, or clear that $75,000 debt you have been carrying.

However, as you are looking for guidance from the universe and collapsing waves, a notion to keep in mind from several spiritual thought leaders: the answers you seek from your higher power may not always be the ones you want, although they will always be the ones you need. Those directives may come in ways you never expected over a period not imagined.

Faith helps you realize what *is* in a situation and allows the universe to guide you in the right direction, even though there may be some painful bumps along your path.

Centering Thought. My friendly universe.

Affirmation. The universe safely guides me.
I am open and listening.

Faith Snapshot No. 3:
Clarify Your Intentions

While I believe an intelligent universe guides us, I also think we must help that cause. Have at least a clue where you want to go, so you can spot when being guided in the right direction, out of harm's way, or make sense of obstacles and disappointments that will inevitably happen.

In his MasterClass, Emmy-winning creator of NBC's *West Wing*, Aaron Sorkin, teaches writers to clarify their character's intentions and obstacles, what they want and what is getting in the way. They want the money. They want the girl. Whatever the character wants, it is something they desperately desire, and whatever is standing in their way is formidable. As in life, we want something and feel blocked. Other times we are stuck because we do not know what we want. We have no intentions or purpose. When one of Sorkin's character's intentions is unclear, he slips into the comfortable habit of just writing witty dialogue that does not add up to anything nor move his story forward. Similarly, when we are unclear about our lives and our next move, we fall back into what we have always done, not getting any traction toward something worthwhile. Not until a clear intention is set does one's story begin.

However, it is not enough to set an intention. You have to understand why your intention is important. When you have that answer, ask why *that* why is important. Keep drilling until you clearly understand your intention, the why behind the why. The clearer you are, the more aligned with life you will feel and the more likely to realize opportunities coming your way. Your awareness widens to include noticing people, events, and situations you would have otherwise missed. You become aware of the synchronicity and meaningful coincidences at play around you.

Ideally, clarify your intention until you pinpoint your purpose: why you are here. Your why gives life meaning and the ability to cope in the face of adversity or trauma, helps you grow spiritually, and enables a fresh viewpoint. It motivates you to get up in the morning, have the strength to face the impossible, and the will to keep hope when disappointments happen. When I do not get hired to be a producer or director on a project I wanted, or when someone else sells an idea similar to mine, I keep going because I have Faith in my path and a clear intention. Moments like this are when I remind myself that God is watching over me and is leading me in the right direction.

When you seek advice from a friend, parent, teacher, or mentor, the clearer you are with an ask, the better they can help you because they know what you want. The same goes for when you consult your higher power: be specific. When seeking guidance from above, I often use three questions inspired by the teachings of Marianne Williamson and *A Course in Miracles*:

Where should I go?

Whom should I meet?

What should I say and do?

Then, I set the intention to be open to what or who shows up to support me. Also, something else slides into play, and that is gratitude. When I am more conscious of the right people, book, or class coming along, I find myself saying, "Thank you." Encourage and nurture this gratitude.

What you appreciate appreciates.

Where the energy flows, it grows.

Now we are back in the land of quantum physics. Remember the Observer Effect from earlier and know that you can make real changes in your life by being the cause of the effect you want, and this is why you must be clear about your desires. As the author of your story, you can choose any intention to create the life you want.

Centering Thought. Clarify intentions.

Affirmation. I help the universe help me
by setting clear intentions.

Faith Snapshot No. 4:
Make Faith Bigger Than Your Fear

It is 1988. Yuppies are still in vogue, and so are denim jackets. Table tennis has become an Olympic sport. The number one show on television is *The Cosby Show*. *Die Hard*, starring Bruce Willis, hits theaters, while Stephen Hawking's *A Brief History of Time* reaches the bestseller list. The world is on the move, yet corporate marketer Martin Dugard could not be more bored. He loves endurance sports and has a knack for writing so starts doing magazine articles in the mornings and on weekends for *Competitor* and *Runner's World* to be engaged in at least one thing he enjoys doing. After five years of this routine and getting the opportunity to cover the Raid Gauloises adventure race in Madagascar, Marty feels it is time to muster the courage to go at it as a full-time writer. He has a long-considered conversation with his wife about trusting God and tightening their belts while he gives this writing thing a real go. Another six years go by before landing a consistent gig covering the annual Tour de France. However, money is still tight. His house mortgage is due, and he does not have it. Despite the fear of losing his home, Marty keeps his Faith and writing.

Then, an unexpected assignment comes up to write a behind-the-scenes book for a new reality competition show on a little island in the South China Sea. Executive producer Mark Burnett commissions the book and the show is CBS's *Survivor*. There was no negotiation for writing this book. However, it was the exact amount Marty needed to save his home. Coincidence? Maybe. God at work? Definitely, if you so believe, and I certainly do. The epilogue to this story is that, as of this writing, Marty has gone on to write sixteen bestsellers, mostly nonfiction narratives about history—this is what can happen when you make Faith bigger than your fear.

Faith is another word for courage. Over the years, in the unfolding of my spirituality, one of the remarkable things I noticed was that the stronger I became in my Faith, the less I feared. My Faith gives me confidence—the confidence that things will go as they should—and I feel buoyed by this, even when life does not go as I originally planned. Many times, it turns out better than I ever imagined. So, now when I set an intention, I end it with a phrase I learned from my first two Happiness mentors, Marci Shimoff and Debra Poneman, "This or something better."

Faith pushes out my fear, replacing it with feelings of love, hope, peacefulness, gratitude, or forgiveness. Faith replaces the fear of the meaningless with the confidence of meaningfulness. "God has a reason" is often cited by those enduring difficult, traumatic times. However, this should not be seen as a state of non-reactivity on your part, that you passively do nothing while God does everything. Another critical piece is "God helps those who help themselves." Keep taking action toward the outcome you want. Faith brings the courage to move onward and upward because your life matters. Your hard work, sacrifice, love, gratitude, forgiveness all matter a lot. Those who believe in a higher power rely on it as an organizing force that harmonizes with one's efforts to improve their lot in life. They work with and call upon this higher power to affect a positive result.

When things seem not to go your way, take comfort in knowing that a higher power is holding you and will eventually course-correct you in the right direction. "No" could very well mean "yes," though not just yet. Use Faith's courage to knock on doors you would have otherwise shyly walked by. Ask the difficult questions that were once stuck in your throat. Say goodbye to situations that, on the surface, seem reasonable and okay, though genuinely not serving you well, like Marty's uninspiring corporate marketing job. Take the courage that comes from Faith to propel you to go beyond your fears to say, "Yes, I want this and will do what it takes, and do it in the best way possible."

Centering Thought. Faith trumps fear.

Affirmation. My Faith gives me the courage
to take leaps into the unknown.

Faith Snapshot No. 5:
Take the Leap of Faith

His eyes anxiously dart around an imposing dark cavern with his hand on a heaving chest as if he is cradling his breath. In *Indiana Jones and the Last Crusade*, Indy faces a ravine so wide and deep that it takes everything to make that first seemingly impossible step to get to where the Holy Grail is hidden. When he finally gathers the courage to defiantly stretch his foot forward and down into what appears to be only air, a bridge appears to support him across the unimaginable. That is also what happens when we lean into our Faith. An invisible force guides and protects us. I think this is true even for the nonbelievers in the crowd who genuinely trust their path (more on this soon). Supportive opportunities and people will and do present themselves.

Although believers and nonbelievers can be fooled into thinking they are taking action, only to find themselves staying in the same place, in reality, they are just repeating the same behavior, not getting anywhere, not getting any better. Why? Because it is comfortable, it is what they know, maybe have ever known. It can be extremely uncomfortable to think of doing anything different. Yet, that is exactly what they, *we*, need to do: something different. You may have heard that the definition of insanity is doing the same thing over and over and expecting a different result. *So, stop the madness.* Instead, lean into your Faith for support in making healthier, more loving, more self-compassionate choices, especially when it is scary. Faith can help you break old patterns that no longer serve you in exchange for ones that do, or give you the nerve when it fails you.

I see Faith as the ultimate karma code cracker. When I studied Primordial Sound Meditation, a form of Transcendental Meditation, at

Deepak Chopra's center, I learned, good or bad, karma is essentially making the same decision over and over, repeating actions with the same consequences. When does this change? When you become aware enough to create a new choice. If you look up this Sanskrit word, *karma* means action driven by intention, which leads to future outcomes. These intentions are formed by the memory of past actions stored over time deep within us, spiritually speaking, held at the level of the soul. However, something else is going on as well and is happening inside your head.

In your brain, memory is neurons and synapses acting together, creating a pleasant or unpleasant memory, good or bad. Memories then get stored with others that are similar. There is a saying in neuroscience, "Neurons that fire together, wire together." Neurons are your head's messengers that travel along synaptic highways, transmitting information to different areas of the nervous system, producing neural feedback that is negative, positive, or neutral. This messenger service allows you to preserve and create memories. When you repeat any action, you bring up its associated memories. Whether positive or negative, they will remain so until you consciously change them. You can use the brain's neuroplasticity to create a positive experience in your mind. So, consider constructive thoughts or experiences to redirect the negative ones causing you to feel in a way you do not want. Hold a new Happier experience in your mind for twenty to thirty seconds, enabling it to imprint in your memory. Juxtaposing two experiences in your mind, one negative, the other positive, and deliberately focusing on the constructive one, the other will fall away from lack of attention and a positive neural pathway will be built. When you consistently take in good experiences, the brain's neural networks eventually get reprogrammed, and positive neural pathways become your default mental state.

By becoming aware of what is not serving you well, you can shift your energy toward making choices that feel good, creating Happy memories, changing unproductive thoughts, and breaking habits that hinder you. You can let go of the fear to change to take a chance at something new, and what can give you the strength? *Right, Faith.* Even though your heart is pounding, sweat is on your brow, and the next step in front of you seems impossible, think about how you can be like Indy. Believe an invisible bridge will appear as you consciously take a leap of Faith.

Centering Thought. Leap.

Affirmation. Confidently, I make the leap of Faith,
knowing that the universe cradles my feet.

Faith Snapshot No. 6:
Look for Kisses from the Universe

A new line of painted red hearts is on the sidewalk in front of the Alcove Cafe in my Los Angeles neighborhood reminding me that love is always the way, even though it may not seem like it now.

A white feather lands at my feet as I paddle in a canoe through a hippo-infested channel on the Zambezi, a message that angels protect me because it is my job as a wellbeing adventure travel designer (my other business) to try scary things.

On a dusty dirt road in Malawi, I drive by a roadside coffin store, triggering a feeling of gratitude that I am alive and must always fully embrace it.

I look at these seemingly random occurrences as kisses from the universe. I take them as whispers from above that I am being guided and everything will be okay. When I do this, I feel comforted, supported, and hopeful. There is a passage in Paulo Coelho's novel *The Zahir* that muses on how the universe speaks in signs and is only understood when your mind is open to reading its language—the language of seeing hidden meanings in what is happening around you. If you pay attention, you will come to know everything needed to support you. "Lessons always arrive when you are ready."

Within the cosmic realm of possibilities, the universe contains infinite pathways you can experience. You experiment with this and that, tumble into a few rabbit holes, hit some dead ends. Do this enough, and you come to understand that another avenue is available when one way gets blocked. One door closes and another one opens, be it personal or professional. When something is impossible, view it as the universe telling you it is not the direction meant for you; instead, be open to a different possibility. Consider that when something is unclear, daunting, or upsetting, something fantastic could be just beyond your current field of vision. Even scientists can only view the natural world within the limits of their knowledge, the questions they ask, and the instruments to measure a phenomenon. As you gain more sensitivity in observing your world, coupled with clear intentions, you will eventually be able to read the universe's language of signs, get those *ah-ha* moments, and see things and situations in a new, more nurturing light. This understanding also helps put upsetting stuff into a better, healthier perspective. Perhaps there are some lessons you need to learn. There is a saying, "Whatever gets you through the night," and this way of seeing things does it for me.

When you learn to read the language of the universe and listen to its whispers, the miraculous happens. Your path in life becomes more focused, impacting your big and small decisions. You know what is a full body "Hell yes!" and what is a "Hell no!" Although, you may face challenges before realizing your priorities and what you truly want. Often this happens after surviving a life-threatening disease, a major injury, a near-death experience, or a catastrophic event. People made significant priority shifts after 9/11 and the Covid pandemic. The Great Resignation partly happened because many realized they wanted a better quality of life.

So, when you feel scared, disappointed, or unclear, be open to those kisses from the universe channeled through your inner voice offering guidance and wisdom. Like Dorothy in *The Wizard of Oz*, she possessed the ability to go home all along. With a bit of help from Glinda, the Good Witch of the North, Dorothy realizes this for herself. Direction comes in all forms and is available to you. Only three clicks of your ruby red slippers, and you can be on your way.

Centering Thought. Cosmic kisses.

Affirmation. I am open to seeing, hearing,
feeling the universe's kisses that guide my way.

Faith Snapshot No. 7:
Trust the Process

"Ugh! Why does everything seem to take so frickin' long and be so frickin' hard?"

Early in my television career, I was a media-time buyer for KRON-TV, the local NBC affiliate in San Francisco. I had lunch one day with a radio ad salesman who kept lamenting how much effort it took to do anything and everything. Finally, after ranting for several minutes, he stopped talking and let out a resigned sigh, saying, "Life just takes time." These words have often come back to me, especially when frustrated by day-to-day living, the lines you stand in to buy food at the market, sitting in commuter traffic, or being put on an endless hold with your credit card company. Yes, all this does take time. However, so do other aspects of life, such as getting an education, developing a career, mastering a talent, cultivating relationships, and many other things. To put this in perspective, humans have a long maturation process because of the energy our brain requires to function, even while at rest, which slows the growth process.

This slow growth process has its own intelligence and timing. It knows how to grow, in what sequence, and when. Like a bud knows how to flower, a tree knows how to sprout, the human organism knows how to create fingers, toes, arms, legs, reproductive organs, a torso, a beating heart, and a brain while in the womb, and continue once born into this world. An organic, intelligent process from developing to maturing and operating knows just what to do. However, things can get wonky when the brain that had organically come into being becomes occupied by consciousness, when your brain and mind become intertwined to run the show. One hypothesis is that the mind is what the brain does. In their book, *Buddha's Brain*, neuropsychologist Rick Hanson and medical doctor Richard Mendius put forth that "an awakening of the mind is an awakening of the brain." So, when your mind, at whatever level of consciousness, does not trust the progression of life, of a situation unfolding in due time, that is where you fall into framing thoughts with:

"It is taking too long."

"I will never get there."

"It is always so hard."

This overwhelmed point of view relates to what you believe are the available choices and the consequences that will result, including how you view the load you bear and your ability to carry it. Some loads are breezy, easy-peasy. Others feel like you are Sisyphus, forced by Zeus to push a massive boulder up a hill, only to have it roll back down, causing you to start over. If this is you, try on:

"God will not let you be tried beyond what you can bear. But when you are tried, He will also provide a way out so that you can endure it." —1 Corinthians 10:13

The secular version of this is to "trust the process."

To believe in your ability to carry life's load and achieve your set intentions, you must first believe in yourself. Otherwise, nothing will happen, or it will be a very long struggle. So, every time you see your life progress through a negative lens, think about what you are reinforcing and instilling in your mind and brain. Ask how much of your thinking is framed in fear, a lack of confidence, or unwillingness. Then, seek to change it. Use meditation to settle and clear your mind. As you sit in stillness, ask: What am I believing that is keeping me stuck? What can I let go of to move forward? Pay attention to what comes up during and outside your dedicated meditation time.

Here's the other thing. We all have an inner voice that tells us what to do, go left or right at the fork in the road, though what happens when you choose one way over another and realize that you should have chosen its opposite? What do you say? "I knew I should not have chosen this way." How do you know that it is true? That the other path would have been better? You do not know, nor will you ever know. That diversion could have been a blessing in disguise. The message is to trust that detours are part of your journey and the unfolding of perfect timing.

Surrendering to the process gives you the courage and confidence—those two words again—to have Faith that when things are not working out, it is for a good reason. Instead of begrudging the way things are going down, appreciate it as an opportunity to become a better human being. There is always room for that. So, accept that life can and does take time. Let it happen, seek to learn, appreciate the process, and above all, trust it.

Centering Thought. Trust.

Affirmation. I trust that the universe is guiding me
in the right direction in perfect timing.

Faith Snapshot No. 8:
Tune In to Become Aware

Done, done, done! I lost it.

My mind, my sense of humor, my sense of self. I came into meditation when I was wholly off-center and overreacting to just about everything. I was coming off an exhausting ten-month television series headquartered in London. The concept of the show was very appealing. It was a competition about driving the most dangerous roads in five countries. The travel part I loved. The actual running of the show, well, *not so much*. It was an emotionally rough go (more on this later). By the time I wrapped the project, I felt so much of my inner work to become a Happier me was left tattered in pieces across Australia, Brazil, Canada, Mongolia, and India, and it was my fault. I had lost sight of my inner Happy place and desperately wanted it back. So, I went to Bali to find it.

I tried meditation for the first time in the middle of a mountainous jungle on that idyllic Indonesian island. It was just what the spiritual doctor ordered. I stayed at a place that was indeed a little slice of Eden, COMO Shambhala Estate, outside of Ubud. I had a room with only a bed enclosed on three sides with floor-to-ceiling windows that faced out into the jungle overlooking a ravine with a river below. I forewent air-conditioning, wanting every window open so I could feel the humid jungle air wrap around me like a soft flannel blanket. I drifted off to chirps, caws, and siren insect sounds at night. Each morning, I showed my body to the jungle, closing my eyes, feeling myself gradually healing and returning to my inner Happy place. While my surroundings did a lot to soothe my off-kilter spirit, my meditation time put me back on center.

A wise voice is living in the spaces between your thoughts and connected to the cosmic universe. Meditation helps you access this space. The gap between your thoughts is where the real, purest you exists in union with the infinite possibilities available for you to observe and become. Sitting still enough to listen will tell you which job to choose or to tough out a situation that seems to not be working. There is a saying, "Praying is you talking to God. Meditation is you listening." Trust the wisdom of that cosmically inspired inner voice like you trust the process; that is why you meditate to fine-tune the ability to listen.

Although, with so many meditation traditions and practices, it can quickly get confusing for a beginner. Meditating simply means spending time in quiet thought for relaxation, contemplation, or religious purposes. Meditation is about shifting your attention to release one's thundering waterfall of thoughts. Generally, the attention is on your breath, a mantra, or an object. This focus quiets your mind and body so you can spend quality time in stillness. Meditation can be a spiritual pursuit, or not for those who are more interested in the physiological benefits. This practice offers help to everyone. The overarching way is that it calms your mind and body, allowing for an opening into higher awareness and alertness. Any time in stillness will have a calming, relaxing effect on the brain's parasympathetic nervous system. The calm moves through your brain and mind, helping to create a neural pathway toward positivity, greater clarity, and a healthier acceptance of your present reality.

There are many other compelling reasons to have a daily meditation practice. It helps manage stress, reduces anxiety, lowers blood pressure, enhances sleep quality, boosts creativity, creates inner peace, awakens intuition. All this is to say, you will find yourself moving from automatic and unconscious behavior to accessing a wider field of conscious possibilities and a less judgmental life filled with greater contentment, wisdom, and harmony. Meditation, specifically Mindfulness, is a way of training the mind to be attentive to your inner and outer worlds to take in positive experiences. Over time, this focused attention reshapes the brain's neural circuits, making the goodness you appreciate part of your being. Ultimately, you feel more connected to your higher self, *ergo*, your connection to God for the non-secular. I call meditation the "Wholebeing Silver Bullet."

Meditation's real magic is the wiping of your lens of perception, the widening of awareness that happens outside your formal sitting practice. You become more fine-tuned to observe, to realize a new reality. With experience, you will be able to maintain a calmer center and avoid being chronically over-reactive, which, if left free to roam, can cause disease and age you far too quickly.

Sitting in stillness allows the mental cacophony to settle, which I discovered during my Balinese retreat from the world. I have been meditating ever since, usually in the mornings to start my day. Most meditation traditions suggest practicing in the morning when your mind is the least cluttered with mental activity and most receptive. However, the best time to meditate is when and wherever you can fit it into your day. Whether it is for five minutes or fifty, consistency counts most. A 2018 behavioral brain research project revealed that after eight weeks of thirteen minutes of guided meditations, beginners saw decreases in negative moods, anxiety, and fatigue while increasing their attention and memory.

So, do what you can because how well you take care of your mind (and body) will determine how well you can tune in to the mental frequencies that create a healthier and Happier you. Think of a radio. The better the receiver, the better the radio frequency will come in. The more you meditate, the more exceptional your ability to tune in to the guidance, opportunities, and people who show up to support you. Allow yourself the gift of tuning in to become more aware.

Those who think they cannot meditate because their minds are too chatty or are too busy with their daily lives, consider the act of meditation itself: the act of focusing your attention on something. Most anything can be a meditation, including the view right before you. I thought a lot about this when I spent a month traveling through South Africa, Botswana, Zimbabwe, and Kenya. I realized when I meditated, I did not want to close my eyes to the majesty in front of me. Instead, I wanted to savor the sights and sounds of Africa in unison—the hippos snorting and bobbing their heads in and out of the water, baboons chasing each other up and down trees, the impala grazing on the plains. I wanted to witness and use these moments as a focal point during meditation. This type of meditation is called "Open-eyed" and helps you be aware of your surroundings. It keeps you present to the moment, thoughts, and emotions as they arise, and, ultimately, more connected to your inner being. However, you do not have to be in a far-off land to create a specific meditation for yourself. I once spoke with someone who wanted to meditate, though she felt she had little time for it in the morning before work and was too tired at night. She mentioned having a cat she cared for in the mornings, and I suggested petting the animal she loved could be her morning meditation. Some find walking in nature to be their meditation. Others sit mindfully with a cup of coffee.

I also believe you can use different meditations for different purposes. I teach and practice three types. I use Mindfulness when I want to stay present by paying attention to my breath, felt sensations in my body, or sounds in the environment.

Primordial Sound Meditation, the Transcendental Meditation style I mentioned taught by Deepak Chopra, is my practice when I want to transcend my current thoughts by silently repeating a mantra based on when and where I was born.

Then, the Prayer of the Heart, also known as the Jesus Prayer, is when I want to feel closer to God by focusing on these words: "Lord, Jesus Christ, Son of God, have mercy on me."

The takeaway here is to notice what you need and use whatever will bring you into stillness by making one thing your point of focus and to do it consistently—this is when you will see the best results.

Centering Thought. Be aware.

Affirmation. I tune into the wisdom of my inner voice
that is always present to encourage me.

♥ ♥ ♥

Faith Meditation Prayer

I still my heart, my mind, so I may know you.

I pray for the whispering of your wisdom and guidance.

I meditate to hear and accept the
direction you are leading me.

I know that you may nudge me in ways I
do not understand or want to go.

Yet, I know I will be safe and comforted
in times of challenge.

Through You, I know I will be uplifted to
times of victory and celebration.

Through you, all is possible.

And so let it be.

DEVELOPING UNWAVERING FAITH

Like Indy's invisible bridge, Faith is your unseen safety net, there to catch you if you ask the universe for guidance, watch for signs, and trust the process—although cultivating or deepening one's Faith can and often does take effort. You make an effort to pray or meditate, take time to go to places of worship, participate in rituals and holidays. While research supports the benefits of being close to a higher guiding entity, Stanford anthropologist Dr. Tanya Luhrmann adds one more provocative idea into the mix—a thought I have often had as I file into line with other parishioners for communion, opening my mouth to take in the body and blood of Christ for the cleansing of my soul. She suggests that many have Faith and are believers because they worship, not the other way around. Worshiping makes people feel close to God and keeps their Faith alive. Dr. Luhrmann's work explores using prayer or meditation, similar to how cognitive behavioral therapy (briefly mentioned earlier) helps shift thoughts from what is going wrong to what is going right. What is right is that those who believe in a loving and supportive Divine or universal source tend to live longer and feel healthier than those who do not.

The physical benefits are improved blood pressure, a more resilient immune system, and reduced rates of stroke, cancer, and heart disease.

Emotionally, you can experience less anxiety, stress, depression, and loneliness. Those in a relationship with God tend to have more fulfilling relationships and fewer mental health problems. Brain MRIs have shown that talking with God resembles chatting with a trusted friend.

Overall, Faith helps one's habits to be constructive versus destructive. You are more loving, forgiving, hopeful, and optimistic. Relationships in all forms are often tighter. If you go to church or some version of this, there is a greater sense of community, supporting feelings that you are not alone in this world. Thank God for that.

So, can I literally believe as they do in the Greek Orthodox religion that communion bread and wine are mystically transformed into the body and blood of Christ for the cleansing of my soul? Well, I struggle with that one. Yet can I consider it metaphorically? Yes, I can, and in doing this, it reminds me of how Christ teaches me to be a good human and is what religious Faith does for many others. It is what Buddhism and every spiritual philosophy teaches—a way to live in love and harmony with ourselves, each other, and the natural world.

The strength of Faith comes down to one's reason *to be* and the feeling that God has your back. Giving over to a higher power, trusting that things will work out for the best, is peace of mind and the bedrock for your Happiness and Wholebeing.

Journaling with Faith: What Does Faith Mean to You?

Now that you have read my thoughts about Faith, I invite you to journal how you can bring more Faith into your life. The following questions include my reflections in italics and space for you to fill in yours.

How do you define Faith, regardless of any religious affiliation, and its benefits?

The most significant benefit of having faith is that it offers me hope and solace. In the quiet hours of the night, when I feel the pangs of a panic attack coming on, worried about sustaining my businesses, having enough money to live somewhere safe with good health care, and enough money to live out my life, I remember that God has my back, and all will be well. Of the eight essential virtues and qualities that I believe create a happy life, faith is the alpha and the omega.

_____

_____

_____

What role does Faith currently play in your life?

Faith is the fuel in my Happiness and Wholebeing tank that delivers me in love, health, gratitude, forgiveness, peace, detachment, and ultimately, abundance in all aspects of my life.

_____

_____

_____

How do you perceive your ability to welcome and accept Faith into your life?

I am open and curious about any kind of spirituality. God is everywhere and of a thousand faces.

_____

_____

_____

How are you, or will you, support your Faith to experience a greater sense of Happiness and Wholebeing?

I have a strong, supportive, prayerful, meditative, and mindful daily practice. My next steps are to keep it this way.

_____

_____

_____

Take a photograph of what Faith looks like for you. Give it a caption. Then journal about your thoughts and feelings.

God is in the details and brings a sense of happiness in everything I see.

Journal Entry: *When I make faith my focal point, I see God in everything. Even the most delicate white flower cradled by a green, life-giving staff shows how God creates the miraculous in everything. Einstein said, "There are two ways to live your life. One is as though nothing is a miracle. The other is as though everything is a miracle." I choose the miracle.*

Faith Photo Ops and Action Opportunities

After journaling your thoughts on Faith, use the following Photo Op prompts to inspire you to find images reflective of your beliefs. Many are meant to be done along with the Action Opportunities designed to guide you through the chapter's central ideas. The Centering Thoughts and Affirmations I offer within the chapter can help you delve deeper into bringing more Faith into your everyday life. I have given you space to write your reflections; this will help anchor the teachings and your epiphanies.

Do the practices that are most significant to you. While you do not need to complete every one, the more you do, the more impactful the teachings in this chapter will become. Remember, there is no right or wrong way of doing these assignments, just your way. Do not worry if you feel you are not a photographer. The Photo Ops are not about capturing perfect images. They are about embodying what you see and feel. The ideas here can feel abstract, so allow yourself creative freedom of exploration and expression to understand better what you are learning.

You also might like to make prints and place them where you will often see them: on a bulletin board, desk, nightstand, or use them as a screensaver or wallpaper on your phone, tablet, or computer. I encourage you to share your pictures and thoughts with our *Take a Shot at Happiness* community on social media or our app. Above all, delight in the process.

Everything just said here will be true in the coming chapters too.

Faith Snapshot No. 1: Believe in Something Beyond Yourself

Photo Op. *A Force Greater Than You Is Always There to Support You.* As you move through your day, capture images of spiritual or uplifting words, passages, or sayings that are meaningful to you. A building's billboard with the word "Believe." A neon road sign that reads "RELAX UR OK." These are two images I took in the past. The words were meaningful to me because, at the time, I needed to feel stronger in my Faith, believing the challenges I was facing would resolve positively and that there was guidance all around me. You may find a passage from a book or a saying on a commemorative plaque. Look for and capture what causes you to think about Faith and how it plays out in your life.

Action Opportunity. The invitation here is to try different spiritual traditions, read books, listen to talks, and go to places of worship. Or try a secular practice, like Mindfulness. Start by reflecting on the Centering Thought: "Believe." Then, see what resonates, whether secular, non-secular, or some aspects of both. It could very well awaken something surprisingly good inside of you. Reinforce your spiritual exploration using the Affirmation: "The Creator of all things is the supportive guiding force in all I do." Use the lines below to write your thoughts and feelings about Faith.

Also, consider using your phone to record an inspirational talk on Faith. Then, listen to it when you need a bit of motivation.

_____

_____

_____

Faith Snapshot No. 2:
Choose to Live in a Friendly Universe

Photo Op. *Why Does This Keep Happening?* Consider a situation in your life that seems to be reoccurring or not resolving. There is probably something there that needs to be addressed. Capture an image that reflects this situation. The following is the second part of this activity.

Action Opportunity. Meditate on the Centering Thought: "My friendly universe." Then, sit with the reoccurring situation you are contemplating and honestly address the question, "What am I not seeing or doing?" Allow yourself to free-form write, continuously writing without stopping or editing yourself, for at least fifteen minutes. You can go longer if you wish. You may hear some surprisingly wise words come from your inner voice. You can always invoke the Affirmation "The universe safely guides me. I am open and listening" to support you.

_____

_____

_____

Faith Snapshot No. 3:
Clarify Your Intentions

Photo Op. *I Am Made to Do This!* Start with doing the following Action Opportunity, then stick the list to a mirror you look into daily. Choose one thing on the list, close your eyes, and imagine yourself doing that one thing. Then, open your eyes, look at yourself, and say, "I am made to do this."

Try to take several photos reflecting some of the things you love doing, showing off your talents and natural abilities. These images will help clarify your intentions.

Action Opportunity. This practice is especially good if you are unclear about what you want or your purpose in life. Start with the Centering Thought: "Clarify intentions." Then, spend time listing all the things you love doing and looking where your talent and natural abilities lie. Use the Affirmation "I help the universe help me by setting clear intentions" to ask what you would do if time and money were not issues. The seeds of your desires will be found doing this reflection.

_____

_____

_____

Faith Snapshot No. 4:
Make Faith Bigger Than Your Fear

Photo Op. *Fear Has No Place Here.* Capture or find images that represent how inspired you feel about taking risks because your Faith gives you the courage to say, "Yes! I am going for it!" You may want to do the Action Opportunity first.

Action Opportunity. Take some time to ask some tough questions. You may be surprised by the answers.

How have I contributed to an unfulfilling situation?

What do I want to do, yet am afraid to do?

What am I willing to do to change my current circumstances?

Before answering these questions, meditate with the Centering Thought: "Faith trumps fear."

Next, lean into your Faith. Use it as courage to overcome your fears, along with the Affirmation: "My Faith gives me the courage to take leaps into the unknown."

_____

_____

_____

Faith Snapshot No. 5:
Take the Leap of Faith

Photo Op. *I Did It!* First, do the Action Opportunity. Then, capture an image or video of you doing a victory dance each time you succeed in changing an action, behavior, or habit. Write photo captions for each image or video.

Action Opportunity. Call to mind the Centering Thought: "Leap." Use it to support creating a new picture of life by taking a moment to write all the actions, behaviors, and habits that are not serving you. Be honest with yourself, even if it is embarrassing just sitting all by yourself. This reflection will only work if you genuinely come clean. So:

One, list all the decisions you are making where you experience the same not-so-great result.

Two, choose the top ten actions, behaviors, and habits that are not serving you well. Then, narrow these down to your top five, next to three, then one.

Three, focus on the one action, behavior, or habit that needs to change most in your life. The one that will send you in a radically positive direction. Then, work on the next thing you want to change. Eventually, you will make your way through your list.

Four, think of one action you will do today to create the habit or change you envision. Invoke the Affirmation: "Confidently, I make the leap of Faith, knowing that the universe cradles my feet."

Five, take that first leap. Although there will undoubtedly be instances when re-envisioning life as you know it will seem daunting, do it anyway. Have Faith that the universe will catch you should you fall. If you do fall, trust that it is possible, truly possible, that you will eventually rise like a phoenix, stronger and more brilliant. Now, capture your victory moments.

Faith Snapshot No. 6:
Look for Kisses from the Universe

Photo Op. *Kiss Me.* Notice the signs around you and photograph them: a billboard that says "Believe," your lucky number showing up in an unexpected place, two different people suggesting you read the same book. Keep these images in a photo album or as a slideshow on your computer, tablet, or phone. Use these images to do your Action Opportunity.

Action Opportunity. Start with the Centering Thought: "Cosmic kisses." Then, be alert to the hidden meanings in what is happening around you. Meditate using the Affirmation "I am open to seeing, hearing, feeling the universe's kisses that guide my way" to support widening your field of awareness. As you do this reflection with images from the above Photo Op, ask, what could they mean? What lessons are meant for me?

Faith Snapshot No. 7:
Trust the Process

Photo Op. *Trust Yourself and the Universe's Timing.* Capture an image of something that will be a nurturing reminder to "trust the process." It could be a picture of a long road, a helping hand, rays of light. It is an image that reassures you that all will unfold when and as it should. Anytime you need a reminder to trust life unfolding, take a reflective photo that encourages this for you.

    Action Opportunity. Focus on the Centering Thought, "Trust," as life unfolds. First, spend time clarifying your dreams. You may already have a good start on this by doing Action Opportunities No. 3: Clarify Your Intentions or No. 4: Make Faith Bigger Than Your Fear. To support this reflection, use the Affirmation: "I trust that the universe is guiding me in the right direction in perfect timing." Then, sit in stillness to notice what thoughts and emotions arise. Journal about these afterward.

Faith Snapshot No. 8:
Tune In to Become Aware

Photo Op. *Be Still.* Find an image that represents how you feel while you meditate or have someone take a photograph of you. Perhaps share it and your Action Opportunity reflections with our *Take a Shot at Happiness* community. People often find it helpful to discuss their experiences. Many meditators, especially ones new to the practice, think they are doing something wrong because they have too many thoughts. However, being aware of your thoughts is actually letting you know you are on the right track. We are thinking beings. Thoughts will arise during meditation. It is what you do with them as they come up that matters, and what you do is see thoughts as trains that you do not have to board.

Action Opportunity. If you do not have a meditation practice, I encourage you to start one. Your meditation practice can begin simply with just one minute once a day, ideally twice, focusing on your breath coming in and out your nose. Gradually you will be able and want to increase this time. Remember, it is not the length of time that counts. It is the consistency that yields its benefits over time. Before beginning a session, become present by invoking the Affirmation: "I tune into the wisdom of my inner voice that is always present to encourage me." Close your meditation with the Centering Thought: "Be aware." You may find it helpful to journal about your experiences and progress.

_____

_____

_____

PICTURING LOVE

Love
\\'ləv\\

noun
: strong affection for another arising out of kinship or personal ties
: attraction based on sexual desires
: warm attachment, enthusiasm, or devotion
: unselfish loyal and benevolent concern for the good of another

"We need Love in order to live happily, as much as we need oxygen in order to live at all."
—Marianne Williamson
Bestselling Author, A Return to Love

SNAPSHOT OF LOVE

In My Viewfinder

My father used to say that Love does not keep a scorecard. He was right.

Love is nurturing, appreciative.

Love is forgiving.

Love is supportive, non-judgmental.

Love is calm, gentle, ardent all at once.

Love is open and connects us to each other, to God, to the universe, and back to ourselves.

One of the greatest lessons many realized during the pandemic was that we are each part of the human race no matter where we reside or what we believe in. We are connected as global brothers and sisters, sharing the same Mother Earth and Father Universe. We are each a wave in the ocean of humankind. What happens in the sea in Antarctica impacts the ocean off the coast of California, now and tomorrow. What you do as an individual impacts everyone around you, who then affects everyone around them, and so on to future generations. Love is the way to go and the most beautiful form of self-preservation.

I love Love in all its nurturing forms. I think most issues in the world can be solved by it. When you hold Love as an idea in your mind and an intention from your heart, thoughts and feelings of hate, anger, and resentment simply cannot coexist. When I feel Love toward anyone—a significant other, a child, a friend, an animal—it radiates a sensation of warmth throughout my body. The only way I am compelled to react is by extending this sensation outward in the form of Love and kindness. Often when I am feeling upset about a person or situation, I pause to close my eyes to take a slow deep breath. Then, as I breathe out, I silently say the word, "Love," sending those molecules into the universe. Almost immediately, a calmer, Happier feeling washes over me. I continue breathing in, breathing out Love until the upset passes.

Love impacts your acceptance of others, willingness to understand and collaborate, and, most importantly, the sense of acceptance of yourself, the recognition of your uniqueness and contribution to life.

Love encompasses everything from your relationship with those you most cherish to resolving issues between warring nations. So, I guess there is something to the adage, "Love makes the world go round." Yet, Love is one of those things that when it is working for you, it is the highest high. When it is not, *oh boy*, it is the bottom of the pit, and we all know it.

If you spend any time looking at what causes suffering, you realize that it is indeed a lack of Love in a situation, toward a person, or even toward yourself. When you apply Love to where it hurts, it feels so much better. I think Love is pretty much the answer to all things, all situations in life. When you are loving, it makes you feel Happier. When you project Love and kindness, it usually comes back to you. Why? Because Love is a universal emotion. Being Loved is something we all want regardless of race, creed, gender, religious practice, spiritual orientation, or no orientation at all. Love is inclusive for and to all. It supports and connects everything, all matter, all beings across the planet and throughout the universe, and it all begins with you.

This sentiment is among many of the real gifts I have received from traveling the world, the realization that we all share some core needs. Whether you are living in a mud hut in Kenya, on a farm in Nebraska, or in an apartment in London, we all want the same basic things: food, shelter, clothing, safety, and, most of all, Love and acceptance. These are common wants. How we are with ourselves about these basic needs extends to how we are in the world about them. It has a ripple effect within our global consciousness that translates to how we care for each other and our planet. I, for one, would rather cultivate harmony instead of anger. Spread Love above hate, and I want everyone on board with this.

Snapshots on Developing Your Loving Heart

Love Snapshot No. 1:
Embrace What Makes You Uniquely You

Think of how different the world would be if:

Mother Teresa feeding the hungry and nurturing the poor…

Martin Luther King, Mahatma Gandhi, changing the tide of nations against racism and tyranny…

Neil Armstrong taking a walk on the moon…

Steven Spielberg re-envisioning how films are made…

Steve Jobs innovating how we process information, view videos, and listen to music…

…had not shown up?

If any one of these individuals had not followed their calling or dream? How would the world be altered had these people decided to stay home, living in some unfulfilled version of themselves? If they had said it is enough to have a normal life, *whatever that is?* Go to work, come home, eat dinner, watch a little television, play some video games, and do it again the next day, the next day, and the day after, eventually bleeding into years of wishing they were doing something else? Had each not tapped in and stepped out into what uniquely made them a person? We all have choices. What separated these folks was that they Loved themselves and followed the dreams and desires that pulled at them. At the very least, they Loved their vision enough to embrace and run with it. Each may not have used the word Love to describe their ambitions. However, that is what it was. Love for humanity. Passion for what is socially right. The Love for exploration, storytelling, technology. There were likely other ego emotions at play as each of these people progressed in their success, though the initial and underlining driver was Love.

Love yourself enough to run with what makes you uniquely *you*, to live out your greatest desires.

We are all called, called differently and at different times. You just have to pause long enough to listen, to think highly enough of yourself to answer your call. Some are called to serve their country on foreign soil, to protect our local communities. Some to open minds. Others to make peace. For many, it is to be a good parent, raising children to be productive human beings. The invitation is to stop living a life of quiet frustration and desperation.

Some find a direct path early on, while others take a longer, circuitous journey, which I think is most of us. Though the *when* is less important than the *do*. The *do* of finding and realizing your dreams. The sooner you define your desires, the sooner you will live the life you want and the more meaning it will have. Do this, and you are less likely to dwell in regret, resentment, anger, jealousy, apathy, or frustration, allowing it to fester and negatively impact you. Studies show that people who find meaning in their lives feel more satisfied, have healthy habits (*ergo* are healthier in mind, body, and spirit) have stronger relationships, greater prosperity, sleep better, live longer, and are Happier.

So, be bold enough to live the life you want. Martin Luther King, Neil Armstrong, and everyone else listed here came into the world the same as you, naked, crying, and into a world of possibilities. Yet, they chose to make life happen on their terms. This choice is always available to you, too. There is no reason you cannot start the next global tech company in your bedroom like Steve Jobs, or shoot your first 8mm film using your dad's movie camera like Steven Spielberg. You can now use your phone's camera to create stories. Think about how much access you have to so many resources right in your back pocket, though the most important one is what is already inside you—your Love and desire to make things happen for a vision you hold of a life you want to live.

Centering Thought. Embrace my uniqueness.

Affirmation. I realize, accept, and put
into action my unique talents.

Love Snapshot No. 2:
The Oxygen Mask Goes on You First

It was a wasteland of dry, brown dirt, void of any tall, majestic pine trees found elsewhere on the mountainside. I had days, not weeks, to lock in the last location for this leg of our road competition in British Columbia. Other options were limited. What was I going to tell the network? We cannot do this episode because our endpoint is just too frickin' ugly to shoot. That was not going to work, so instead, I lost it on my unfortunate location scout, going off about how unacceptable the spot was for our race finish line. To his credit, he let me vent. He knew I was exhausted from the weeks we had been working on the road. I was so frustrated with the crew I inherited when I was asked to take over running the show, who seemed to prefer beers after work versus working during the day. I was worried about delivering a series the network wanted without the budget it needed. Sleepless nights were wearing on me as I tossed and turned, stressing about how I would make everything work. Production was having its toll on me. I was not taking care of myself, nor the most pleasant to be around. In hindsight, it was a painful lesson in what happens when I do not show up for myself.

After your relationship with a higher power, the most important Love relationship to nurture is the one with yourself. Think of when you are on a plane. Before you take off, the flight attendant announces that an oxygen mask will drop in front of you in the event of an emergency. The instruction is first to cover your face with the mask, then to take care of those around you. This advice goes for life too. Okay, maybe you have heard this analogy before. It a good one because it is true. We are all flying on Air Life. How can you be there for others if you do not take care of yourself and do things to develop the best and healthiest you? We all need a good dose of self-love.

For a long time, I struggled with what self-love meant. Like many of us, I equated it with self-centeredness, selfishness, ego, and vanity, all of which have negative connotations that can bring on a negative self-image. It can be all these, though it does not have to be so. Self-love can have a positive and productive purpose in the form of self-care, self-directedness, self-compassion, and self-forgiveness. The rewards for caring for your mind, body, and spirit are kinder, Happier, and more fulfilling relationships on all fronts.

When you prioritize developing self-love as a positive attribute, you also share the good that comes of it with others. My location scout in Canada would have appreciated being the benefactor of this.

On one trip to Kenya, I visited the Ol Jogi Montessori School located about 140 miles north of Nairobi atop the six-thousand-foot Laikipia Plateau, near Mount Kenya. Pretty remote. My heart was touched by a very self-aware and self-actualizing song the second graders sang. "I am special. Look at me, you will see someone very special. That is me." Then, I noticed the framed sayings hanging on the classroom walls.

"If you want to fly, give up everything that weighs you down."

"Integrity is the most valuable and respected quality of leadership."

"Accept no one's definition of your life. Define yourself."

I wish my young mind had been given this kind of nurturing and these messages in elementary school. However, it is never too late. Learning to be your personal coach, best friend, companion, and healer is a great place to begin this inward journey toward self-love. Going for walks with yourself, taking time to think, making a nutritious candle-lit dinner, meditating. The options for activities you can do on your own are limitless. For many, this is a challenging step because it could mean one, Loving yourself for the first time, two, seriously committing to caring for your wellbeing, and three, spending time alone; although, this alone time can be terrifying if you are not used to doing this. Eventually, you will come to embrace and covet time with yourself. I look forward to evenings when I can make dinner by myself while watching a favorite television series or hiking through the foothills. Most of my travels are solo.

The other benefit of Loving and showing up for yourself is that you are with people because you want to be, not because you need to be. Tom Cruise was wrong when he told Renee Zellweger in *Jerry Maguire* that she completed him. You do not need someone else to complete you. You already do that for yourself. Right now, say, "I complete myself."

Centering Thought. Mask on first.

Affirmation. I take care of myself to
better meet life's challenges.

Love Snapshot No. 3:
Love Another Day and Be Grateful for It

Now, this may not seem likely when your heart is in shattered pieces all around you, be it from a friend, family member, or lover. In every moment of despair lies a moment of hope, especially if you come from a place of Love and faith—Love for yourself and faith in a higher power. I am genuinely and profoundly grateful for the pain I have experienced in past relationships. Would I rather not have had the pain? Well, of course, though I can put the pain to use and grow from it. My heart was broken so I could understand that Happiness is an inside job. I have learned to reframe my thinking and have become a better person for it. My pain caused me to ask:

What do I truly want both in a relationship and in life?

How am I going to get it while emotionally remaining intact?

That *what* was Happiness and the *how* was faith. Then, the real work began, figuring out what would make me Happy and how my faith could be cultivated to support this. So, take these moments of darkness and turn them into moments of lightness, self-evaluation, and personal growth. This choice is the most Loving action you can take for yourself and those around you. I am a much better daughter, sibling, friend, and co-worker for having applied just this one lesson about Love and being grateful for all my relationships.

In romantic relationships, I think there are those times when you come across that person whose energy is so intense that, without a shred of doubt, you feel that the clouds have parted, and a ray of Love's light has shone upon you two. Those times you feel so strongly that someone is meant to be in your life, they are passionately there for a bit. Then *bam*, they make an unexpected left turn without using a blinker. *Poof!* They are gone as if they were never there, and you are left utterly bewildered by what just happened. Your energetic feeling toward that person was probably right. However, they did not fully recognize it, want to develop it, or open up to the energy that was present between you. In short, they were not ready for that relationship. Their ability to see, feel, or accept it was not there, whether they say it was for emotional, geographical, financial reasons, or a combination of these.

One of the best *ah-ha* explanations I have come across on why a man decides to move away from a woman, even when he initiates interest, is what I call the "Picture Frame Theory." A guy meets a girl and says he is crazy for her, like no one before. He is saying that he likes her picture frame, what he sees. As he gets to know her, he fills in the picture frame, listening to what she has done and wants to do in life, looking at where she lives, what she drives, how she dresses, and who she associates with. Then, he makes a calculated decision as to whether he can afford her both emotionally and financially. He moves on if he feels he cannot afford her in either of these areas. When I heard this explanation from a man, I might add, it certainly gave an insight into the times a guy told me they could not give me what I wanted. A comment that always left me confused, especially when I saw some of the ladies the guys would go on to date. Not that they were horrible. They just did not appear to be a better match. However, instead of comparing yourself, ask, do you really want to be with someone who does not want to be with you? Why would you? It just hurts to keep Loving and being rejected. It is so unkind to yourself. Take this rejection as protection, let go, and move on. Use this as a sign that there is a higher power at work.

I think the Picture Frame Theory applies to any relationship. It is what we humans do. We size things up, decide whether it is suitable for us, and move on if it is not—some move on more gracefully, more kindly than others. Despite the way things go, try to find and be grateful for the lesson you received from the person who suddenly vaporized.

Centering Thought. I Love me.

Affirmation. My picture frame is
Lovingly and unapologetically me.

Love Snapshot No. 4:
Thank Your Soulmate, Even When It Hurts

"A true soulmate is probably the most important person you'll ever meet, because they tear down your walls and smack you awake."

Another Love relationship to be thankful for is the one with your soulmate. The dictionary defines a soulmate as a person ideally suited to another in temperament or strongly resembling another in attitudes or beliefs. However, author Elizabeth Gilbert offers an alternative view of soulmates in *Eat, Pray, Love*. Instead of someone similar, a perfect fit, they reflect all the ways you are putting the reins on yourself, living small, the obstacles, the addictions, the ego. Their sole purpose is to twist you up so much it forces you to have those awkward, tough Love conversations with yourself. Then, vanish. While Elizabeth feels a soulmate may be your most important relationship, thank God, they are not meant to be forever. *"Nay! Too painful."*

To Elizabeth's description, I have had two soulmates come into my life, both very painful to reconcile after they were gone. One was with a man I thought I would always be with. However, our lifestyle differences were too vast for us to stay together. His family obligations with a young child from a previous relationship kept him at home. I was the opposite, free to travel the world. After one too many times leaving on a jet plane to parts unknown, he told me he wanted to be in a relationship, and right now, he was not in one, not with me. When I protested and said I would not travel so much, he looked deep into my eyes. "Aw, honey, I can't ask you to do that. It would break your spirit." He knew me so well, and that was that.

The other was with a colleague, a fellow producer. I felt we had so much in common—the type of work we did, our love for travel, our ideas about life, and even what we ate and drank. We commiserated about the same things when we worked together. However, after about a year of hanging out, he moved on to another relationship without telling me. I found out when I saw him across a stadium arena, sitting cozily with someone else at a taping of a boxing match show for the production company we worked for. Like that, I was now in a cliché scene from a romantic comedy when the girl discovers the boy does not share her feelings about their relationship, and I was not laughing. I felt betrayed, embarrassed, and devastated by the person I thought had become my best friend and love interest. How ironic, that this scene took place at a boxing match.

Both relationships motivated me to profound inward turns as a human being. When I got on the other side of my hurt emotions, I realized their leaving was a blessing. It took them coming into my life and then going for me to work through what I wanted in a romantic partnership—that and in so many other significant areas of life. Had I stayed with either of these men, I would not have the life I do and Love so much now. I bet if you think about it, by Elizabeth's definition, you have had a soulmate or two in your life. So, if you Love your life now, thank them for tearing open the space to realize it.

> *"This is a good sign, having a broken heart.*
> *It means we have tried something."*
>
> —ELIZABETH GILBERT

Centering Thought. Thank you, goodbye.

Affirmation. Thank you for coming into my life and thank you for leaving. I have learned much.

Love Snapshot No. 5:
How Others Show Up May Be How You Show Up

"Magic mirror on the wall, who's the fairest one of all?" Okay, so you may not be like the evil witch in *Snow White*. Nevertheless, in an age of selfies and narcissistic tendencies, you might consider the person you are looking at in the mirror and what the people around you are, perhaps, reflecting back to you. What do your relationships say about you?

Seriously, contemplate how characteristics of others within your close quarters may, in some form, be showing up in you. When someone is upsetting, bugging, or frustrating you, look to see if those irritations are your traits getting mirrored back. You may not be the fairest one of all and may even be a bit of an evil queen who needs to do some cleaning up with themselves.

There is a story producer I have worked with for years. We were doing a particularly challenging show. The location was challenging. The talent was challenging. The network was challenging. The timeline was challenging, and so on down the line. I never get the easy shows. However, no matter what was going on or how crazy it was, this story producer was always kind. Every person she met, every email she signed, and every phone call was enveloped in kindness, and she always got cooperation. As I kept noticing this about her, I started to look at how I communicated with people and the reactions I was getting. I cannot say I scored as high as that story producer. She was far more patient than I was. So, I tried to emulate her, and guess what? I started seeing that people were much more receptive. I was getting back what I was putting out—this seems like a simple and obvious lesson. Yet, like myself, it is not always easily practiced for many, especially when feeling rushed and stressed. Grace under pressure is a good one to keep trying to master for everyone's sake, something I realized after standing on that mountainside I described in British Columbia, going off on my location scout. That is one part. The other is noticing when people are consistently showing up...

With inaccessible feelings,

Not fully disclosing their feelings,

Acting toward you in a way that has you feeling used,

With judgment, criticism, and lack of support,

As envious, selfish, and self-centered in a hurtful way.

Take a beat to ask yourself...

Are my feelings inaccessible?

Do I withhold my feelings?

Do I use and abuse myself? Do I do that to others?

Am I too judgmental, critical, and unsupportive of myself and others?

Am I envious?

Am I selfish and self-centered in a hurtful way to myself and others?

Chances are that the answer is a resounding "yes" to at least one of these. Those who show up in your life often reflect how you show up for yourself and others. They are a mirror for how you behave and an insight into how Loving you are to yourself.

If you view someone as critical and unforgiving, take a good look at where this exists inside you. When you search and find that part, ask if you can Love enough to forgive yourself for being critical and judgmental toward yourself. Can you forgive those around you for being critical and judgmental toward you? Once you forgive yourself and them, let all the criticism and judgment go because it is not serving you. It never did and never will. This release is essential. It is the key to self-acceptance, self-esteem, and, ultimately, self-preservation.

When I started doing this self-reflection, I also spent time looking at all my relationships. I thought long and hard about the kind of people I wanted in my life, and more importantly, those I did not because they were unhealthy for me to be around. Disconnecting from some of those relationships was a tough yet necessary choice. The company you keep affects how you Love and view yourself, which impacts your level of Happiness, and, in turn, influences how you interact with the world.

This relationship assessment includes considering your family. Think about with whom and how you define family. You may discover there are people you feel close to yet are not blood related. While you cannot choose your biological parents and siblings, you can choose whom you call family. The community around you can create a pantheon of those who will care about your Wholebeing and support your personal and professional endeavors. Love yourself enough to create your version of a nurturing family. Keep those who make you feel good and lose the rest. That does not mean you do not talk to these people if they come around. You just do not go out of your way to engage them. If you must engage them professionally, if they are related to you, you will now know how to deal with them and have boundaries. There will be a term of engagement and a value set on their words and actions.

Learn to see who you are dealing with, are they friends, family, or foes? More importantly, what are they reflecting back to you? Both are acts of self-love and self-preservation. Save yourself from the evil queens inside and around you.

Centering Thought. Show up Lovingly.

Affirmation. I Lovingly show up for myself and
others who care about me and lose the rest.

Love Snapshot No. 6:
Be Accountable in All Relationships

His eyes are vacant except for the remorse that fills them. "There comes a time when one must take responsibility for one's mistakes." The flamboyant, irreverent Captain Jack Sparrow in *Pirates of the Caribbean: Dead Man's Chest* momentarily steps out of himself to offer a bit of true insight. Cosmically. Karmically. On some level, both sides share the outcome of things. No situation is entirely your fault, nor is it solely the other person's fault. It does take two to tango, literally and figuratively. In healthy relationships, each party must own up to their transgressions and issues. However, you cannot make someone take responsibility in a given situation. You can ask, then the rest is wholly on them. More importantly, you take responsibility for your thoughts, emotions, and actions. Mind your business and leave others to mind theirs. Others have gremlins that tease and torment them, which have absolutely nothing to do with anyone else, including you. That is life. We all have gremlins to contend with. God knows I keep working through my parade of these guys. So, stop trying to take responsibility for someone else's inner work, or in some cases, excuse their bad behavior, and stick to being responsible for your inner work. You have enough of your own gremlins to deal with, let alone someone else's. This release of feeling responsible for someone else's inner work applies to colleagues, friends, siblings, parents, significant others, and even kids after coming of age to care for themselves. Their issues should not become yours, and vice-versa, I might add.

When I was still in San Francisco working as a local television station media-time buyer, I was with a guy who seemingly had everything. He was so brilliant, so beloved, and with an abundance of financial resources available to him. Yet, instead of all this being a gateway to a joyful, healthy, productive life, it was his prison. He could have been and done anything he wanted. Yet he often expressed envy that I had a job to go to every day, which at first mystified me. My yearly salary was exactly the amount he had paid for the Persian rug covering his living room floor. How did he envy me??? I was spending hundreds of thousands of dollars in the market buying media space, not making it. Eventually, it registered why he envied my workaday world. I had a reason to get up, to be someplace where I was expected to be productive. It was not about earning a paycheck. It was that I had a purpose for rising out of bed, showering, putting on a suit, and going to an office where people were accomplishing things. He did not have that in his life, and it was driving him to drink, often and heavily. Indeed, finding a sense of life meaning is often difficult at best, rooted in how you think, feel, and process your experiences, which certainly proved out with this guy.

The tipping point came the morning after an all-night drink-fest when he thought he was having a heart attack and an ambulance arrived screaming to the house for what turned out to be a panic attack. As I watched the paramedics hover over his body, I suddenly got that was it. I was done with the relationship. This guy put himself into his current position because he did not want to change his drinking habit. In fact, he did not want to stop smoking either, his other not-so-great habit. Nor find a life purpose that would give him a reason to stop drinking and smoking. Apparently, I was not enough of a motivator either. I realized then that if someone does not decide to change for themselves, no amount of crying or pleading will have an impact. The decision to change must come from within and only from there. A person cannot break a pattern if they are unwilling to do the emotional and physical work. If they do not do this, it will not happen. It is that simple, and if my boyfriend were not taking responsibility for himself, I would take it for myself.

Your spiritual growth and personal evolution come when you take responsibility for all aspects of your life—when you take the time to view the events, relationships, and circumstances that did not work, are not working. I am not talking about doing the blame game, "You did this; he did that." I am talking about viewing the events in your life from a broader perspective. This bigger picture viewpoint is for everything in life.

Where are you accountable for a particular scenario not going as hoped?

Where did you go from supporting a partner's emotional needs to becoming an enabler?

From being physically comfortable inside your body to being overweight?

From paying your bills on time to accounts getting canceled?

When you take responsibility for all that happens in your life, you are moving into a command position with empowered feelings of being in control—a much more productive place to live. So, how does this story and these questions reflect an area in life where you need to be more responsible, be it a relationship with someone else or a habit you need to change for the betterment of your Wholebeing? I hope you take Elizabeth Swann's lead and not Jack's.

> Elizabeth Swann: "There will come a time when you have a chance to do the right thing."
>
> Jack Sparrow: "I love those moments. I like to wave at them as they pass by."

Centering Thought. One hundred percent responsible.

Affirmation. My Happiness is measured by the choices I make and the responsibility I take for living a good life.

Love Snapshot No. 7: Find Time to Experience Joy and Love

The year 2000, about twenty minutes north of San Francisco: sitting in two armchairs in the middle of a room, amid bootleg Miles Davis and John Coltrane CDs, photos of a legendary music man's wife and parents, a shelf of jazz books, and a Spider-Man pinball machine are Carlos Santana and Chris Heath, a writer from *Rolling Stone* magazine. As their interview begins, Carlos takes a piece of yellow paper from his pocket and reads:

"If you carry joy in your heart, you can heal any moment. There is no person that love cannot heal; there is no soul that love cannot save."

I let these words sink in before reading the rest of the article. I think they are true and can apply to how we view each day as we live it. Yet, how often do we not even consider the joy and Love we could be experiencing in the present moment that could be easing our troubled minds and spirit?

We can find fault with and complain about so many things in life. Why is that? Why do people seem to fixate on what is wrong rather than right? Making life more complicated and miserable? It is because of something that we all possess: a "Negative Bias." It is what triggers us to fight, flight, or freeze. This bias caused our ancestors to lean toward overestimating threats and underestimating opportunities. If they did not accurately read a danger, they could have found themselves as a saber-tooth tiger's afternoon snack. Unfortunately, this autopilot reaction prevents us from Loving the moment we are experiencing.

As we evolved, one part of the brain, the limbic brain, has remained the same regarding our reactions to the people and events in our lives. We still overestimate threats and underestimate opportunities; although now, it causes us to be afraid to take risks, play it safe, and not see life's joy. We are wired to think of the worst instead of the best. Thankfully, we are not stuck here. Choices are available in how we see and respond to the world around us. One invitation is to find something to Love in the moments you live. Create a positive bias to temper the negative and do it every day.

Back in San Francisco, though a few years earlier than Carlos's interview, I was feeling like daily life was taking so much effort. I found the city cold and windy. I hated walking uphill with my arms loaded with groceries, standing in long lines at every restaurant, waiting forever for buses. I was not enjoying life in one of the most beautiful cities in the world, and that had to change. So, I started looking for at least one fun thing to do every day to help me feel better. Finding something fun did not have to be anything big. It could be as simple as walking through my favorite neighborhood and treating myself to a cafe latte afterward or making popcorn and watching a romantic comedy at home after an intense day at work. It just needed to be something that I acknowledged felt even a little fun. Soon, it made an enormous difference in how I felt about my days.

As I moved from media-time buying to television production, I went from being on staff to freelancing. This professional shift was when I realized I could choose my projects. It was liberating and scary. The liberating side of being a freelancer is also what can make you afraid, the instability of work and having enough of it to pay bills. Fear compels many in this unpredictable world to take any position, especially when faced with recessions, acts of mother nature, and global pandemics. Often people get stuck accepting jobs that leave them feeling unfulfilled, making money replacing life satisfaction. You worry that another job will not come your way if you do not take the one being offered. It can be a lot to manage emotionally, and I found myself applying the same principle of finding something fun each day to the television production jobs I took on, even at the entry level. I still do this today, find something to Love in everything I do. *Well, most everything.*

Remembering to find those one or two things you Love about whatever you are doing will fuel you to face more days with a healthy attitude than not. Life is so much better when you find something to Love. Of course, you will still have those moments when this is difficult to do, as I would later experience being responsible for shows with larger crews, budgets, and, not to leave out, egos. However, if I could pull focus on something to Love that day, slight as it might be, it made all the difference in my worldview and morale. It helped me realize the shifts I needed to make to level up the quality of my life.

Reflecting again on Carlos Santana's words, the heart healed and soul saved by Love was mine; this can be true for anyone.

Centering Thought. Love everything.

Affirmation. Everything I do has a dose of Love
added to it, making my tasks more joyful to do.

Love Snapshot No. 8:
You Can Always Choose Love

"Can we all get along? Can we stop making it horrible for the older people and the kids?" Three days into the 1992 Los Angeles riots, ignited by the acquittal of four police officers beating Rodney King within an inch of his life, King himself makes this public plea to bring peace. Twenty-eight years later, the siblings of George Floyd and Breonna Taylor, also victims of police brutality, call for the end of violent demonstrations. Their calls for peace were calls for Love, for all to come together and fix what is systemically broken in our country. These were victims of a horrific and socially unjust world. Yet they were not asking for revenge. Instead, King and the siblings of

Floyd and Taylor wanted a non-violent solution. I believe they understood that we all share an invisible bond, Love, which is the flowerbed for peace.

You can only give away what you have. What you have and what you are at your very essence is Love. This Love is always accessible, and you can choose it in any situation. This choice is true for every one of us. Just for some, their Loving essence is a bit more covered up, in fact, downright buried deep within the recesses of their being. Though it is there, it is what we are as sentient beings.

Love is the basis of every spiritual philosophy, Eastern or Western. The Bible, Torah, and Qur'an teach, "Love thy neighbor as thyself." The Dalai Lama, "My religion is kindness." These are all similar ideas. You seek to Love all of humankind, not just some of humankind.

Loving-kindness is one of the Four Immeasurables taught by the Buddha, which is to want all beings to be well and Happy. Yes, even your enemies. Hurt, anger, and frustration are really just Love gone missing. If you choose and apply Love to the areas that hurt, the pain stops. This application of Love comes in all forms. The easy ones are to Love a cooing baby, Love a mother's warmth, a father's support, a friend's kindness, a lover's kiss. Then it gets more complicated. Still Loving someone who has slept with your spouse, beaten you senseless, or killed a brother—in these instances, of course, it is unquestionably more difficult to feel, choose, and give Love, if not seemingly impossible.

When someone does something dishonorable in South Africa's Babemba tribe, everyone in the village stops what they are doing to gather around this person. Instead of accusing this person, everyone in the community recalls the good things about them. All their positive attributes and contributions throughout their lifetime are remembered. This communal recounting can go on for days. In the end, there is a celebration welcoming this person back into the fold. This act is described in Jack Kornfield's *The Art of Forgiveness, Lovingkindness, and Peace* as a forgiveness ritual. I think of it as a Loving ritual that shows we are not only our misdeeds. The sum of any person includes the good they have done that gets forgotten when one does something terrible.

The challenging times are when you need to dig deep, deep, deeper than you ever thought possible. To be clear, applying Love to a painful situation is never about condoning harmful behavior of any sort, ever. What you do is eventually recognize another person's essence, which is Love, who they are underneath all the bad stuff, the selfish, unscrupulous, unconscious behavior, which is what the Babemba tribe does. If you can find it within you to Love that universal essence that threads us together, what you are doing is remembering to Love at the level of the soul. It is the kindest, most compassionate, and ultimately healing thing you can do for your sake. Give yourself the grace for this to happen. Any situation in itself is neutral. What gives it its charge is you, and it is well within your control to affect.

When you think about it, what are you angry and struggling with? It is the physical embodiment of an action that someone has taken toward you in what they said or did to you, not their spiritual embodiment where Love still resides, the spiritual expression of Love that your enemy has forgotten, has pushed into the turmoil at the surface of their hurt, anger, frustration, or resentment.

These ideas can seem quite fantastic, especially when you are in the mix of something incomprehensible, as was the case with Rodney King. I am not saying this is easy to grasp, much less put into play. I am challenged by this time and again. You may be, too, when going through a contentious divorce, a business partner embezzling company funds, or someone stealing your idea. Yet, I know when I release feelings of anger, hurt, betrayal, or blame, when I allow Love to come in, I can breathe again. I can function in the world again. You choose, show, and give Love so you can move on with your life, no longer treading in the stagnant waters of hurt and pain. I found releasing the upset toward the guy who moved on to another relationship without telling me and replacing it with Love stopped the heartache and put things into a healthier perspective. I felt my heart turn pink again. Maybe there is an area of your life where Love is the answer. Be open to it.

Centering Thought. I choose Love.

Affirmation. I choose Love over anger and
resentment, freeing me to live joyously.

♥ ♥ ♥

Love Meditation Prayer

In the name of Love, I choose Love.

In the name of Love, I choose to Love my brothers and sisters.

In the name of Love, I choose to Love myself.

*In the name of Love, I choose to Love
that which is greater than I.*

In the name of Love, we are all one.

And so let it be.

DEVELOPING YOUR LOVING HEART

With Love, there is no darkness, only a lightness of being. It is the essence of every person. Love eases pain, trumps fear, and is always the answer. Your thoughts create a physical change in your brain, sending electrical charges that cause chemical reactions throughout its synapses, which ends up as an emotion, your feelings. So, thoughts become emotions and vice-versa. Both are energetically charged. So, Love is comprised of thoughts and feelings that create an energetic frequency.

Unconditional Love is the highest frequency of all. The more you seek this state, the more natural, the more automatic it will feel to live in the energy of Love. Thoughts infused with Love can act as a powerful energy source, capable of having a significant impact. Love in your mind creates Love in your heart. Love in your heart creates Love in your words and deeds, healing most problems. The more you live in this energetic state, the more you send out that Loving energy to others. Love expands you while its opposite contracts you. Even though we are predisposed to gravitate toward the negative side of things, we are also predisposed to positively connect with ourselves and others. Love is an essential cause of Happiness and uplifts your Wholebeing.

Journaling with Love: What Does Love Mean to You?

Now, I invite you to journal about infusing more Love into your life. I have additional reflections about Love in italics and have given you space to write yours.

How do you define Love and its benefits?

Love enables me to have healthy relationships with others and myself. It keeps me in a state of harmony, which keeps my mind-chatter in check and my heart beating to the rhythm of life. Love and faith are my two bedrocks for happiness. I feel that health, gratitude, forgiveness, peace, and ultimately abundance are built on these Happiness Essentials, which is why I put them as the first two in this book. I cannot think of anything good that happens without love and faith being part of the equation.

_____

_____

_____

What role does Love currently play in your life?

Love is an uplifter, consoler, reconciler, nurturer. It is the glue that binds me to people, places, things, events, activities, and myself.

_____

_____

_____

How great is your ability to Love?

I would like to think that I easily give love. Yet, I know that I can be icy cold and not all that empathetic when I feel irritated toward someone or righteous about my stance on an issue. In these moments, I wrestle with my ego to open my heart. Eventually I come around, accepting that others will have behaviors and points of view that will not always reconcile with mine. What is more significant is that I remember that we are all one and that I love another person despite our differences. It is not always easy to do, although I try.

How are you developing, or will you develop, more Love in your life?

Loving more is being attentive and responsive to the needs and desires of others in a way that is meaningful to them, to be less quick to judge and shut out someone for one reason or another—especially important is that I choose to be open and loving.

Take a photograph of what Love looks look like for you. Give it a caption. Then, journal about your thoughts and feelings.

I choose a path paved with love and kindness.

Journal Entry: *Every day I feel I have the choice of the path I want to walk that day. I try to choose love and kindness consciously. Admittedly, I am not always successful; many times, I fail miserably. However, the baseline intention is there. When I become aware that I am wandering and suffering in darkness, I guide myself back to the light through love and happiness.*

Love Photo Ops and Action Opportunities

Like the previous chapter, you can create or find photographs reflecting your ideas about Love using the following Photo Op prompts. The Action Opportunities help you develop Loving habits that will enhance your Happiness. You can choose one or more of these assignments and the spaces below to journal your experience. Then, for supportive encouragement, share your pictures and reflections with our *Take a Shot at Happiness* community on social media or our app.

Love Snapshot No. 1:
Embrace What Makes You Uniquely You

Photo Op. *I Realize and Accept Myself.* First, do the Action Opportunity.

One, make a collage or series of images that reflects your interests and talents. Once you choose something to focus on, go to the next step.

Two, capture images as you develop one specific interest or talent into something meaningful. Place them somewhere your progress can inspire you.

Action Opportunity. This Action Opportunity is similar to Faith Opportunity No. 3: Clarify Your Intention. However, the focus is on identifying and getting comfortable with what makes you like no other. Start with the Centering Thought: "Embrace my uniqueness."

One, make a list of all your interests and talents.

Two, pick your top ten. Out of that ten, select your top five, then the top three. Finally, the one thing that would energize and empower you.

Three, every day, do a little something to develop your interest or talent. Those small steps will become bigger and bigger and turn into something that meaningfully excites you. You can use the Affirmation: "I realize, accept, and put into action my unique talents" along with the Photo Op images to journal about your progress.

_____

_____

_____

Love Snapshot No. 2:
The Oxygen Mask Goes on You First

Photo Op. *Reservation for One, Please.* Notice and take photos of settings where you enjoy your own company: seated in a favorite chair at home, at a local cafe, a nearby park. Use them as reminders that it is okay to spend time on your own, taking care of yourself. You may even start looking forward to going to these places to sit and reflect. This can be very meditative and soothing.

Action Opportunity. Meditate on the Centering Thought: "Mask on first." Then ask if being alone is daunting to you. If yes, start by taking five or ten minutes a day to do something kind for yourself by yourself, even if it is to sip a cup of coffee while you think about some of your positive attributes. Increase this alone time as you feel more comfortable. You may find helpful the Affirmation: "I take care of myself to better meet life's challenges."

Love Snapshot No. 3:
Love Another Day and Be Grateful for It

Photo Op. *I Am Loving Me Today.* Capture images of you giving yourself big hugs. Notice how you feel and what thoughts are coming to mind.

Action Opportunity. Use the Action Opportunity to write about this experience. Consider how these moments propel you beyond your hurting heart because you are taking care of you. Start with the Centering Thought: "I Love me."

In addition to journaling about your images, look at the lesson in what hurts or confuses you. Make an effort to look at a now-defunct relationship in a more productive, confident, Loving light. When you emotionally struggle, as you will, leaning into your faith will eventually get you to the other side. Use the Affirmation "My picture frame is Lovingly and unapologetically me" to help you feel good about yourself.

_____

_____

_____

Love Snapshot No. 4:
Thank Your Soulmate, Even When It Hurts

Photo Op. *Healthy Mate.* Make a collage or series of images that reflects the things that define a healthy relationship for you. You might even consider opening a conversation about this with our *Take a Shot at Happiness* community. What defines a good relationship? When is it time to break it off?

Action Opportunity. Begin with the Centering Thought: "Thank you, goodbye." Then, look at the romantic relationships you have had and are having, the soulmates who turned your life upside down.

Besides you, what was the constant in each relationship?

Why did the relationship hit a dead end and cease to be a source of Happiness in your togetherness?

What were the consistent issues? Are these issues that you want to change? If yes, make a plan and get busy. If you do not wish to change anything, stop looking for the right partner in the wrong places. Yield to the red flags that are telling you to go no further.

Seal this reflection with the Affirmation: "Thank you for coming into my life and thank you for leaving. I have learned much."

_____

_____

_____

Love Snapshot No. 5:
How Others Show Up May Be How You Show Up

Photo Op. *Mirror, Mirror.* Capture or find images of relationships that you consider to be supportive, as well as one that is not. What are they reflecting about yourself? Do this Photo Op along with the Action Opportunity.

Action Opportunity. Call to mind the Centering Thought: "Show up Lovingly." Then, using the images from the Photo Op, start noticing how people in all parts of your life are showing up.

How are people showing up for you?

How are you showing up for them?

How do you treat others who are vying for your attention?

What personal traits do you need to adjust to attract healthier relationships into your life?

Sometimes observing someone else in your sphere can help you see things about yourself that could use an adjustment, as I saw through my observation of the story producer working on my show. It could also show you who is not emotionally healthy to be around. This noticing requires complete honesty with yourself. Use the Affirmation "I Lovingly show up for myself and others who care about me and lose the rest" to nurture yourself.

_____

_____

_____

Love Snapshot No. 6:
Be Accountable in All Relationships

Photo Op. *Taking Responsibility.* This Photo Op is done along with the Action Opportunity. As you work through the list of steps you are taking to turn around an unsatisfactory situation, capture an image representing how you feel each time you succeed at taking responsibility for your life.

Action Opportunity. Look at one situation that you view as subpar. Consider where and how you played a role in creating that situation. What decisions did you make or not make that landed you where you are today? Objectively do this assignment without judgment, a story, or justifications. This questioning is a mindful exploration, not a beat up on yourself exercise. Start with the Centering Thought: "One hundred percent responsible."

Next, list all the actions you can do to turn things around, steps both small and big. Then choose one you can do today. Tomorrow, pick another. Keep working your way through your list. Each time you complete one of the action steps, celebrate and capture the moment with a photo. The Affirmation "My Happiness is measured by the choices I make and the responsibility I take for living a good life" will support you.

Love Snapshot No. 7:
Find Time to Experience Joy and Love

Photo Op. *See the Joy around You.* Take a daily photo of something that makes you Happy. Write a caption for it. Notice how it makes you feel. This practice is one that can live far beyond the pages of this book.

Action Opportunity. Start with the Centering Thought: "Love everything." Then, every day, try to find at least one experience, one thing, and acknowledge it as enjoyable or something you Love. It can be as simple as stopping to savor the warm end-of-the-day sun on the sidewalk in front of you. It will make a difference. As you do this Action Opportunity, seal the moment with the Affirmation: "Everything I do has a dose of Love added to it, making my tasks more joyful to do."

Love Snapshot No. 8:
You Can Always Choose Love

Photo Op. *Love You, Love Me.* Make a collage or series of hearts in every size, shape, and form you come across. Someone wearing a heart on a t-shirt, an image of the world shaped like a heart, a cloud that looks heart shaped. Do this Photo Op alongside the Action Opportunity.

Action Opportunity. Begin by recalling the Centering Thought, "I choose Love," and consider Love across all areas of your life by doing a Loving-Kindness meditation. This meditation may not heal all your hurt and pain, though it is a place to start.

Sit or lie down and close your eyes.

Silently, think of someone you Love and say, "May you be well, may you be happy."

Next, think of someone you are struggling with and say, "May they be well, may they be happy."

Think of someone who may be struggling with you, and say, "May they be well, may they be happy."

Now say for yourself, "May I be well, may I be happy."

Think of all the people around you, and say, "May all people be well, may all people be happy."

Think of the whole world, all beings, and say, "May all beings be well, may all beings be happy. Just as I, too, wish, may we all be safe, healthy, and live with ease and happiness."

Close with the Affirmation: "I choose Love over anger and resentment, freeing me to live joyously."

Then, journal about the images you captured. How meaningful are the hearts you find?

_____

_____

_____

PICTURING HEALTH (MIND, BODY, AND SPIRIT)

Health

\'helth\ also \'heltth\

noun, often attributive

   : the condition of being well or free from disease

   : the overall condition of someone's body or mind

   : the condition or state of something

♥ ♥ ♥

"You are never too old to set another
goal or to dream a new dream."

—LES BROWN
Motivational Speaker

SNAPSHOT OF HEALTH

In My Viewfinder

I was once developing a show around a team of doctors who would fly their private jet into small rural areas in Central Nebraska. The reason was to bring patient care to people who would otherwise drive great distances to get medical help. Over time, they noticed that many of these people would get better more quickly than those suffering the same injuries, the same sickness, and the same treatments while living in urban areas. They attributed this largely to the fact that their loved ones surrounded them. They were part of a community that cared for them while sick instead of being isolated in a sterile, unfriendly city hospital room. The doctors thought the other part of their speedier recovery was that despite some hard living, these people were physically better equipped to heal. Their bodies were stronger from the manual work they did every day, compared to their urban counterparts who sat behind desks throughout the week. The last part of this story is that they knew that if they were not Healthy and back home, tending to their farms and stores, nothing was getting done. That meant no income.

So many of these folks in Central Nebraska, possibly unknowingly, were taking care of their Health in a three-dimensional way. How? By focusing on what was essential to their survival, working their bodies daily, and caring for each other. Of course, this is a very broad brushstroke. I am using this example to convey that good Health revolves around three fundamental concepts:

Take care of where you focus your mind.

Mind what you do with your body.

Have the comfort of knowing that someone or something is supporting you.

Truly, the best Health insurance, the best investment that anyone can make, is the one that involves you taking care of yourself in a three-dimensional way—mind, body, and spirit—instead of spending your money on medical care, doctors, and hospitals. If you do not take the time to be Healthy, you will be forced to take the time to be sick, and by then it could very well be too late. If you are sick, really ill, all the money, all the privilege, all the objects of desire mean nothing, a big zero. You are of no use to yourself or anyone. Being Healthy should be a critical focal point in your *Take a Shot at Happiness* journey. From good Health comes the physical and mental ability to do everything else, including managing one's life well, having a sustainable work-to-play ratio, and tending to relationships between family, friends, and self.

This means you are not spinning all the plates simultaneously. That is too exhausting. Instead, you make wise and measured assessments of when and where you need to give attention and extra focus to your life. Maybe you need to emphasize more on your family because one of the kids is struggling in school. Perhaps you need to give more effort to your career to make a deadline. Maybe you must devote more time to exercise because you have been in the work tunnel making that deadline. You put your point of focus on the area of life that needs particular attention for a time. It should be an amount of time that does not throw the rest of your life so out of whack you can barely recognize it as yours, putting you into a state of overwhelm—not the place you want to be for extended periods. Chronically being overwhelmed leads to chronic stress. Chronic stress leads to sickness. If you fall sick, one of the best sources of healing comes from having a loving support system of family and friends, like the folks in Central Nebraska.

Snapshots on Developing Your Mind, Body, and Spirit

Health Snapshot No. 1:
Think Healthy Thoughts

"You are not your thoughts." I promise this is true, unless you choose to believe them.

If you meditate and practice Mindfulness, you have often come across this statement. While it can be challenging to wrap your head around this concept initially, it is valuable to understand.

So, what does this statement actually suggest? It sounds good and even hopeful in some instances. You mean I am not a frustrated driver on the 405 Freeway in Los Angeles who wishes for a James Bond car that can spit bullets at the vehicle that just cut me off?! I am not a sad girl because another guy said he could not give me what I want, *whatever that means???* I am not a disappointed producer feeling slighted that another producer got the show I wanted? That would be fantastic. Yet, my reality does not feel this way, and if I am not my thoughts, then who am I...really? The answer is complicated because you feel so connected to your thoughts, which create your emotions. The images in your head seem very real. Your thoughts create your perceived reality and felt senses in the body.

However, consider how would it be possible to be something that is impermanent? You can feel frustrated. You can feel hurt. You can feel angry. All these feelings eventually go away, especially if you acknowledge, accept, and constructively manage them, and the sooner you do, the better. Who you are, and only are at your essence, is love. Remember Love Snapshot No. 8: You Can Always Choose Love? Love is always there, even when you cannot see or feel it.

Thoughts and emotions are like passing clouds against a blue sky. Some days you have dark foreboding clouds that can block out the blue sky: your unhappy thoughts. On other days you have white puffy clouds that dot a blue sky: your Happy thoughts. Either way, there is always a blue sky behind the clouds. So, thoughts do not have to mean anything significant or defining about you. What gets in the way is your natural tendency toward a Negative Bias that holds your mind, intellect, and ego tightly to limiting thoughts, affecting how you feel and see the world. Then, add that your negative thought patterns may be so habitual that you are not even conscious of how often, how automatically, you choose the negative over the positive. Pay attention to your thinking. Become aware of being aware.

Another way to view thoughts is as trains. You can choose to ride them, or not. If you do hop on a thought train, you can also choose when to get off. Learn to reframe the thoughts that are not serving you well to those that do by being curious about your reactions to thoughts versus the thoughts themselves.

What felt sensations in your body and outward behavior are your thoughts motivating, and is that okay?

Part of the difficulty of viewing your thoughts, meaning yourself, comes from the way you phrase your self-talk.

"I am mad."

"I am unlovable."

"I am not good enough."

When you say or think "I am," followed by a negative description of yourself, your subconscious considers it true. It is important to praise instead of criticize yourself at all times; be kind and gentle. Knocking yourself locks into your brain a negative pattern that will not serve you. If you consciously separate yourself to become the observer of this negative self-talk, you will probably find that your statement is not valid. You understand that your ego is talking in the form of a limiting belief instead of the real boundless you.

Negative messaging, when left unchecked, will cause you to start breaking down after a while, maybe even years of being in a constant state of unconscious high alert. Long ago, I bought into the belief that most diseases begin in your head, how you think, and your perception of the world. It is critical to your Wholebeing that you remove the mental and emotional energy that prevents you from living vibrantly. Your mind and body get tired of being battered around, sending out distress signals that cause your fight, flight, or freeze mode to be permanently switched on. Eventually, it can manifest into illness, from a mild cold to the advanced stages of cancer.

Disease, *dis*–ease, is your mind not at ease. When your mind is not at ease, guess who becomes sick? Think about some of the following illnesses and ailments and how they may relate to you or someone you know.

Cancer could stem from deeply held resentment, the pain eating away at the body. A few research findings suggest a link between suppressed anger and breast cancer, in particular.

Lower back problems may come from worries over money, or from feeling unsupported financially.

Stomach issues may result from feeling dread, or the fear of something new.

You can help counter some of these diseases, ward them off, or in some cases, reverse them altogether, by getting into the practice of observing your thoughts and reframing the negative ones into constructive ones. Scores of doctors, health practitioners, contemplatives, and first-hand witnesses endorse the power of the mind's ability to heal itself. I watched my mother do this to overcome ovarian cancer.

When they put my mom on the operating table and opened her up, she was already at an advanced stage of cancer. The surgeon kept her for three hours, losing a lot of blood. I arrived at the Cleveland Clinic from Los Angeles the day after her surgery. When I walked into the hospital room, there she sat next to her bed instead of in it. She never once asked for pain medication when she was in the hospital. What was an angry red, rope-sized incision that ran from her navel to her pubic bone eventually became a barely perceptible thin pink seam. With ease, she made her fifth cancer-free anniversary. The doctors claimed her recovery was miraculous.

During that period, I often saw my mom reading passages from a book by New Thought minister Dr. Joseph Murphy, *The Power of Your Subconscious Mind*. I know she applied his positive thinking principles and prayer to beat cancer. I am convinced that doing these two things was a significant part of what pulled her through. Witnessing my mom's recovery from cancer taught me a profound lesson about the power of observing your thoughts, faith, and what goes on in the subconscious. Whether you are religious, spiritual, atheist, or agnostic, faith can play a role in healing. The power of your subconscious to affect outcomes in life is proportional to your belief, your faith; the quality of your thoughts matter. You can change your limiting thoughts. When you obsess about the past or worry about the future, shift your focus to what is going on now and what is right about it.

Often when I notice I am having thoughts I do not want, I interrupt them by clapping my hands once and saying, "Stop it!" out loud if I am alone, silently if not. This way of interrupting thoughts is called "Thought-Stopping." What you are doing is literally startling yourself out of your negative thinking to shift your thoughts onto something different that constructively serves you. I will often put my mind on something else, like the movie I am looking forward to seeing.

Even though being present and aware of your thoughts takes vigilance, it will become your habit, like how you automatically do a specific sequence of actions when driving a car: start the car, check your mirrors for other vehicles or people, put your car in gear, foot on the gas, and go. When unproductive thoughts come, you automatically hit the brakes.

Centering Thought. Think constructively.

Affirmation. I am the observer and choice-maker of
my thoughts and I choose to be loving toward myself.

Health Snapshot No. 2:
Mind Your Environment

At the time, Christina Pascucci was a reporter and anchor for the independent news station in Los Angeles, KTLA. She went out in the trenches every day, often posting her thoughts about news reporting on social media. One post in particular got to the heart of what I am talking about here.

"It's been a really intense week. I covered a lot of death. I hugged sobbing family members of fallen police officers, saw footage of two women's bodies after they were killed in a street takeover, went to knock on a door of a shooting suspect and realized I was standing on his trail of blood. And yesterday, I spent the day covering the Capitol riot hearing which was draining in a 'worried about the future of my country' kinda way. Today, I covered former President Trump's first public response to it all. It's. So. Much. News peeps, I hope you are looking out for yourselves, your minds. We take in a lot. Take care of yourself."

Christina is right. We do take in a lot, perhaps not to this extent, though the bombardment of information and people we are regularly exposed to can be taxing, and we do not always realize it. This conversation is another shade of "think Healthy thoughts." Here, the focus is on becoming aware of the messaging in your environment and how you internalize it. Do you modulate the barrage of news, information, and marketing on all your internet devices, television, and radio?

We spend about a third of our waking lives across various internet-powered devices. Our global internet consumption hit five billion users in April of 2022, almost two-thirds of the world's population. Of this number, four billion seven hundred thousand were social media users, spending an average of 147 minutes daily on their devices. That is a lot of information consumed throughout the day, and the type of content directly impacts you.

Think about your people consumption as well. Who is around you? To what kind of conversations are you exposing yourself? How often do you allow the peace of a moment to be overtaken by someone else's drama? If you are sitting in a restaurant overhearing someone at a table complaining endlessly, do you move to another table?

Now, add in the presence and awareness of your thoughts. The two operative words here are *presence*, as in being present, and *awareness*, as in being aware of your consciousness. In several articles, Stanford Professor Fred Luskin is credited with publishing research showing the average person having more than sixty thousand thoughts per day. Eighty percent are negative, of which 90 to 95 percent are repeated from one day to the next. However, a new study from Queen's University in Canada several years later showed this number to be much lower, around 6,200 thoughts per day, by developing a way to detect when one thought starts and stops, called "Thought Worms." Regardless of which research number you accept, every facet of life shapes your thoughts. The news media you take in, the content of the films and television you watch, the books you read, the types of conversations you allow yourself to engage in, everything you absorb, and how much of it, matters a lot. The list just mentioned creates your environment and informs your beliefs. The brain changes through our experiences. How you mind your outer world will influence how you care for your inner world and vice-versa. Both influence what the Buddha, Gandhi, and the Bible refer to in their wisdom about creating a Happier life—the how and where you focus your thoughts matters.

> Buddha: "Our thoughts shape us; we become what we think. When the mind is pure, joy follows like a shadow that never leaves."

> Gandhi: "Your beliefs become your thoughts. Your thoughts become your words. Your words become your actions. Your actions become your habits. Your habits become your values. Your values become your destiny."

> Proverbs 23:7 (NKJV): "For as he thinks in his heart, so is he."

Centering Thought. Mind my environment.

Affirmation. I control my environment.
It does not control me.

Health Snapshot No. 3:
Eat Clean and Mindfully

"Your body is not a temple. It's an amusement park. Enjoy the ride," a cavalier statement from the late chef and travel documentarian Anthony Bourdain, and *ah, wrong* partial answer, sir.

Your body is the temple of your Wholebeing. It will take care of you if you take care of it, starting with what you put into it. Then, you can enjoy the ride. Sounds obvious enough, though obesity is considered an epidemic in most parts of the world, including the United States, where 36.2 percent of the population was labeled as obese in 2022. Even if you are not obese, carrying excessive body fat affects almost every aspect of your Health, including your memory and mood. Think being at greater risk for type 2 diabetes, heart disease, high blood pressure, arthritis, sleep apnea, cancer, and strokes—all potentially preventable Health issues. So, not only are we impacted by what and how we manage our thoughts, we are also affected by what we eat.

Here I give a lot of credit to my Greek mother, who instilled Healthy eating early on in life. Many of her dishes use simple ingredients. Often, they included olive oil, lemon, oregano, salt, and pepper. Long before it became a mainstream conversation, she fed us fresh fruits and vegetables, lots of fish, whole wheat bread, 2 percent milk, and used honey instead of refined sugar. Rarely were there soft drinks and potato chips in our home, and she fried very few foods. This diet is essentially an anti-inflammatory one: little to no refined carbohydrates, fried foods, sugar-sweetened beverages, red meat, or margarine. And why do we care about this? Like excess weight, inflammation of your body, when left unchecked, can lead to a host of diseases you do not want, including the ones already listed, as well as depression and Alzheimer's.

There are many diets to choose from, the vegetarian diet, the Mediterranean diet, Ayurvedic, intermittent fasting, keto, paleo, and the list goes on, each with its pros and cons. The first thing to consider is what your body's needs are and then determine which diet to follow. Some diets are geared toward general Health; others are for specific issues, controlling heart disease, cholesterol, diabetes, hypertension, or weight loss.

Reading across different diets and hearing what various nutritionists say, you will be okay in most cases if you follow some basic guidelines.

Eat as close to a clean source as possible, meaning unprocessed, fresh, organic, wild-caught, or free-range foods. As much as possible, avoid anything in a box or fried, fatty or processed meats, creamy sauces, processed sugar, and soft drinks. Follow my mom's advice to eat fruits and vegetables in all colors of the rainbow throughout the day. Using alternative medicine advocate Dr. Andrew Weil's anti-inflammatory diet as inspiration, meals are ideally based around these:

Legumes, beans, al dente pasta, and whole or cracked grains.
If you are an omnivore, favor fish and poultry over red meat and pork.

Include edamame, tofu, tempeh, soy nuts, soy milk, and lots of cooked Asian mushrooms.

For cooking, either grill, bake, broil, steam, or sauté your food items.

Use vinaigrettes, lemon, and olive oil.

Have eggs and dairy in moderation.

Red wine, coffee, and tea are also okay in moderation. Herbal teas are good.

Water is vital. Drink lots of it.

You can get a blood test to determine precisely the vitamins and supplements you need and in what amounts, although do not rely on them as your primary nutritional source. Vitamins and supplements are not replacements for a Healthy diet. They augment it.

How and when you eat is important too. Mealtimes are best when they are just that. No phones. No television. You are not reading the newspaper. You are not sitting at your desk working. Nor are you in a heated debate with someone. Instead, you are present to your meal, enjoying the taste of each bite, *slowly breathing in*, allowing your body to relax as you mindfully chew, then slowly *breathing out*. This quiet eating time practice helps with the digestion of food. That said, I confess to enjoying listening to talks or watching a favorite show when I cook dinner and eat alone.

There are also various theories on when you eat. I think much of that has to do with your culture. Europeans tend to eat a later, lighter dinner. If you are from the subcontinent of India, many prescribe a window of time to eat, usually with your last meal around 6 p.m. Many Americans often skip breakfast and have a big lunch, though breakfast helps set up your body for the day. You are less likely to eat larger meals later because you become too hungry. Overly big meals can trigger a rush in blood sugar; doing this too often can lead to an increased risk of high blood pressure, high cholesterol levels, heart disease, diabetes, and obesity.

The afternoon is a good time for a large meal. It fuels the body for the rest of the day when you still may need a lot of energy.

Ideally, evenings are your lightest meal of the day, eaten about three hours before bed. A meal too close to lights out can make falling asleep difficult because of the blood sugar and insulin injection you are getting from whatever you are eating. Plus, you are storing fat instead of burning it off.

Two big notes before leaving this section: seriously knock off eating processed meat and sugar. No good will come of it.

For those who enjoy eating meats that are smoked, cured, salted, or chemically preserved, the World Cancer Research Fund has found strong links between processed meats and colon and rectum cancers. Enough said.

Excessive sugar intake not only causes tooth decay, you also risk a greater likelihood of obesity, inflammation, type 2 diabetes, heart disease, liver disease, cancer, dementia, and depression. The upside of not eating processed sugar is how you feel and look. When I stopped eating almost all processed sugar, it changed my body shape. I looked slenderer and no longer got sugar hangovers from eating too much of it.

If it helps, as a general guide, focus your shopping on the store's perimeter when you are at the grocery store. That is where fresh produce, meats, and fish are most often found, with the bulk of boxed and processed foods you want to stay away from in the center aisles.

Bottom line, you become what you think and eat. So, think and eat well, and you will be well.

Centering Thought. Eat well, live well.

Affirmation. My body is my temple, and
I honor it with nourishing foods.

Health Snapshot No. 4:
Drink Lots of the Elixir of Life

"Water is precious. Sometimes may be more precious than gold," utters Howard in *The Treasure of Sierra Madre* film classic, and so does a ton of research about the benefits of staying hydrated.

Animals need it. Flowers need it. Trees need it. Our planet is it. Seventy-five percent of the Earth's surface is covered in water. If you want a miracle elixir that gives life, water is it. Your body is 60 percent water for men and 55 percent for women, which needs to be replenished to help eliminate toxins and waste when you sweat or go to the bathroom. It flushes bacteria from your bladder. Water helps keep the balance of your body fluids and your temperature regular. It improves circulation and blood flow. It prevents muscle cramping, lubricates and cushions joints, and protects sensitive tissues. Water keeps your heart pumping blood and normalizes blood pressure. It aids in digestion and prevents constipation. It transmits oxygen to your cells, enhancing your energy level. So, if you are feeling tired, drink some water. Plus, water keeps your skin more radiant by plumping up the skin cells and reducing fine lines and wrinkles. If nothing else, drink water so you maintain your youthful good looks.

Water also aids in managing your stress levels by keeping your brain tissue, which is 73 percent water, hydrated. Your brain function begins to suffer from dehydration, affecting mood, concentration, reaction time, and memory—another compelling reason to keep sipping this magical elixir.

How much you need to drink depends on your size, age, diet, health, weather, level of activity, and where you live. You will need more water during warmer times of the year or in hotter climates, if you are at a high altitude in the mountains, flying, or exercising heavily.

As we age, our body's fluid reserve reduces, and so does our ability to conserve water and sense thirst, making paying attention to your water consumption even more important.

Harvard Health claims four to six (eight-ounce) cups are good for generally Healthy people, yet that will vary if you sweat a lot, are exercising, or if the temperature is hot. Then, you may need two or three cups of water per hour. However, the US National Academies of Sciences, Engineering, and Medicine ups the daily amount to 11.5 cups for women and 15.5 for men, quite a big difference. I think the easiest guide is to look at the color of your urine. If it is a pale yellow and odorless, you are doing well.

If you are wondering, it is possible to drink too much water, especially when taking medications that make you retain water, or when you have health issues with the thyroid, kidneys, liver, or heart. So, be attentive to the color of your urine and consult your healthcare advisor.

All this said, many find getting enough water a challenge and helpful to know that it is not just water that keeps you hydrated. Any beverage containing water helps in daily water consumption. Even caffeinated beverages and alcohol can be part of a net positive contribution to the day's total fluid consumption, although caffeine can make you jittery and keep you up at night, and alcohol should be limited to one or two daily drinks. Several studies show that red wine is rich in antioxidants and that drinking in moderation can help fight inflammation and lower the risks of heart disease, autoimmune disorders, or certain cancers. You can also eat water-rich foods. Here are some simple ways to create a water drinking habit:

Sip water throughout the day. It can help to use an eco-friendly straw.
Flavor your water with oranges, lemons, cucumbers, or berries.
Carry a water bottle with you.
Eat apples, melons, peaches, cucumbers, celery, tomatoes, lettuce, zucchini, and watercress.
Attach drinking water to a routine: every time you eat a meal, when you get up in the morning, take vitamin supplements and medication, brush your teeth, or use the bathroom.

So, when you feel thirsty, reach for the life-giving elixir that is more precious than gold.

Centering Thought. Water is life.

Affirmation. Water, the elixir of life,
nourishes and replenishes me.

Health Snapshot No. 5:
Get Up and Move Every Day

"I hated every minute of training, but I said, 'Don't quit. Suffer now and live the rest of your life as a champion.'"

The addendum I would make to the greatest heavyweight boxer Muhammad Ali's pearl on living life like a champ is that physical training never ends. We all know that exercising is a Healthy choice. Whether you adhere to any regular activity or regimen is another story. Unfortunately, many do not, and it costs us individually and collectively. Health-care estimates in

2013 suggested the price tag for individuals not getting at least 150 minutes of moderate-intensity physical activity per week (exercises that get your heart rate up 50 to 60 percent higher than when at rest) burdened our global health care systems by $53.8 billion, making physical inactivity one of the world's major non-communicable diseases and the fourth leading cause of death. Shocking, right?

Studies show that adults typically sit for nine to ten hours a day. One of the many reasons you do not want to sit for hours on end without offsetting it with physical activity is that it is linked with the risk of depression, a mental affliction often headlined during the Covid pandemic, undoubtedly fueled by far too much time in isolation sitting in front of computers and too little time moving our bodies. How much time sitting is too much has yet to be determined, although a meta-analysis of research data reveals one's sitting time to health risk tipping point could be around seven hours.

An extensive study of over one million individuals showed a significant connection between daily sitting time and the risk of death caused by any disease in adults with low or moderate physical activity levels. What can you do to offset this? Sixty to seventy minutes of daily moderate to vigorous-intensity activity: exercises that get your heart rate higher than 60 percent of its resting rate.

Other benefits of daily exercise are the endorphin *feel-good* hormones that reduce one's pain perception, increase positivity, and create a greater sense of Wholebeing. Seeing yourself improve and get stronger and faster gives you a sense of self-worth. It also gives you a pause during a stressful day, a distraction from worries and hamster-wheel thinking, helping to relieve some of the anxiety. You just feel more in control.

Research supports that exercise is critical to maintaining brain Health and preserving your cognitive performance as you age, particularly in the hippocampus, associated with memory and learning. It boosts mental functions by improving blood flow and reducing inflammation in the brain. You feel more productive when you feel physically good and perform mentally well. Feeling productive gives a sense of meaning and purpose, helping you live longer, more vibrantly, and with less risk of debilitating diseases like diabetes, cancer, obesity, or heart disease. Your bones, joints, and muscles are

Healthier. Exercise can help lower cholesterol and blood pressure. All pretty compelling reasons to get your body moving.

Although, as with nutrition, there are a lot of prescriptions for exercising based on averages. The question is, what is average? Is it average for your age? Average for your weight? Average for your environment? Average for your body type? My suggestion is to find the physical activities you enjoy most and consistently do them, be it hiking, biking, yoga, dancing, surfing, or whatever gets you to move your body. You are more likely to be motivated to keep doing whatever gives you pleasure instead of forcing something you do not look forward to doing. We do things we enjoy and avoid what we do not.

Throughout the week, include activities to improve and maintain your endurance, strength, flexibility, and balance.

Jogging, biking, and swimming are aerobic endurance activities that increase your heart rate and breathing, improving the Health of your heart, lungs, and circulatory system.

Lifting weights, doing wall push-ups, using resistance bands, and even carrying kids strengthens your muscles and improves your balance, which will keep you climbing stairs and getting up from chairs well into more mature decades.

Balance exercises could save you from bad falls that would impact the quality of your life, so try standing on one foot, walking heel to toe, or repeatedly standing up from a seated chair.

Finally, stretching improves your flexibility, so you will always be able to do things like bending over to tie your shoe or looking over your shoulder. Sounds simple until they become more difficult over time.

On the days you cannot get a workout at a gym, go to a dance studio, or hike around some foothills, you can still get some exercise. Help your cause by parking your car further away so you walk a bit. Work your arms by carrying your groceries. Try for ten-minute walks three times throughout the day. Build your legs by taking the stairs instead of an elevator.

Once, when I was doing a demanding series on location, I could not get to a gym for months. To intentionally get exercise, I walked whenever

I could, to meetings outside the office or restaurants. Also, I lived on the fifteenth floor of my temporary home. Rarely would I ever take the elevator. Can I tell you how strong my legs and lung capacity became? This brings me to your breath—pay attention to it.

Your breath will tell you a lot about your emotional state. Fast and shallow usually means you are anxious or excited. Long and deep usually means you are calm. Try to live in the latter breath. It will help keep your mind and body in relaxed alertness by releasing tension throughout your body, making you more effective at responding to life as it happens. There are many breath practices, though my go-to when I feel anxiety rising is the "Ocean Breath" or "Ujjayi Breath" for the yogis out there. It is simple and can be done anywhere, anytime.

Close your mouth to breathe in and out of your nose. Slightly constrict your throat muscles, which causes an ocean wave-like sound when you breathe out. This breath activates the parasympathetic nervous system that triggers your mind and body to relax, helping you focus and concentrate better.

Another part of the body you may not have considered exercising is your eyes. While there is inconclusive evidence that this will help improve vision, it can do a lot for eye strain, especially after looking at a screen most of the day. Two practices I have consistently seen written up on medical websites and practice myself are:

"The 20-20-20 Rule." When you are doing close-focused work, every twenty minutes, stop to look twenty feet in front of you for twenty seconds. The practice can significantly reduce eye strain and help with watering or dry eyes and blurred vision. Some studies also show that it relaxes the eye's focusing muscles.

"Palming." This practice also helps relax the eyes. Cup your hands and place each one over an eye. Allow everything to go completely dark. Stay there for at least thirty seconds. I like to rub my hands together to create warmth, then cover my eyes. I will often rest here for about three minutes.

You exercise to improve and keep the quality of your life, so you can always live like a champ.

Centering Thought. Think Wholebeing Health.

Affirmation. I am good to my mind, body,
and spirit, and they are good to me.

Health Snapshot No. 6:
Take Time Out to Rest and Recover

Honor sleep. Honor rest. Honor time off.

The United States is a country of workaholics; however, this mindset shifted some during and after the Covid pandemic. Still, this point is where the rest of the world has it on us—well, at least the Europeans. They work to live versus the average American who lives to work. Americans work more than any other industrialized nation. We work longer days, vacation less, and retire later. Many feel there are complaining bragging rights, saying they have not had a holiday in two, three, four years. This vacation deficit is not something to brag about; it just tells people you do not know how to draw work boundaries. More, as in more hours at work, does not equate to better. Instead you are putting yourself in the crosshairs of major burnout. You need time to rest, reflect, and renew. All these are critical to your ability as a decision-maker.

It is not about the hours you put in; it is about the value you put out to be the best version of yourself. You want to be Healthy, and that includes the quality of your thoughts, the fitness of your body, and the harmony of your feelings. When you are at your best, you are more focused, think more creatively, make clearer decisions, and lead more effectively. However, this does not happen unless you take time out, pause during the day, get enough sleep at night, and take vacations.

For those in a constant state of sleep deprivation, you are stressing out your body. Looking at various lists of torture techniques used worldwide, you will see sleep deprivation is consistently near the top. That should be evidence enough of the importance of rest. Studies show that you need seven to nine hours of sleep each night.

The importance of getting enough sleep became crystal clear during my years as a supervising producer on *Survivor*. The type of television production I do is physically and emotionally grueling. During the seasons I was on *Survivor*, I worked crazy long days. I would stand on the beach for hours, watching the contestants. Conduct interviews. Direct the camera teams on what stories to follow. Call in the helicopter when I wanted aerials of the camp. Make sure everyone on the crew got their break. I had an earpiece in my right ear to hear an audio feed of what the contestants were saying—another one in my left ear to listen and relay information to production. There was usually someone standing in front of me, asking questions. A lot of chatter was funneled directly, nonstop, into my head, all day long. Add the sweltering heat, the torrential rain we were working in every day, and the bugs! I was exhausted by the end of the day. What I learned during that time was the importance of honoring sleep. I needed seven hours, maybe six, of sleep to function.

Many studies and productivity coaches suggest that you will operate best when you move between periods of focused activity and rest instead of going in for long work sessions. Alternating between *work, rest, work, rest* helps you stay more alert and emotionally buoyant. Plus, there is something psychological about accomplishing massive projects in bite-sized chunks, particularly challenging ones. It makes its completion seem less daunting and far more doable.

Success mentor Darren Hardy speaks a lot about doing focused work for ninety minutes in "Jam Sessions" inspired by the athletes who do interval training—this means doing an intense period of work, followed by a recovery period. The suggestion is to go at it for ninety minutes, then take a ten to thirty-minute break.

Why ninety minutes? After that you become less efficient and tend to make more mistakes. Therefore, you need regular breaks to remain at your peak performance level.

Also, your body tends to cycle in ninety-minute waves. After one of these cycles, you tend to get fidgety, lose concentration, or feel sleepy. When you push through this fatigue to keep working and do this regularly, your body starts to defend itself by shifting into its fight, flight, or freeze mode, releasing stress hormones that cause you to become more reactive and less effective. As a result, it impairs your ability to see the bigger picture. Do this long enough and you will shut down.

The invitation is to figure out a way to manage your work life and stress instead of it managing you. There will always be a pressing matter to handle. There will always be another email to write, phone call to make, and item to tick off your never-ending checklist. You need to rest and recover to keep showing up as the best version of yourself—to be more effective and creative. Throughout history and today, even the famous have taken time out during their days. Many were big nappers. Aristotle, Leonardo da Vinci, Albert Einstein, Margaret Thatcher, Jacques Chirac, Chris Martin, Lady Gaga, Benedict Cumberbatch—look where having intentional rest periods got them. So, make it a priority to hit the pause button during the day. Make it a priority to get the hours you need at night.

As a little incentive to get those necessary hours of sleep, use a good night's rest for problem-solving by setting "Bedtime Intentions"; this is a technique I learned while studying spiritual psychology with Drs. Ron and Mary Hulnick. Before going to sleep, think about the things from the day you are grateful for and say "thank you." Then, ask your higher power to clear any negative charges or thoughts by offering to see things differently—all judgments, misperceptions, and misunderstandings. Close with a request for guidance in whatever you are working on or trying to manifest. Ask that it comes in a way you will clearly understand and that whatever it is you do is for the highest good. Spiritually, you surrender to your higher power, and it goes to work as you rest.

While writing this section, I did an internet search about the subconscious mind, the unconscious, while sleeping, for those wanting something more concrete. About 4,970,000 results came up about this topic, and I learned that your subconscious mind commands your conscious mind. Some write that it is thirty thousand times more powerful than your conscious mind. New science developmental biologist Dr. Bruce Lipton claims your subconscious determines 95 percent of your actions. Whether or not these numbers are accurate, the takeaway is that your subconscious mind runs your emotions, hopes, and desires based on your worldview and the actions you have taken in the past. So, when you ask for guidance to achieve what you want before sleeping, it triggers your subconscious to work unfettered by the conscious mind critically judging what you should and should not be doing. It allows the subconscious to shift the thoughts to drive actions that can help to resolve issues, and it is why you often wake up the following day with the solution to a problem. So, the next time you say, "I'll sleep on it," know this is productive time.

Whether you take a physical or spiritual perspective, calling for your mind to quiet before you close your eyes at night works. Protect and honor your sleep, like you protect and honor the people you love most, including yourself.

Centering Thought. Rest to recover.

Affirmation. Every pause helps me return
refreshed, renewed, and better than ever.

Health Snapshot No. 7:
Intentionally Open and Close Your Day

Store sign: "Closed for the day. I need a break and a martini."

Intentionally open and close your day to regulate the overwhelm you can experience because you are always on and available. We are so connected by technology that if we allow it, we can easily be open for business 24/7. Physically and emotionally, it helps to create boundaries around your availability and accessibility. These boundaries will give your body and mind the time we just talked about to recharge. As a result, you will make wiser, more thoughtful decisions, and be a better leader in life overall.

Having clear "on" and "off" times also serves relationships. The Academy of Management in New York, running a study of 142 couples, found that being expected to respond to emails during non-working hours often leads to dissatisfaction and conflicts in relationships. Not a hard conclusion to believe. Think about all the times you have been annoyed by friends and family always seeming more interested in an email or social media post on their phone instead of the conversation they could be having with you.

Or is it the other way around? Are you the culprit, not keeping clear boundaries between available and unavailable? What is it costing you? Researchers at Charlotte's University of North Carolina found that those in relationships with workaholics are twice as likely to get divorced.

When you are accessible all the time, even if it is because you are trying to survive, putting bread on the table, and keeping a roof over your head, there is still an opportunity cost to your personal life. If you genuinely care about yourself and your relationships, you will make it a priority and set boundaries around the workday. Otherwise, you could find your partner resentful that they are not a priority or that they are left to carry the burden of keeping the household together.

Before executive producer Mark Burnett and actress Roma Downey were married, Mark promised Roma always to be home by 6 p.m. to have dinner with their kids as they grew up. They also promised never to be separated for more than a few days. They consciously made each other a priority. Having been a producer for Mark over many years, I know how busy he was during his courtship and early marriage to Roma. I have tried to emulate this lesson in my life, although I was not always as successful, and it has cost me many missed opportunities to create memories with people I care about because I did not put out a closed-for-business sign.

Unavailable for work should mean available for your closest relationships, including the one you have with yourself. Take time for meals, hikes, massages, meditation, whatever will support your mental, physical, and spiritual Wholebeing.

Before a store opens for business, the owner goes through a specific sequence to get ready for customers that day. They turn off the security alarm, activate the cash register, put the finishing touches on the displays, and finally go to the door and flip over the open sign. At the end of the day, it is the reverse. They flip over the closed sign, clear the cash register, sweep the floors, and restock inventory. Create your version of this. Start with a promise not to contact or respond to anyone during certain hours of the day or night.

Then:

Set a cut-off time for doing emails and texts.

Use the Do Not Disturb function on all your devices.

Use Out of Office messages during off-hours and when on vacation.

Let people know your unavailability ahead of time.

Temporarily delete the email and messaging apps when you do not want to be in contact with anyone.

Before you put out your open sign in the morning, have a croissant and a cup of coffee with someone you love, even if that just means yourself. Respect your open and closed boundaries, and you will discover that others will too.

Centering Thought. Respect boundaries.

Affirmation. I open and close each day
with a peaceful and joyful mind.

Health Snapshot No. 8:
Age Is Just a Number

"As long as God gives you life and gives me strength, I will have to keep doing it."

I felt a warm smile cross my face as I watched a petite, soft-spoken woman being interviewed on *Good Morning America*. She grew up in the house belonging to her grandfather who had been born into slavery. Ninety-five years later and still full of energy, Dr. Melissa Freeman is practicing internal medicine at her Harlem office with no thoughts of retiring after more than six decades of service helping people, especially those with drug addictions. And, like most other New Yorkers, she takes the subway. So, inspirational.

Over the past century, our life span has notably increased and will continue to do so, even though we saw historic dips in life expectancy during the pandemic years. However, looking from an optimistic viewpoint, in just one decade the 2019 US census shows that the sixty-five and older population grew by 34.2 percent (this includes the Baby Boom generation). That equates to almost fourteen million more people living beyond the previous generations, partly because of advances in science and technology, and partly because of Healthier lifestyle choices.

I feel fortunate to have been raised by parents who have consistently exercised throughout their lives and remained curious and engaged. They have been great role models for aging gracefully. One of their secrets is regular physical activity, along with a willingness to try new things. My mother began skiing in her forties. My father practiced and taught self-defense all his life.

My background in producing television in remote places led me to join the Explorers Club, an international organization dedicated to keeping alive the spirit of exploration. They are the ones who go to the moon, dive the deepest parts of our ocean, save our wildlife, and protect our environment. When I joined, the average age was sixty. There was a time when retirement happened at fifty-five. That seems so young to be rolling up the carpet on life. Yet, in my career and through the club, I have met outstanding examples of people who did not let age stop them from climbing mountains, literally. One of the most inspiring people I met was a very hearty, beloved Alaskan whose motto was "dare to fail," meaning within failure lies success as long as you keep trying.

I was a producer on a wildlife series and was sent to Alaska to do a story on a famous Iditarod trail dog musher, Colonel Norman Dane Vaughan. He was born in 1905 and died a hundred years later. His first claim to fame was bringing dogsleds to the South Pole during Admiral Byrd's first expedition in the late 1920s. By the time I encountered Norman, he was ninety-four. It was apparent that this man lived life on his terms in the best of ways.

My favorite Norman adventure was when he learned to climb a mountain at the young age of eighty-something. On his South Pole expedition, the admiral named a mountain after Norman as a thank you for safely managing their dog sleds. All of Norman's life, he wanted to climb his mountain, Mount Vaughan, a 10,302-foot peak in Antarctica. Being a dog musher, he had no idea how to climb a mountain, so he got someone to train him in his Alaskan backyard. That alone was a great challenge and the start of many more to come along Norman's journey to his mountain at the bottom of the world, including running out of money in Punta Arenas, Chile, their launch point to the white continent. However, he did not give up, nor did he ever stop training to climb his mountain. As he waited for more money to be raised, Norman kept his legs strong by wearing ski boots to climb the stairs at the lodge where he stayed. After almost a year, the needed funds arrived, and he finally reached the base of his mountain. He could now put those boots on to climb for real. On December 16, 1994, just three days before his eighty-ninth birthday, Norman fulfilled his lifelong dream and summitted Mount Vaughan.

I sat with Norman in his pickup truck, listening to his story. In the distance, the end-of-the-day sun was kissing the top of Alaska's Denali, the highest mountain peak in North America. At that moment, I realized that age was just a number.

Recent research from Singapore's biotech company Gero suggests that the maximum lifespan could be between 120 and 150 years. This age window seems to be the current outer limit of our body's ability to continue restoring itself. The supposed world's record holder for the longest lifespan is Jeanne Calment from France, who made it to 122 years and 164 days.

While these numbers seem hopeful for those wanting to live longer, the real question is not about lifespan, which is your biological resilience to ward off diseases, stress, or injury. Instead, it is "Healthspan," defined as the number of years you can live vibrantly, free from chronic diseases and disabilities. Once again, I return to the quality of one's thoughts being a significant driver of how we view and live life, *ergo*, our vibrant longevity. Those with a higher baseline of optimism tend to have longer, Healthier lifespans, Healthspans, by 11 to 15 percent more than the average.

I think optimism, gratitude, and purpose are some of Dr. Melissa Freeman and Colonel Norman Vaughan's secrets to remarkable active lives well into their nineties. So, let us all take note.

Centering Thought. Ageless.

Affirmation. I am not daunted by age,
only by erroneous thoughts about age.

♥ ♥ ♥

Health Meditation Prayer

I ask for the willpower to heal myself.

May my good thoughts be my best medicine.

*May my body move with ease and my
heart beat to the rhythm of life.*

*Allow me to see, feel, and wrap myself
in what is good and nourishing,*

*And push away that which does not feed
my mind, body, and spirit.*

For I am a beautiful vessel to be cherished.

*I take care of myself so that I can take
care of those around me.*

And so let it be.

DEVELOPING YOUR MIND, BODY, AND SPIRIT

At the start of this chapter, I suggested that your best insurance plan is the one that involves taking care of your mind, body, and spirit. Think of your Health as an integrative lifestyle: it all matters in the short and, most assuredly, in the long run. You will be less worried that you are teetering on the brink of having some terminal disease. Save money on Health insurance, bills, and medication, not to mention the time spent on appointments and being sick, and you will be more productive and think more clearly.

Ultimately, you will spend more time in action instead of out of action, enjoying your overall lifestyle, doing the things you love, being with the people you love, having more profound relationships with yourself, those around you, and with your spirituality. All compelling reasons to care for your mind, body, and spirit, and it all starts with what is going on in your head.

Every second, thousands of natural chemical reactions explode in your brain. Many can boost your Happiness when you pay attention to your thoughts, attitudes, and perceptions.

Endorphins are the brain's pain sedative. Result, feelings of relief.

Serotonin calms anxiety and relieves depression. Result, feelings of relaxation.

Oxytocin creates bonds with others. Result, feelings of love.

Dopamine is what you feel when you accomplish a job well-done. Result, feelings of reward.

What you eat, the number of hours you sleep, the amount of water you drink, the air you breathe, the types of exercise you do all influence your thoughts and emotions, *ergo*, the brain chemicals that are getting released throughout your body. There is a lot within your conscious power to affect your Health, Happiness, and Wholebeing.

Journaling with Health: What Does Health Mean to You?

Now that you have read my ideas about Health, take some time to journal how you can create a Healthier lifestyle. I have provided additional personal reflections in italics and space for you to do the same.

How do you define Health and its benefits?

Health is a three-dimensional state of being: mind, body, and spirit. Taking care of my health is my best insurance, full stop. As long as I have my health, my options are only limited by my beliefs.

_____

_____

_____

What role does Health currently play in your life?

Most days, I consciously do some form of exercise, meditate and pray, and watch what I eat and drink. However, I do not shame myself when I fall off the healthy habit wagon. I know I will always return to taking care of my health—nothing good will happen without good health.

_____

_____

_____

How Healthy are you in mind, body, and spirit? What areas need to be fortified?

I am very healthy and consistently good about meditating, exercising, eating well, and honoring sleep. However, I am not so good about the hours I eat or the time to go to bed. According to much of the research I have read, both are often too late in the day, and especially eating and sleeping soon after—this is a constant struggle.

How are you, or how can you, develop Healthier habits?

Because of the schedule I keep and enjoy, I try to do a modified version of 16/8 intermittent fasting at home (eating within an eight-hour window and fasting for sixteen), attempting to eat between 12 p.m. and 8 p.m. a few times a week. When I travel, I limit my intake of processed sugars, meats, desserts, cream sauces, and fried foods. At home, I rarely eat any of these items. It makes a significant difference in how I feel.

Take a photograph of what Health looks like for you. Give it a caption. Then, journal about your thoughts and feelings.

Good food, good people, good life.

Journal Entry: *Eating lots of fresh veggies, legumes, and fish, daily walks, morning meditations, and thinking productive thoughts are all part of my daily health regimen and are a large part of what keeps me buoyed and happy.*

Health Photo Ops and Action Opportunities

What photographic reminders can you create or find representing how you might make Healthier choices? Look for images using the following Photo Op prompts. As you learned from the chapter, good Health only happens when you take action; so, here are Action Opportunities to help you develop Healthy habits to increase your Happiness and Wholebeing. Share your experiences with our *Take a Shot at Happiness* community on social media or on our app.

Health Snapshot No. 1:
Think Healthy Thoughts

Photo Op. *Get Off the Thought Train.* Take an image of a train and write a caption for it. Use it to remind yourself that you can hop on or off a thought train at any time.

   Action Opportunity. Sit with the Centering Thought: "Think constructively." Then, lean into the Affirmation: "I am the observer and choice-maker of my thoughts and I choose to be loving toward myself." Pay attention to your thoughts throughout the day, so you can choose what to do with them.

_____

_____

_____

Health Snapshot No. 2:
Mind Your Environment

Photo Op. *What You Surround Yourself with Matters.* Create a collage or series of photos of how you plan to safeguard your environment. What are you saying "no" to from here on out? No complainers. No gossipers. No violence. Whatever it is for you, think about why you are saying, "No, not now or ever again."

Action Opportunity. The real work is managing the thousands of thoughts that you have each day. Start with the Centering Thought: "Mind my environment." Set boundaries to safeguard your environment. How will you be mindful of the people around you? What you talk about, the way you speak, for how long, and how often? Be aware of the time, the content, and the amount of information you consume. Remember the Affirmation: "I control my environment. It does not control me."

Health Snapshot No. 3:
Eat Clean and Mindfully

Photo Op. *Savor Each Bite.* Two parts to this one.

First, go to an outdoor market to capture images of fresh fruits and vegetables. Notice how deliciously inviting these images are and whether that motivates you to want to eat more of them.

Second, buy ingredients to make a healthy recipe. Photograph the finished dish. Then, eat while mindfully savoring your dining experience.

Action Opportunity. Reflect on the Centering Thought: "Eat well, live well." Then do some homework to see what diet is best for you. At the very least, apply the basic advice given in this Snapshot. If it helps, use the Affirmation: "My body is my temple, and I honor it with nourishing foods." Notice how you feel when you eat Healthily.

Health Snapshot No. 4:
Drink Lots of the Elixir of Life

Photo Op. *Water Log.* To help you develop the habit of drinking more water, each time you have a full glass or bottle, take a photo and caption the date. It will help you notice how much you are drinking daily.

    Action Opportunity. Recall the Centering Thought: "Water is life." Use it to remind you to drink water, lots of it, every day. It may help to carry a water bottle or set reminders on your phone. As you drink, you can use the Affirmation: "Water, the elixir of life, nourishes and replenishes me." Journal about the difference you notice by drinking more water. Notice your challenge to make it a habit and consider what you can do.

_____

_____

_____

Health Snapshot No. 5:
Get Up and Move Every Day

Photo Op. *Bend and Stretch.* If you are beginning an exercise program, take a photo of yourself in your birthday suit on day one. Then, every week, capture a new image.

    Action Opportunity. Spend some time with the Centering Thought: "Think Wholebeing Health." Using the weekly images from the Photo Op, journal about how the changes in your body make you feel and the confidence you gain by having a Healthier body. Affirmation: "I am good to my mind, body, and spirit, and they are good to me."

_____

_____

_____

Health Snapshot No. 6:
Take Time Out to Rest and Recover

Photo Op. *Take a Pause.* Create a side-by-side photo of you working on one side of the image and relaxing on the other side. Use this as a reminder that both are equally important to your Happiness and Wholebeing.

Action Opportunity. Consider the Centering Thought "Rest to recover" as you set aside focused time to get work done and get plenty of rest. Schedule focused work periods on your calendar as you would any other necessary appointment. Same with rest periods. On your breaks, say the Affirmation: "Every pause helps me return refreshed, renewed, and better than ever."

Also, set an alarm that tells you it is time to go to bed.

_____

_____

_____

Health Snapshot No. 7:
Intentionally Open and Close Your Day

Photo Op. *Set Work Boundary Intentions.* Capture or find an image that tells people you are open for the day. Create one that says you are now closed. You can post this on social media, text, or email, whenever it is useful to do so.

Action Opportunity. Start with the Centering Thought: "Respect boundaries." Create a morning and evening routine that tells you when you are open and closed for business and when you are available to the world. Next, reinforce your daily boundaries with the Affirmation: "I open and close each day with a peaceful and joyful mind."

_____

_____

_____

Health Snapshot No. 8:
Age Is Just a Number

Photo Op. *There Is No Try, Just Do.* Find an image of something you genuinely want to do. The New York Marathon. Climbing Everest. Launching into space. Keep this image somewhere you will frequently see it as inspiration. Commit and announce your intention to our *Take a Shot at Happiness* community. Publicly verbalizing your plan makes it more real. It motivates you to live up to your aspirations. Dream big and do it!

    Action Opportunity. Focus on the Centering Thought: "Ageless." Use it to keep dreaming, no matter your age. More importantly, never stop acting on those dreams. Reinforce this with the Affirmation: "I am not daunted by age, only by erroneous thoughts about age."

_____

_____

_____

PICTURING GRATITUDE

Gratitude

\\ˈgra-tə-ˌtüd, -ˌtyüd\\

noun

    : a state of being grateful, thankfulness

♥ ♥ ♥

"The expression of Gratitude is a kind of meta-strategy
for achieving happiness."

—Sonja Lyubomirsky
Bestselling Author, The How of Happiness

SNAPSHOT OF GRATITUDE

In My Viewfinder

It was sweltering by 8 a.m. during the filming of *The Australian Outback*, season two of the television competition show *Survivor*. I always showed up at camp around first light. By now, the two competing tribes had already merged as one. Several players were still left. The *Survivor* contestants were so hungry and lazy that they did not want to do anything. I mean nothing, not even sitting along the river holding a fishing pole to get some much-needed protein. They desperately needed food, yet all they could do was talk about it. Nothing was going to budge them except the arrival of Tree Mail, which announced their next challenge. Even then they were pretty slow-moving.

It was an unsteady climb up a sandy bank to get out of camp and on their way to that day's challenge. The tribe had built their tented, makeshift home on a dry riverbed at the base of a wide gully open to the edge of a river. Its banks were steep. The earth was so dry that the leaves, branches, and dirt quickly gave way as the Survivors struggled to keep their footing getting to its top. Once there, it was a journey to get to the location of their challenge, having to cross several more rocky, dry riverbeds.

Finally, they arrived, only to find out they would be doing a physical endurance challenge. The test was to see how long each could stand while holding a wooden rod across their back with sand-filled buckets at either end. Given how lazy and food-deprived the Survivors were, we thought things would be over quickly. However, the idea of winning an evening of hot dogs and hamburgers shared with real Australian Outback Cowboys, and a warm cot inside four-structured walls, was a strong motivator. So the challenge went on and on and on, lasting the entire afternoon, with Colby Donaldson winning out. During the challenge, the cowboys stood by on horseback, holding the reins of an empty-saddled horse reserved for the winner. It now had Colby's name on it. Being a ranch-raised Texan and dying to eat those hot dogs and hamburgers, Colby suddenly found the giddy-up to get into the waiting saddle and set off with his newfound cowboy friends.

As the remaining Survivors watched the backs of Colby and his posse get further away, drops of rain started to fall. Then, the skies released a deluge of rain, though it did not last long, and soon we were returning to the Survivors' camp. However, the previously dry riverbeds we had crossed coming to the challenge were now raging with water. We had already made a couple of crossings, and we were working on the next and biggest one when I saw our production helicopter flying in the general direction of their camp. The pilot did not radio me as he passed over, and I did not think much of it.

Next came an explosion of radio chatter in my ear. Someone was calling my name. I walked away from the Survivors and put my head down to respond. A near-hyperventilating voice on the other side of the radio announced that a flash flood had just hit the contestant's camp. Everything was washed away, including their home, on the no longer dry riverbed. The cameraman waiting at the camp had called production's base camp with the news. That explained the helicopter. I was asked to hold off from bringing the Survivors back to camp. Production wanted aerials of the flood. As the radio chatter continued, I slowly lifted my head to see all the Survivors holding hands that formed a line as they struggled to help each other across the white water swirling around their legs. I would not have to do anything to keep them from entering the camp. I looked at the sky. It was still cloudy and getting darker as our daylight started slipping away.

When they got to the top of the gully and saw the remains of their camp, the Survivors' faces were shocked and resigned. They were like ghosts moving through space for a long moment, making their way into camp.

Picking up a fishing hook here, a fleece jacket there, each registering how little they had left of their already meager existence. Finally, Tina Wesson broke the silence when she saw their only food. A can of rice lodged between fallen tree branches and rocks on the other side of still raging water.

Now sitting on the edge of light with no time to waste, Tina plunged into the freezing water to rescue the can. By the time she reached it, it was dark. The calls after Tina to "be careful" cut through the blackness of the night. Another Survivor, Keith Famie, tried to go after her, crossing a slippery log and alarming everyone even more. Now, two people were at risk of hurting themselves over a can of rice. After several moments everyone sighed with relief as both safely returned with the rice can in hand. Cheers and hugs went all around—though their euphoria came crashing when they realized they had no matches to make a fire with; there was still no food. The heroic save of their only sustenance was for naught. At that point, their spirits completely broke.

Mechanically, they each plunked down onto the wet sand. One of the Survivors found a somewhat dry blanket. They huddled together under it with their backs to each other for warmth. For a moment, they wondered how Colby was doing, eating hot dogs and burgers near a warm fire, probably hearing great cowboy stories and singing songs. Then, Elisabeth Hasselbeck remembered what day it was, Thanksgiving. As she finished saying the word, I felt a notable shift. The television competition show had stopped. The Survivors were now really surviving. I do not recall who started it off, one by one, they went around their circle, saying what they were thankful for at that moment. It was the most touching moment I ever witnessed in all my seasons of producing the show. To this day, every Thanksgiving I think of that night when there were no alliances, no secrets about who would get voted off. They were just like one. You could feel the bond between them. They were so grateful for having so little. That moment taught me so much about appreciating and being thankful for what I already have in life, even when it does not seem like much.

All this may sound trite. After all, it was just a television competition show and an act of mother nature within a controlled production environment. However, maybe consider viewing this story in its relative context—

the Survivors' feelings of despair and Gratitude for what few things they still had were real to them. It was cold and dark, their bellies ached from lack of food, they had to endure their circumstances away from home on Thanksgiving, and they did it with grace.

Snapshots on Developing an Attitude of Gratitude

Gratitude Snapshot No. 1:
Live Gratefully

"Thank you, Lord, thank you. Thank you for everything. I hate to ask this, but I was just wondering when exactly the meek will be inheriting the Earth?" So asks Meryl Streep as Ellen Martin in *The Laundromat.*

Early in my television career, I worked for a start-up production company owned by two thirty-something guys. They were renting out their cameras and sound gear to keep the lights on while developing and pitching shows in hopes of a sale. Two things about one of the owners impressed me then and still do today, centering around his ability to live Gratefully. First was his Gratitude for any sale made to any broadcaster. No matter what the show was about, he was not only Grateful to be in production, he also made the best content possible with the resources he had at that time. The second was his lack of envy and show of support for someone else's success. When he would hear about another production company selling a show, he would always say, "That's really great!" He was genuinely excited for them, even though they most likely sold to a broadcaster he had been recently pitching. He knew that someone else's success was not at the exclusion of his. While applauding a competitor's success, he felt Grateful for what he had already accomplished while looking toward achieving more.

Over the years, I watched this fledgling television production company flourish into one of the most successful in the unscripted broadcast arena, Renegade 83, the producers of Discovery's *Naked and Afraid.* I think a cornerstone of their success was Gratitude. When you energetically appreciate what someone else has, along with being Grateful for what you have, it generates a positive circular flow and expansion of goodness. For some, living Gratefully comes naturally. For others, they have to develop it. If you want to know how, you do it daily with yourself, with friends, with family, with anyone who comes into your path until Gratefulness becomes your habit and way of living.

To live Gratefully is to see the gift within every moment. The gift of the moment is to understand the opportunity that is always there. What is always there is a choice—a choice to be positive or negative, of seeing the light instead of darkness, seizing the moment, and not shrinking away.

When you live Gratefully, you act from a mindset of having versus one of lacking. When you live Gratefully, you are not as scared of life, events, or outcomes. You are not out to hurt others or yourself. Instead, you are willing to share what you have, appreciate people's differences, and respect others.

When you feel Grateful towards someone or something, you feel connected to it, especially in relationships. You both feel supported and more forgiving. As a result, your unions are stronger.

When you are Grateful you are Happier, more content, less likely to be envious of what someone else has, and more likely to appreciate what you already have. A Grateful world is a joyful, Happier world.

So, if saying thank you and expressing Gratitude is a sign of meekness, let us all be just that.

Centering Thought. Live Gratefully.

Affirmation. I appreciate the gift in
every moment of every day.

Gratitude Snapshot No. 2:
Get High on Helping

In 2009, I happened to be in New York doing a press tour for one of my new television series and walking down the street when I heard the news. The winner of *Survivor: Africa*, Ethan Zohn, had been diagnosed with cancer. That hit home. One, he was a friend. Two, my mother had overcome the latter stages of ovarian cancer just a couple of years earlier. So, I genuinely wanted to do something supportive. It turned out that Ethan was a spokesperson for the Livestrong Foundation, one of the recognized charities for that year's New York Marathon. I asked him to contact the organizers for me. Within hours, I became one of their fundraisers, excited about participating in my first marathon.

Feeling on purpose and having a fuller heart is the byproduct of what happens when you show Gratitude by giving back. In this case, I was Grateful that two people I cared about were still around and for a natural talent I could use to help others.

Grateful people are more helpful, generous, and compassionate; therefore, they are more prone to helping others with problems and offering emotional support. The Dalai Lama says helping others is really helping yourself because we are interconnected. So, if you genuinely want to look out for yourself and feel happy, be *wisely selfish* instead of *foolishly selfish*. Gratitude helps this choice by motivating you to help others in a meaningful way. You find yourself helping because it feels good. Often this help is in the form of volunteering or fundraising. You may have heard of a "Runner's High," an energizing, euphoric state of joy many athletes experience during or after a long run. Well, another version of this is "Helper's High," which comes from the same endorphins produced in the brain when you actively make a charitable contribution.

I began noticing my Helper's High when I started fundraising for the Livestrong Foundation. All my life I have enjoyed long, long walks. When I would hike in the foothills near my Los Angeles home, I almost always passed a man partially paralyzed on his left side. He could not bend that side's knee, and his arm was permanently in the same bent position near his waist. His eyes were set only high enough to take his next step. I admired that neither the steepness of the path nor the heat of day ever daunted him. Step by step he would drag his left foot forward until he reached a plaza area, a steady mile or so upward from the trailhead. Each time we passed one another, I said a silent prayer for him. He reminded me to be Grateful that I had two legs in perfect working order. Seeing him eventually motivated me to want to do something constructive with my ability to walk for hours on end. It seemed as soon as I had this thought, an opportunity I never expected in a context I never anticipated presented itself, and that was fundraising as a distance walker in the New York Marathon.

Over the next five years, I walked a marathon on every continent, each for charity. Still, almost every mile I walk today contributes to a nonprofit I care about. During our two-plus Covid pandemic years, I walked over two thousand miles in the foothills where I had trained for my marathons. As of May 22, 2023, I have logged 7,583 miles using an app called Charity Miles, and there are hundreds of miles not logged.

Wanting to help, and seeing where I could, inspired me to focus my ability to walk distances in service of a greater good. This desire directly comes from feeling Grateful for my mother and Ethan surviving cancer, and that I have the legs and endurance to do 26.2 miles in one go. The Helper's High I received is from being able to pay forward a natural gift in a meaningful way.

Centering Thought. Giving is my high.

Affirmation. It is in the practice of giving that I receive.

Gratitude Snapshot No. 3: Use the Language of Gratitude

Johanna pats Michael's shoulder affectionately, acknowledging his great job pitching a limited series to the network (touch).

Johanna looks intently into Susan's eyes, nodding as she describes a scene she wrote for her (attention).

Johanna gives Sandra a 14k gold Emmy charm pendant as a thank you for her performance in their last series (gift).

Johanna offers to work weekends in Bill's homeless soup kitchen because he secured the production financing on her last project (service).

Johanna tells Emily, "I appreciate you more than you will ever know" for the long hours worked editing her television pilot (kind words).

Bestselling author of *The 5 Love Languages*, Gary Chapman, says that people respond to expressions of love differently. Some like a reassuring touch of a hand. Some like your undivided attention. Some prefer a gift, others an act of service. Another only wants to hear a kind word. These five love languages apply to expressions of Gratitude as well. As the giver, you set aside your ego to show thankfulness in a meaningful way for the receiver in a way that you know will make them feel cared about. I think this makes you feel even closer to the person who is the focus of your appreciation. So, you both feel good.

However, the language of Gratitude generally includes the use of words. We can talk about our inability, adversity, misfortunes, and lack. Or we can talk about our gifts, blessings, fortune, and abundance. Clearly, one feels better thinking, feeling, and expressing. Words release an energetic vibration from your brain which travels through your body and out into the world. What we think and feel informs how we communicate with others. The first set of words listed reflects a lack of Gratitude for what one has in life: inability, adversity, misfortune, lack. The second is a show of it: gifts, blessings, fortune, abundance. Your verbal tone and words will either magnetize people towards you or polarize them. When you focus on channeling appreciation, you are in the energy of Gratitude. So, Grateful thoughts become Grateful words that become Grateful deeds, making the world a better place.

People are less likely to feel underappreciated when the language of Gratitude is used. In the workplace, people are more likely to experience greater satisfaction in what they are doing. Consistent, meaningful expressions of Gratitude shown by any leader help increase productivity, enhance creativity, encourage cooperation, and decrease turnover, which ultimately translates into greater company teamwork and customer loyalty, and higher net sales. Do the same at home and you will find a similar result in healthy, loving, fulfilling relationships.

An often-cited reason someone will leave a relationship or a job is that they feel a lack of appreciation. I was once working on a television show where the executive producer constantly reminded the producers and camera teams how much he did for them and how he made their careers. Rarely was there a "thank you" or "good job" for bringing back a great story. It caused most of the production team to feel resentful, unhappy, and less willing to go the extra mile. We worked long hours under extreme conditions, often in dangerous locations, and our efforts usually went unrecognized. Several left the show because of this lack of appreciation. Those who stayed spent a lot of time complaining about the boss. This executive producer never realized we would have all walked on water for him. We loved the adventures we had traveling the world and doing stories. We just wanted our boss to show some Gratitude. Indeed, you will go miles if you just say a heartfelt, "Thank you, I appreciate you."

Centering Thought. Thank you, I appreciate you.

Affirmation. I express the language of
Gratitude in meaningful ways.

Gratitude Snapshot No. 4:
Celebrate Your Present Moment

They just could not shut up for five minutes. Standing on a hardened, smooth, black lacquer lava field, watching a broad, dense, pillowy, white plume of steam gloriously ascend into the sky took my breath away. I could feel the warmth of the distant molten lava flow underneath my feet as the electric orange stream slowly reached the water of the Pacific. All I could think was we were watching a piece of the earth forming. Lava creates new land as it seeps into the ocean and solidifies along Hawaii's Big Island coast. My production crew and I were privileged to see it, or I thought so. Gracious, how many times and places will anyone be able to experience such an extraordinary sight? None of them could manage even three minutes of silence to appreciate the awesomeness of that moment. It was like they could not help themselves and had to talk and joke around, trying to outwit each other. They could have been anywhere doing the same thing. I had to walk away from them, so at least I could etch the moment into my mind.

How often have you thrown away what could have been meaningful moments, not being present to them, distracted by irrelevant conversations, stuck dwelling on the past or thinking about the future, mentally being somewhere other than where you are now? Celebrating events like standing in the middle of a lava field, or birthdays, anniversaries, graduations, are not the only times worthy of acknowledging; the smaller ones are too—waking up, finishing a satisfying project, getting an unexpected compliment. Each moment is worthy of celebration because we are breathing and here. Yet many times, we are not aware or appreciative of our presence.

Likewise, most people, myself included, are guilty of giving up the serenity, excitement, and enjoyment of their present moment by being caught in the past of *I should have*, the future of *what if*, or just being upset about one thing or another. All this truly does is cause some form of suffering. You are dwelling on either what was lost or what could potentially be lost. The past is gone. The future, no one knows. All you really have is now. Within every moment of *now* lies your ability to be a choice-maker. You can choose to be in the positive or negative realm. You can choose to be present or checked out. How you deal with the present, your thoughts and actions will determine your future outcome. That is why the present moment is a present, as cliché as this sounds.

Right now, pause reading to take a deep breath and feel where you are. Allow the breath to flow in and out of your nose gently and listen. Listen and delight in the sound of the breath, the morning birdsong outside the window, the distant buzzing of gardeners tending to the neighborhood lawns, the warmth of the clothes you are wearing, whatever this moment is for you. I just shared the moment I am in. I love it for the busyness outside and the quietness inside as I sit. It affords me the time to think and write this book. Take in all the fine details of your present moment now. Then, do the same for the next and the ones after that. Do it throughout the day, include the people you meet, the things you do, and the objects you touch. Eventually, notice the cumulative effect of all your celebrated present moments in a day. More importantly, how does it make you feel when you afford yourself the space to do this? Likely, pretty darn good. You may even be glowing from the day celebrating.

The root word for Gratitude comes from Latin, *gratia*, meaning graces, goodwill, kindness, thanks, all descriptors for generosity and appreciation. By valuing a moment in time toward someone or something, you are less likely to take it for granted, leaving you open to having a more exceptional, magnified experience with it. Positive emotions can be short-lived, and

Gratitude is what extends their lifespan. So that contentment you feel sitting in a lounge chair, the excitement of a new relationship, or the joy of a recent trip will feel alive longer when you celebrate the moment you are experiencing them and feel Grateful for it. Gratitude will create a stronger connection to whatever is the focus of your appreciation, keeping you anchored in the present as you celebrate and staying in your heart and mind long afterward.

When I celebrate the present and express Gratitude for it, my heart swells as if it will burst from uncontainable joy. Colors are richer, sounds are crisper, and smells more intoxicating, though even while consciously looking to stay present, I could still do better relishing these times of Grateful celebration. It is and will always be a constant practice.

Centering Thought. Celebrate now.

Affirmation. Every moment I breathe,
every step I take, every sight I behold,
every sound I hear is a moment to celebrate.

Gratitude Snapshot No. 5: Life Is in the Details

Sitting on a bus stop bench, talking to some random person who is doing their best to ignore him as he digs around a variety candy box, stuffing his cheeks with chocolates, Forrest offers one; they keep ignoring him. "I could eat about a million and a half of these. My momma always said life was like a box of chocolates. You never know what you're gonna get." Sweet, sweet Forrest Gump is in the moment, savoring it while sharing a bit of *aw, shucks* wisdom about life's surprises. The person next to him in the film does what many of us do: keep our noses buried in a book or our phones instead of realizing the specialness of a moment. From this scene, I get Forrest was genuinely present and probably had experienced and appreciated about a million and a half of these small moments in his life.

Stopping to smell freshly cut roses. Pausing to acknowledge a friend's "I Love you" text. Enjoying holding hands with your sister as you stroll together. Doing a Happy dance when you find twenty dollars in the lining of your coat pocket. All the small things that make you smile when you experience them as they happen. As we saw in the previous section, the small things in life are also indeed big.

Take time to admire the beauty of something in and of itself, the significance of what someone is telling you. Most of our lives are made up of small events. Yet, these details equal a fulfilling and eventful life when appreciated and summed up.

Just saying "thank you" can make you feel warm and content with your momentary life circumstance.

One of the best things I learned from neuropsychologist Dr. Rick Hanson is the concept of "Taking in the Good." Your mind is created, shaped by the flow of experiences you take in, the felt sensations that take hold in your memory at the subconscious level, good or bad. When I had the privilege of going on that month-long trip to Africa I mentioned earlier, there were countless times I consciously thought, "Remember this moment." Remember the early morning sounds of the Cape turtle dove, a red and violet sunset lighting up a river's edge, the feeling of hot wind forcing itself against me as we drove through the bush. The idea is that when you experience something wonderful, even if it is merely smelling a fresh garden rose or listening to someone's casual observation, you savor that moment for twenty to thirty seconds. Long enough for it to become a memory and a felt sensation in your body. The longer you enjoy it, feel it, the stronger it will live on in your memory, which you can later call upon when you are experiencing an unhappy situation, feeling angry, hurt, or even bored. Consciously calling up a positive memory while experiencing a negative emotion can help retrain your brain toward the positive. More importantly, taking in the good, appreciating the remarkable details of an experience—especially the unexpected ones—and recalling them when you are feeling unhappy not only makes you more optimistic, it becomes your way of being. Taking in the Good has truly helped me live more Gratefully.

Gratitude gives importance to what we would otherwise take for granted or ignore. Unfortunately, the woman sitting next to Forrest missed a bit of profound insight. Try not to be like her.

Centering Thought. Details matter.

Affirmation. I find joy and happiness
in the goodness of my life.

Gratitude Snapshot No. 6: Count Your Blessings

It is the middle of the night. I have no idea what time it is, just that it is still dark. For the third time, as I lie in bed, I hear police sirens blaring through the streets, followed by the neighbors' dogs crazily barking. Further down the road, an argument explodes, a car door slams, wheels squeal and speed off. I do not think it is a full moon, although it sure is a busy night around my neighborhood. However, as the orchestra of chaotic sounds plays outside my bedroom window, I feel at peace inside. There is a slight smile on my face as I make a mental list of all the things I am Grateful for at that precise moment: my warm bed, the thick cotton duvet that covers me, the fact that I even have a roof over my head when others sleep in tents and cardboard boxes under the freeway. While it may seem like an odd time to notice my blessings, it is actually the perfect time to do just that. It is always the ideal time to be Grateful for what you have.

Be Grateful for every moment and open to life's unfolding. Appreciating what you already have in life gives you a sense of satisfaction and contentment. Put your attention on the many ways you are already supported emotionally, financially, or spiritually. Do this, and you will find countless things to be Grateful for, thus giving you hope for the future. Value what you already have instead of always reaching for something new, thinking it will make you Happier. The more you do this, the more you see through the lens of abundance versus scarcity. This way of seeing things helps during challenging times. You can be more positive and thankful when you consciously see what is working in your life while still realizing your challenges. Remembering the good times in comparison to the tough times makes one Grateful and gives another reason to take in the good when it happens.

I consciously cultivate feelings of Gratitude to navigate challenging times. Emotionally, it helps a lot. Like many, my business went upside down during the Covid pandemic. I produce shows filmed on location in distant lands. Only a few daring souls were venturing beyond their doorstep, let alone crossing borders for over two years. I used part of the time to lay the groundwork for a wellbeing adventure travel business that I had wanted to start for a while—combining my abilities as a television producer and PhD in conscious-centered living. I felt that the travel industry would emerge from the pandemic with travelers wanting more intentionality to their sojourn experiences. However, in the interim of all things waking up again, my bank account was going down instead of up. Faith, detachment (more on this later), and Gratitude were my lens of choice, enabling me to see what I already had and what was working for me. I appreciated my seemingly small business wins, like the money earned from consulting on television and film projects, teaching meditation online, and starting to get more travel inquiries and repeat clients, though none of these added up to put me back in the financial green zone. Nonetheless, these wins gave me hope for the future, and I counted each one as a blessing. In a 1998 Gallup survey, 90 percent of American teens and adults who responded mentioned that expressing Gratitude helped them feel Happier. Had I been part of the survey, I would have been included in that percentage figure.

Also key was remembering the times that excited me, like when I did a show that started in Zanzibar and then traveled the width of Tanzania, the adventure to one of the furthest reaches of Alaska along the Bering Sea, the thrill of crossing my seventh continent marathon finish line in Antarctica to raise money for cancer—counting these blessings and savoring each memory added to feeling Happy, content, and on purpose.

You can start counting your blessings anytime, even right now, reading these words.

Centering Thought. Count my blessings.

Affirmation. I appreciate and delight in what
I already have and say, "Thank you, God."

Gratitude Snapshot No. 7:
Make Gratitude Your Daily Habit

One dainty foot lands on the floor, "thank." Then the other, "you." This is the way Roma Downey begins her days, expressing Gratitude, and she has much to be thankful for: a celebrated actress, producer, and president of her LightWorkers Media company, she has a wonderful family with her husband, their three kids, and a beautiful Malibu home in California. Seems easy to say thank you when you have so much going for you. Yes, now. Although there were many uncertain days without a mom and dad after age twenty, leaving her Irish homeland to take a chance at acting in the States, that Gratitude could not have been so easy to hold in Roma's heart. Yet, it was always there, along with her faith that better days were ahead.

Self-made multi-millionaire motivational speaker Tony Robbins has a daily ten-minute, three-step routine.

One, he thinks about something humble that makes him feel good, like the start of a new day.

Two, he spends a few minutes praying for his family, colleagues, and others who come to mind.

Three, the last minutes are about committing to three results he wants to achieve.

I bookend my days, saying thank you to Big G upstairs as well as throughout the day when the unexplainable brightens a present moment, even when it does not, and then look at it as a lesson I am meant to learn or a different path to follow.

Gratitude is another easy-to-apply practice you can do with miraculous benefits in your daily life. It boosts optimism, joy, pleasure, excitement, and contentment. As these feelings go up, anger, jealousy, envy, resentment, and greed go down. What increases are feelings of self-worth, making you alert, energetic, passionate, attentive, and resilient, even for those recovering from traumatic events or suffering from bouts of depression. Gratitude encourages you to spend more time bonding and less time comparing yourself to others. It just makes you a better human, which is why all the major spiritual traditions practice Gratitude.

We lug around suitcases full of regrets about the past and anxiety about the future. Gratitude helps you drop that emotional baggage. Frequently listing the things you are Grateful for is linked to having a sunnier, more positive outlook on life. Evidence shows that those who write in a Gratitude journal are 25 percent Happier. Of course, if you are not a journal keeper, like me, mentally listing what you are Grateful for, especially before you go to bed, works too. You will also likely have a more restful sleep and feel more refreshed when you wake up.

Indeed, practicing Gratitude every day has proven to be one of the best ways to increase feelings of Happiness and contentment in oneself and overall life satisfaction. Use it to navigate challenging times until they become better times. I often use these periods to reflect on a similar thought as Benedict Cumberbatch's character in *Doctor Strange in the Multiverse of Madness*:

Wong: "Dr. Stephen Strange, are you happy?"

Dr. Strange: "That's an interesting question. Sometimes I do wonder about other lives. But I'm still grateful of this one. Even with its own tribulations."

Centering Thought. My attitude is Gratitude.

Affirmation. I Gratefully acknowledge today,
all its joys, all its sorrow, all its lessons.

Gratitude Snapshot No. 8: Honor Those Who Help You

Poppy: "Thank you."
Branch: "No, thank YOU."
Poppy: "For what?"
Branch: "For showing me how to be happy."

These words are from one of my favorite moments in the animated film *Trolls* because it reminded me how important it is to thank those who have helped you be successful. Thinking about the good things that have happened in your life, you are likely focused on the good that you have done. Maybe consider the good that others have done on your behalf as well. Gratefulness, thankfulness, and appreciation are circular and exponential. What you appreciate comes back to you and multiplies. So, enjoy what you already have and desire more of that. Admire your body and take steps to make it healthier. Appreciate the money you do have and want more of it. Value the relationships that you have and desire to make them stronger. As you appreciate the goodness already in your life, consider where it was encouraged. Many times, it lies outside of yourself.

Sincere Gratitude involves a humble acknowledgment that other people, God, and the universe gave you gifts that helped to achieve all that is wonderful in your life. Consider some of the more memorable Oscar award acceptance speeches:

Adrien Brody, at age twenty-nine, was one of the youngest actors to receive Best Actor for his role in *The Pianist* (2002). "There comes a time in life when everything seems to make sense, and this is not one of those times. What I do know, though, is that I've never felt this much love and encouragement from my peers and from people I admire and from complete strangers. And it means a great deal to me."

Halle Berry was the first black female to receive Best Actress for *Monster's Ball* (2002). "This moment is for Dorothy Dandridge, Lena Horne, Diahann Carroll. It's for the women that stand beside me, Jada Pinkett Smith, Angela Bassett, Vivica A. Fox. And it's for every nameless, faceless woman of color that now has a chance because this door tonight has been opened. Thank you. I'm so honored."

When Ben Affleck and Matt Damon won their Oscar for *Good Will Hunting* (1997), Ben, at twenty-five, was the youngest writer to win Best Original Screenplay. "We're just really two young guys who were fortunate enough to be involved with a lot of great people whom it's incumbent upon us—there's no way we're doing this in less than twenty seconds."

Trent Reznor, Atticus Ross, and Jon Batiste for *Soul* (2021). The composing trio won Best Original Score for their animated film. Overwhelmed with Gratitude, Jon Batise accepts the award. "You know what's deep is God gave us twelve notes, it's the same twelve notes that Duke Ellington had, Bach had, Nina Simone…I'm thankful to God for those twelve notes."

Grateful people who acknowledge and appreciate others get more support from them. They can receive and accept all of life, seeing its gift or potential gift. They can block toxic emotions that can destroy their Happiness with each other and themselves. As we mentioned in Gratitude Snapshot No. 1: Live Gratefully, when you have a high level of Gratitude, you have a low level of envy and resentment. You cannot feel jealous and Grateful at the same time. So, who in your life deserves an Oscar speech?

Centering Thought. Offer Gratitude.

Affirmation. I appreciate and thank the universe and my supporters. It is because of you that I am here.

♥ ♥ ♥

Gratitude Meditation Prayer

Thank you for the clouds above and the earth below.

Thank you for the rivers that flow.

Thank you for every mountain peak and blade of grass.

Thank you for all creatures, big and small.

Thank you for those who care about me, and those who do not, for all are my teachers.

Thank you for the roof over my head and the food in my belly.

Thank you for every breath I take, every sight I see, every sound I hear, and every touch I feel.

Thank you for the love that fills my heart and kisses my soul.

Thank you. Thank you. Thank you.

And so let it be.

DEVELOPING AN ATTITUDE OF GRATITUDE

Gratitude makes you feel good about giving and receiving. It is a vessel for appreciation and hope. Some of the most Grateful and positive people I have come across have also overcome terrible obstacles or grief in their life. There was a colleague during my *Survivor* show years that always seemed to be on the upside of things. Regardless of what production challenges we faced, and there were many, especially in the first few seasons as we worked out shooting a large-scale network production in remote locations with little to no existing infrastructure, he just took things in stride. Generally, he wore a smile, laughed easily and often, and was quick to say thank you. One day, I asked him why he was so positive and Grateful. His reply taught me a lot about perspective. When my colleague was younger, he lost his mother to cancer. He felt when something like that happens to you early on, you learn that many arguments, frustrations, and resentment are truly small and not worth the fight within the larger picture of life. If only more of us could see things this way.

Gratitude builds a wealth of positivity which helps you cope with difficult times. It is pretty much the antidote for the negativity and hardships that distress us. It helps you, your family, and your community better deal with extreme loss. Think of the times you have seen in the news a couple crying over losing their home to a fire or flood and still being Grateful to be alive and have each other. On balance, Grateful people have more positive emotions more often. They are Happier, more energetic, hopeful, helpful, empathic, forgiving, and spiritual.

Gratitude can boost feelings of belonging and decrease feelings of stress. After 9/11, such a wave of Gratitude swept our country. People seemed kinder and more generous towards everyone: friend, foe, or stranger. We saw this again during the Covid pandemic, especially in the first few months of global quarantining. Leading Gratitude expert Dr. Robert Emmons shares in his book *Gratitude Works!* a research summary of the many benefits of expressing thanks, some surprising, some not:

Increased energy, alertness, enthusiasm, and vigor.

More success at achieving personal goals.

Better ability to cope with stress.

Having a sense of closure around traumatic memories.

Increased feelings of self-worth and self-confidence.

Having secure social relationships.

Being more generous and helpful.

Potentially prolonged enjoyment of pleasurable experiences.

Improved cardiac health.

Having a greater sense of purpose and resilience.

How can two one-syllable words, "thank you," have such a far-reaching impact in the present, across time, embedded in all wisdom traditions, here, now, and everywhere? Well, they do. Some wise advice from thirteenth-century German philosopher Meister Eckhart: "If the only prayer you ever say in your entire life is 'thank you,' it will be enough."

Journaling with Gratitude: What Does Gratitude Mean to You?

Now, I invite you to journal how you can bring more Gratitude into your life. As with the previous chapters, I have shared my thoughts on the questions asked in italics and given space for you to share yours.

How do you define Gratitude and its benefits?

Gratitude is the expression of thankfulness. Simply saying thank you throughout the day does a lot for my mental health and resilience, increasing my feelings of abundance, which gives me hope for the future.

_____

_____

_____

What role does Gratitude currently play in your life?

Gratitude is what I use to acknowledge and appreciate the contribution of others to my successes and wellbeing, it supports good relationships with those I encounter, and it gives rise to forgiveness and the ability to detach from a specific result.

_____

_____

_____

How often do you express Gratitude?

I say thank you before bed and when I wake up. It flows from me throughout the day in almost every instance. Not a day goes by without it.

_____

_____

_____

How are you, or will you, bring into your life more Gratitude?

My area to grow is in feeling grateful toward someone I am angry with, upset with, or hurt by. I try to take a moment not to talk, not react, and just breathe. When I finally feel more settled inside, I consider how I could have handled the situation better; I set the intention to do so in the future and say a silent thank you for the opportunity to grow.

_____

_____

_____

   Take a photograph of what Gratitude looks like for you. Give it a caption. Then, journal about your thoughts and feelings.

I feel grateful, warm, and friendly inside.

Journal Entry: *Joyful, cheery, yellow roses. Your color so warm and bright, like a fresh spring day. Giving or receiving yellow roses reminds me of heartfelt feelings of appreciation and friendship.*

Gratitude Photo Ops and Action Opportunities

There is always time to infuse more Gratitude into your life. Use the following Photo Op prompts and Action Opportunities as a guide to becoming more mindful of what causes feelings of Gratitude.

Gratitude Snapshot No. 1:
Live Gratefully

Photo Op. *A State of Thankfulness.* Capture images of the things and people you are already Grateful for in your life. Notice how it makes you feel as you take these photos. Then, look at all of them as a collection and think about why you feel Grateful for these blessings.

    Action Opportunity. Savor the Centering Thought: "Live Gratefully." Notice and tell whoever is supportive in your life, your mom, best friend, assistant, whomever, why you are Grateful to them. Your feelings will genuinely touch them. Likely, they will reciprocate with heartfelt wishes for you as well. Support this action step with the Affirmation: "I appreciate the gift in every moment of every day."

_____

_____

_____

Gratitude Snapshot No. 2:
Get High on Helping

Photo Op. *Be of Service.* Memorialize how you help others through a series of images. Notice how you feel during these moments. Come back to these photos a week or few weeks later. How have your feelings changed or remained the same?

    Action Opportunity. Start with the Centering Thought: "Giving is my high." Then, think about how you can consistently support a worthy cause or help someone. Finally, acknowledge and absorb how you feel helping others, using the Affirmation: "It is in the practice of giving that I receive."

_____

_____

_____

Gratitude Snapshot No. 3:
Use the Language of Gratitude

Photo Op. *What Is Your Language of Gratitude?* Create a photo series that shows the five languages of Gratitude: touch, attention, gift, service, and a kind word. Observe how you feel as you do this Photo Op.

Action Opportunity. Spend time focusing on the Centering Thought, "Thank you, I appreciate you," to show Gratitude toward someone—could be a loved one, a friend, a co-worker. Consider how they would like to be appreciated. What would be meaningful to them versus to you? What is the language of Gratitude that speaks loudest to them? Use the Affirmation, "I express the language of Gratitude in meaningful ways," to support you.

_____

_____

_____

Gratitude Snapshot No. 4:
Celebrate Your Present Moment

Photo Op. *Carpe Diem.* Make a photo album of your favorite moments from the past. Keep adding to it as you collect new ones. When you are feeling down, look at these images to help cheer you up.

Action Opportunity. Affirmation: "Every moment I breathe, every step I take, every sight I behold, every sound I hear is a moment to celebrate."

Come into presence with the Centering Thought: "Celebrate now." Then, journal about one or two moments you celebrated in the past. What were they? Were any of these smaller life moments that became more important because you celebrated them? How is this a practice that could change your attitude about daily life?

Gratitude Snapshot No. 5:
Life Is in the Details

Photo Op. *Find What Feels Good in Your Viewfinder.* For at least a week, capture the images you describe in the Action Opportunity. You will do something similar for Gratitude Photo Op No. 7. However, this Photo Op is about appreciating something now, in the moment. The other is about what you are Grateful for that day. You may find the difference subtle, though notice the significance between the two.

    Action Opportunity. Meditate on the Centering Thought: "Details matter." Then once a day, stop to appreciate something you are experiencing at that exact moment. The Affirmation, "I find joy and Happiness in the goodness of my life," may be helpful as you savor each experience for several seconds. Over time, notice how this daily ritual makes you feel.

Gratitude Snapshot No. 6:
Count Your Blessings

Photo Op. *Blessing One, Blessing Two, Blessing Three.* Make a collage or photo series of some of the most important things you already have and appreciate in your life. Notice how you feel as you collect these images and put them together.

Action Opportunity. Meditate on the Centering Thought: "Count my blessings." Off your meditation cushion, keep counting those blessings. If it helps, write them down. The invitation is to recognize the overall good that already exists in your life. If it helps, use the Affirmation: "I appreciate and delight in what I already have and say, 'Thank you, God.'"

_____

_____

_____

Gratitude Snapshot No. 7: Make Gratitude Your Daily Habit

Photo Op. *What Makes You Feel Grateful?* For at least one week, capture one image of something you genuinely feel Grateful for that happened that day, even when you are not feeling all that Grateful; indeed, especially these days. It will help you to feel better and more hopeful. Caption your images and keep them as a reminder of the goodness around you.

Action Opportunity. Contemplate the Centering Thought: "My attitude is Gratitude." Then use the Affirmation, "I Gratefully acknowledge today, all its joys, all its sorrow, all its lessons," every day; notice what you are Grateful for and how it makes you feel to savor these moments. You may want to keep a journal of these times. Write about one or two of them in depth. Use this as an exploration of your thoughts and emotions.

_____

_____

_____

Gratitude Snapshot Photo Op No. 8:
Honor Those Who Help You

Photo Op. *I Want to Thank....* First, do the Action Opportunity. Then, photograph, frame, and hang the speech you wrote in your home or office.

Action Opportunity. Start with the Centering Thought: "Offer Gratitude." Write a Gratitude speech. Think about who you want to thank in your own life's Oscar speech. For extra credit, write it and deliver it. As you do this Action Opportunity, lean into the Affirmation: "I appreciate and thank the universe and my supporters. It is because of you that I am here."

_____

_____

_____

PICTURING FORGIVENESS

Forgiveness
fər\-ˈgiv-nəs\

noun

   : the act of forgiving someone or something
   : the attitude of someone who is willing to forgive
     other people

"Peace always comes to those who choose to forgive."
—Bishop Desmond Tutu
Nobel Prize Winner for Peace

SNAPSHOT OF FORGIVENESS

In My Viewfinder

While researching a documentary about POWs, I learned a powerful lesson about Forgiveness during an interview with the former 1936 Olympic runner and World War II POW Lou Zamperini. He was a famous elite runner and the top US finisher in the five-thousand-meter event during the Berlin Olympics. After the Olympics, Lou continued collecting awards and worldwide recognition. However, once World War II exploded, Lou exchanged his running jersey for a bombardier jacket when he was commissioned into the US Air Corps as a lieutenant in the Pacific, flying B-24 Liberators.

One day, while on a routine reconnaissance mission, his aircraft took an uncontrollable nosedive into the Pacific Ocean.

Crash!

From that moment, life for Lou forever changed. For the next forty-seven days, he and another crew member aimlessly bobbed around the vast ocean in a small rubber raft with the occasional shark swimming around, keeping them alert. Finally, they drifted into Japanese waters around the Marshall Islands two thousand miles later. The enemy picked them up, turning Lou's odyssey into one of never-ending verbal and physical abuse as he was sent from one POW camp to another. His captors tormented and humiliated him because of his Olympic notoriety. He ended up spending his last two years as a POW in one place, where a guard made it his mission to break Lou. Thankfully for Lou, the war ended before the guard ever succeeded.

However, despite coming home to a hero's welcome, Lou's POW experience was far from over. Nightmares plagued him. He turned to alcohol for relief. Then, he met the Reverend Billy Graham, and his life would forever change again—though this time, upward. Lou found it within himself to Forgive his captors in person. He also became a missionary in Japan, preaching Forgiveness to the very country of people who made his life a living hell.

"I think the hardest thing I've done in life is to forgive. Hate is self-destructive. If you hate somebody, you're not hurting the person you hate, you're hurting yourself." For Lou, having the courage and heart to say these three words, "I forgive you," is what finally stopped the nightmares.

Over the years, since my interview with Lou, I often thought about him, and still do. It turned out we lived in adjacent Los Angeles neighborhoods and occasionally saw each other at the market. Each time I saw Lou, what struck me was his upbeat nature, always with a smile on his face and kind words to match. Seeing him in the produce section, you would never have imagined the horrors he had gone through in earlier years. Lou did not show the pain, the anger, the victimization. As far as I could see, he did not walk through his present life as a shell of a man. Instead, Lou was forever walking as a victor, all five foot nine of him, because he chose to Forgive. In doing so, Lou took back control of his life. Once again, he gave it a purpose—something another WWII survivor, concentration camp prisoner Viktor Frankl, did under different circumstances and then wrote about in *Man's Search for Meaning*. Years later, South Africa's anti-apartheid leader Nelson Mandela would Forgive his captors. Each of these men teaches us that you Forgive so you can go forward in life with strength, dignity, and vibrancy. You Forgive so you can still love and be kind. You Forgive so you can be an example of humanity and dignity. Forgiveness enables you to be kinder toward others, and even more so, compassionate toward yourself. It helps to acknowledge that you are doing the best you can each day and in every circumstance.

Developing Forgiveness may turn out to be the absolute most challenging thing for you ever to do, especially when linked to trauma and directed toward yourself. However, it is so necessary for your emotional Wholebeing, your Happiness. Realize that you may need professional psychological or spiritual guidance. I lovingly encourage you to seek the advice you need. There is nothing shameful about getting help. What is regrettable is when you do not.

Snapshots on Developing Heartfelt Forgiveness

Forgiveness Snapshot No. 1:
The Past Is Just That

"Forgiveness liberates the soul, it removes fear.
That's why it's such a powerful weapon."

—NELSON MANDELA

The relationship with my father was a lifelong issue that beckoned me to move through and get to the other side. As much as I loved and respected my father, I spent much of my life resenting him. It took me years to understand that what was frustrating me was that my father treated me differently from my older brother and sister. My brother had special needs, so tending to those needs was understandable to a certain point. I grew up feeling like what my sister did not want to do and what my brother could not do became an expectation of me—and I resented it. When I would appeal to my father about my feelings, I felt that he did not respond with compassion nor empathy nor take any emotional responsibility; this did not help our relationship.

As I grew into adulthood and became more successful in my career, I genuinely wanted to make peace with my father. I realized that I had come to a place where it was time to stop blaming him and become responsible for myself. While we had an uneasy relationship, I deeply loved my father.

A few years before he passed, I took my father to Russia as a peace offering. I knew he always wanted to go there because of his love of Russian music and literature, his passion for teaching himself to speak the language, and his desire to connect with my maternal grandfather's roots in that country, because he cherished him like he was his own father. So, I booked a cruise ship adventure for the two of us along the waterways from Moscow to

Saint Petersburg, which gave us the time and space to have several heartfelt talks. While there was still more healing work to do after this father-daughter trip, Forgiving my father was huge for me. It felt like I was releasing an emotional anvil off my mind, chest, shoulders, and heart.

What I was able to see from Forgiving my father is that spiraling down into the hurt and resentment of yesterday robs you of today. You are just extending your suffering by hanging on to the old stuff. No matter what the circumstance, there is a way to find Forgiveness. Nelson Mandela, Mahatma Gandhi, Jesus Christ all Forgave their captors and persecutors. That Forgiveness is where they found life, whether it was here or eternal.

Not that I am implying my father persecuted me; he was an admirable man. However, letting go of the tough stuff, the stuff that hurt, the things we feel bad about, and the situations you or I wish would have gone a different way is not about burying it, trying desperately to forget, or pretending nothing happened. It is about recognizing what happened and learning how to coexist with past traumatic events. It is about finding a way around letting it stop you from living today. There is nothing you can do about what already happened. However, there is everything that you can do about today and tomorrow. When you choose to Forgive, you choose life, your life, by taking back control of it. Then that hurtful situation or person no longer has power over you. Even if they or the circumstance does not change in any way, Forgiveness is more about how it will change your life, enable you to go forward, and will involve something we discussed in the Love Snapshot No. 8: You Can Always Choose Love, offering love to where it hurts to stop the pain. Love and Forgiveness are inextricably intertwined, and you will discover in the following chapter Snapshot that so is inner peace.

By choosing Forgiveness, you will once again find peace, joy, compassion, understanding, gratitude, and, most importantly, hope for the future. Nelson Mandela, Mahatma Gandhi, and Jesus Christ showed us how we can Forgive. Let us follow in their ways.

Centering Thought. Free my spirit.

Affirmation. I release the pain of the past and
live to embrace the joyfulness of today.

Forgiveness Snapshot No. 2:
Forgiveness Is Another Word for Compassion

Utensils scraping across plates of food can be heard in the background. Sitting at a quiet local diner eating in the film *A Beautiful Day in the Neighborhood*, Mr. Rogers replies to the reporter he has been speaking with, Lloyd, who has just observed that Mr. Rogers likes broken people—people like himself, a self-proclaimed broken man because of Lloyd's relationship with his father.

"I know you are a man of conviction—a person who knows the difference between what is wrong and what is right. Try to remember that your relationship with your father also helped to shape those parts. He helped you become what you are."

During my first visit to see my mother after the height of the Covid pandemic, one of my intentions was to finally organize and clear out my father's belongings after he passed. Unfortunately, my father collected anything and everything you could imagine. There were moments when I was frustrated and annoyed at him because of the sheer volume of stuff I had to wade through.

However, because I had taken the time to Forgive my father before his death, I was able to transform my annoyance into compassion. Forgiveness allowed me to empathize with my father's experiences as an immigrant, the discrimination he faced and the things he endured going from country to country with a wife and young children and trying to make a better life. Being willing to Forgive brought a new and healthier perspective to our relationship. I was able to take away the layers of anger, hurt, frustration, and resentment and see a man who loved and took care of his family.

Having compassion for someone you feel deeply hurt you may seem counterintuitive; however, it may be one of the most liberating things you can do for yourself. Compassion does not mean the person who hurt you is no longer accountable. It does mean that, on some level, you understand the cause of their behavior. It could very well be that they likely do not have the emotional tools to deal with their issues in a healthy, loving, and constructive way. Then, unfortunately, you just happen to be in the path of their messy emotional fallout.

Mister Rogers: "It's funny. Sometimes it's the hardest to forgive the ones we love."

Centering Thought. Be compassionate.

Affirmation. I understand we are both just humans trying to make the best of our lives.

Forgiveness Snapshot No. 3: Be Kind Instead of Right

"When given the choice between being right or being kind, choose kind."
—DR. WAYNE DYER

One of the reasons people have a hard time Forgiving is they think Forgiving equals condoning. It does not. The bad behavior you experience from someone is never condoned. Instead, Forgiveness enables you to acknowledge what happened and then choose to keep living your life. You have permission to feel every emotion that comes with a lived incident. So, get those negative emotions moving out of your system; yell, scream, pray, whatever it takes to get you through the upset (more later in this chapter's Happiness Essential).

The real point here is that as long as you keep perpetuating the belief, "They did this to me, and it was not fair," you are not free. You are stuck in the past. Forgiveness is a form of self-preservation that allows you to frame hurtful situations in a healthy, healing, and nurturing way. You do not have to keep standing your ground in righteousness and indignation. There are things in life not worth continuing to fight for, feel hurt over, insulted by, or victimized by. Most issues between people are genuinely minor in the grand scheme.

Do yourself a favor and avoid arguing and staying angry, especially when someone can only see their point of view, want what they want, and continue to insist on having their way on all fronts. I have had several people like this in my life. Admittedly, being around them is not always comfortable, easy, or fun, and I found that the path of least resistance is often better for peace of mind. While I am not suggesting you be their doormat, it is to say that as kindly and calmly as you can express your thoughts, state what is bothering you, then let it go. If they persist in bad behavior, it is just as well you let them go.

I was producing a series with an editor who was an extremely talented storyteller, one of the best I had ever worked with, with the ego to match it and an attachment to always having to be right. It would be a cold day in the underworld before he would back down on an opinion. Initially, I would get into heated debates with him; however, it only made my work life on the show miserable. Then I realized whatever drove his need to be right was on him. His issues had nothing to do with me. I also got that this stubborn Greek girl, *me*, did not always have to be right, too. So, I ceased the circular arguments, finished the series much Happier, and never worked with that editor again.

The reality is, you cannot make someone behave a certain way or accept your point of view. If they choose not to respond, ignore, feel insulted, harbor hard feelings, or want to keep fighting, that is their prerogative. If a relationship ends, perhaps it is for the better, at least for the moment. People who are meant to be in your life have a way of coming around again; however, that relationship could take a different form. A broken romantic relationship could return as a friendship mended. A damaged business relationship becomes a restored personal relationship. A fractured friendship is now a stronger, healed one. The invitation is to keep open to a dysfunctional relationship coming back as a functional one in whatever form it takes.

When people always need to be right, it is generally just their ego talking. If you let go of yours, you will feel more in control. Resist being drawn into arguments you know you cannot win, the ones that are more fruitless intellectual gymnastics rather than really trying to solve a problematic situation. Recognize that it is okay to disagree. Understand that certain firmly held convictions are often part of one's core belief system, current culture, or personal experience. The chances are that a single conversation will not change anything, so save your relationship, energy, and frustration for the times that deserve it. Choosing Forgiveness through kindness over being right can be the most loving thing you can do for yourself.

Centering Thought. Choose kindness.

Affirmation. I choose an open heart that does not always have to be right over a closed heart that only feels right.

Forgiveness Snapshot No. 4: Rejection Is Often a Blessing in Disguise

A cable network planned to do a live show during the May 2014 climbing season at Mount Everest. They were going to do live coverage of a ten-thousand-foot wingsuit jump. By the time one of the network executives told me about it, it was already staffed. I felt a twinge of hurt that none of my contacts asked if I would be interested. I had trekked to Everest Base Camp a few years earlier, so I understood the production challenges. The only thing not in my background was doing a live event. I felt I had enough other capabilities at least to be considered for the pre-taped storytelling part of things. At the time, I tried to stay on the upside of things. I was busy with other projects. Yet, it was still in the recess of my mind that no one considered me for the show.

Then, the worst disaster ever on Everest happened. Sixteen Sherpas were caught in an avalanche as they moved supplies at twenty thousand feet through the icefall above Base Camp. They all perished, with another three missing. The shocking news led to the cable network's understandable decision to abort the entire project. It was tragic on all fronts. I felt sad for the lives lost and the family and friends left to grieve. Candidly, I also felt incredibly blessed to be sitting in my living room in Los Angeles and not in a tent at Everest Base Camp. No one could have predicted such an event. However, if you believe in the universe's intelligence and guidance as I do, you feel there was some divine intervention at work, keeping you safe, and that is how I looked at this situation. For those who were at Everest, I believe they were there for a reason, too, though beyond my comprehension.

"When God gives you a 'no,' give Him a 'thank you.' He was protecting you from less than his best."

I do not know who said this, though, from my humble perspective, they were right. And I would widen this sentiment to include protecting you from harm. The universe spared me a lot of trauma, perhaps even saving my life. At some point, I also realized that staying bummed out about not being asked to work on the show would not change anything. So, I chose to let go of my disappointment and frustration. I accepted what happened and reasoned that it was not my path or it would have happened. Instead, I was supposed to do something else or receive protection from some unknown harm, *like an avalanche*. Whatever the case, I Forgave anything related to that show and emotionally moved forward.

The Everest show that did not happen taught me to Forgive rejection instead of harbor resentment toward it. Not getting the job you dreamed about or falling out with someone you loved could be a blessing in disguise, possibly saving you from your worst nightmare. Rejection is an opportunity to be open to something better coming along, and it could be that "no" means "yes," *just not yet*. Love, Gratitude, and Forgiveness are powerful healing thoughts and actions to employ when things are seemingly not going your way; remember to say thank you.

Centering Thought. I am blessed.

Affirmation. I let go of disappointment, knowing
that I am so very blessed in other nurturing ways.

Forgiveness Snapshot No. 5:
Kiss and Make Up

"The first to apologize is the bravest. The first to forgive is the strongest. And the first to forget is the happiest." I 100 percent agree with this insightful quote from motivational YouTuber Ralph Smart.

Those who kiss and make up have stronger, healthier relationships. Forgiving makes you feel better, Happier, especially if the person who hurt you has sincerely apologized and is now making amends. Forgiveness raises your Happiness as it heals people's relationships and draws them closer together, which is significant in the grand scheme. Close relationships play a crucial role in long-term Happiness and Wholebeing.

Over three decades of Forgiveness studies show that the amount of time you spend trying to Forgive will correlate to the actual degree of Forgiveness expressed. This finding is essential to understand and put into practice. It connects your mind and body—psychologically, biologically, and socially. Standing up for Forgiveness builds your self-esteem, lifting feelings of being trampled on and taken advantage of by people. While not always easy, spending time understanding why someone hurt you and being empathetic toward them will go miles toward your overall health. It will reduce the anxiety and depression that compromise your immune system. Releasing anger and resentment, especially when seated in your body, relieves the stress created within your physical frame. Your muscles become supple, energy increases, and your immune system now strengthens.

The other side of Forgiving is dealing with the repeat offenders who know they can get away with misbehaving by just saying a meaningless "I am sorry." Unfortunately, those who are always the ones Forgiving eventually become less and less happy. Apologies only work when they are genuine. It has to be meaningful, and accompanied by an honest effort not to repeat the hurtful behavior. Accountability needs to go along with the "I am sorry." If this person is not taking responsibility for their actions, you need to take responsibility for yourself, which you should do anyway. That could mean distancing yourself or cutting off the relationship altogether. You can Forgive and not continue the relationship, even if they are family or long-time friends. I know this sounds harsh. However, with these repeat offenders, ask yourself whose life you want to live, theirs or yours? Then, do what will support your decision. You reap what you sow.

Throughout these pages, I have shared where letting go, or Forgiving, has given me life-giving breath, turned my heart pink again, and, most of all, eased the churn of unsettling, anxious, angry thoughts that held my mind and body. Only when I Forgave and moved on did I feel strong and now the Happiest I have ever been inside myself and among others.

Centering Thought. I kiss you.

Affirmation. I kiss you today so that we can move
forward with tomorrow stronger than before.

Forgiveness Snapshot No. 6:
Forgive Others, Forgive Yourself

"Forgiving is not forgetting; it's actually remembering—remembering and not using your right to hit back."

Bishop Desmond Tutu's "Four Steps to Forgiving" has profoundly influenced how I navigate those who have hurt, disappointed, angered, or betrayed me. I do a process inspired by his work and it goes as follows:

One, speak your hurt until there is no more to be said.

Two, openly allow the other person to have their peace.

Three, give room and space for a genuine "I am sorry" that shows remorse from the one who wronged you.

Four, without condoning their bad behavior, move on with your life. You can choose to stay in contact with them or not.

These four steps certainly proved out when I was a producer in the early years of *Survivor*. Every season, one of my shows was the last episode, so I was on the beach with the remaining *Survivor* contestants until the very end, day thirty-nine (except the Australia season, when it was forty-two days). It always struck me when a Survivor sat in an interview apologizing for their deceitful behavior in the game. Time and again, season after season, I would hear the same thing. "This is not really me. This is just me playing a game." Every time in my head, my reply was the same. "No, this is the 'real you.' You just have never been put into a situation that brought out, enabled, or pushed forth this aspect of you. It is the real you. How could it not be?"

We all have a darker side. The question is, how do you view and treat this part of yourself when it rears its dreadful head? Those Survivors who humbly and genuinely apologized for their betrayals were often Forgiven.

Those who remained arrogant and unremorseful were not and soon found themselves voted off the island.

While Forgiving others is essential to one's Happiness, it is also necessary to Forgive ourselves. Otherwise, resentment, anger, shame, or guilt will interfere with your life. So many peoples' minds are caught in a nonstop hamster wheel going round and round, reliving the same story of hurt, betrayal, and victimization with an internal voice continually nagging and criticizing their every move, obsessing over why they did what they did, why the other person did what they did, reliving the *should not haves* that creep into your mind, "If I knew then what I know now," blaming others for their circumstance. Instead, say something kind to yourself. Say something loving and repeatedly until that hamster wheel halts, and you know that you have finally Forgiven. Forgiving does not mean that you forget what has happened. Instead it does mean you no longer hate yourself or blame others.

Then there are those incredibly embarrassing times, shameful moments when you did something so wrong to someone else that you cannot bring yourself to talk about it. You cannot kick yourself to confront the person you harbor guilt over. Find a way. Festering shame and guilt makes you feel weak and vulnerable. In these moments, it is essential to understand that while you may have done something wrong, that does not equate to being a bad person. If you need to, write a letter, make a phone call, see that person you hurt. Admit your remorseful feelings. Tell them how you want to make amends. However, be prepared. That person may not accept your apology; at least you know that you tried, and that is a huge step forward in Forgiving and healing yourself.

"Forgiveness is simply about understanding that every one of us is both inherently good and inherently flawed." More wise words to heed from the Bishop.

Centering Thought. I understand.

Affirmation. I Forgive others and myself, accepting
in each the loving essence of whom we are as
spiritual beings having a human experience.

Forgiveness Snapshot No. 7: Breathe into Forgiveness

My body constricted, feeling stiff and cold inside for months. The show idea was mine. I brought together all the players. However, someone somewhere did not like me, did not think I was worthy enough to stay attached to my show, and I was unceremoniously relegated to a passive producing role just like that, no longer able to have creative input on any aspect. Then I was cut out altogether as the show continued the following year. Rage, hurt, disappointment, and jealousy filled me. It was all I could think about every moment of every day, replaying in my head every conversation, rereading every email, trying to piece together why I got sidelined. What did I say or do wrong? I never found out, and I will never divulge who or what the circumstance was; legally, I cannot, and that is not the point here. It does not matter anymore, and that is the point. What matters is that I eventually let go of the negative emotions that consumed me and Forgave. As soon as I Forgave everyone and everything, it was like a high fever broke, leaving me feeling mentally and emotionally well again. It was the best ending to this story I could have ever given myself. Forgiveness brings down the level of resentment, blame, and anger toward someone, including yourself, no longer feeling offended. So instead of being unforgiving and blaming, try to understand what caused a situation to happen. If you cannot figure out what caused a situation, like in the story I just shared, then accept that it is not yours to know and move on. When you Forgive and let go of that psychological bag of rocks you have been lugging around, you feel lighter, brighter, and Happier. "Ahhhhh," is what comes to mind for me.

Each time I Forgive, it feels like my insides change. My lungs feel cleansed. The creases on my forehead and brow become smoother. My over-all body feels suppler, softer. When I Forgive the most, best of all, my heart feels pink again. Peacefulness and contentment wash over me, and I can now savor the lightness of being once again. You Forgive so you can feel the weight of resentment lifting from you.

In an *O Magazine* interview, the late Dr. Maya Angelou said, "It's one of the greatest gifts you can give yourself, to forgive. Forgive everybody… (have) enough courage to stand up and say, 'I forgive. I'm finished with it.'" This from a woman who Forgave the man who raped her when she was seven. You will read more about Dr. Angelou's story later.

Centering Thought. I Forgive.

Affirmation. Each time I Forgive, I
cleanse my heart and mind.

Forgiveness Snapshot No. 8:
Forgiveness Gives Back Your Life

The ocean breeze felt cool and soothing on my perspiring brow. My long hair fluttered in a trail behind my head. I breathed deeply, filling my body with negative ion molecules rushing oxygen into my brain. I felt alive and electric as I walked along the water's edge. It was our first day doing the last one hundred kilometers of the Camino de Santiago Portuguese, the "Spiritual Way of the Apostle James," part of one of the world's most significant Christian pilgrimages, believed to be the way his disciples brought the apostle's remains from Israel to the shores of Spain to end up enshrined inside the Santiago de Compostela Cathedral. Six days later, I would walk through a cathedral door that is only open during the Camino de Santiago's Holy Years, when Apostle James's feast day lands on a Sunday. When you walk through this door as a Christian pilgrim, like me, you receive plenary indulgence: Forgiveness for all misdeeds done throughout life. So, between now and then, lots of ground to cover, literally and figuratively. Every day, as I walked, I would ask who or what I needed to Forgive. Several difficult memories surfaced as I walked for long silent stretches. Some were caused by others in my past, some I caused, and it was time to let it *all* go.

If you are harboring hurt, resentment, and anger, it will manifest somehow, and it is often as a disease in the body, the mind, or both. Let go of all those raging emotions by focusing on what you are grateful for and feelings of kindness. When you count your blessings, also think of what you can Forgive. Sincerely ask, and do not bypass this one. You may want to try Loving-Kindness meditations, which acknowledge the shared desire to have a good life. We are all broken in some way and want to be Happy. "But for the grace of God, there go I." The path forward is through love, kindness, and Forgiveness. You experienced this meditation doing Love Action Opportunity No. 8: You Can Always Choose Love.

"Just as I wish, too, may we all be safe, healthy, and live with ease and happiness."

Most importantly, be patient and compassionate toward yourself as you work through emotional pain and trauma. Once on the other side, life will look different. You will be more flexible and tolerant of how life or people should be and realize that you, too, have a choice about your life. You can create the path you want to walk.

Ultimately, Forgive so you can live life rather than being locked in the past and hostage to it. When you are present and fully living, those around you, who love you, get to share in your absolute wonderfulness too. That is the greatest kind of emotional victory, and it begins with the desire, with you wanting to learn to Forgive.

*"Getting over a painful experience is much
like crossing monkey bars. You have to let go at
some point in order to move forward."*
—C. S. LEWIS

Centering Thought. Forgiving is for living.

Affirmation. I choose to Forgive as an
act that gives me life once again.

♥ ♥ ♥

Forgiveness Meditation Prayer

In Christ. In Gandhi. In Mandela. They Forgave.

May I walk in their way.

*May I be kind, may I be compassionate, may I
be loving even when pain is all I know.*

May I not judge and never mind when I am judged.

The others know not what they do, though I certainly do.

Forgiving is for living, and that is what I am here to do.

And so let it be.

DEVELOPING HEARTFELT FORGIVENESS

Forgiveness takes the weight off both your mind and physical being. As a result, you perceive a less daunting world, moving through it with more grace when under fire. It enables you to heal your heart, to breathe again. Being in a chronic state of negativity can contribute to cancer, heart disease, and other autoimmune disorders—the prescription, a dose of Forgiveness to heal the body and ease your soul. The other benefits of Forgiveness are numerous:

Lower blood pressure and heart rate
Less anxiety and stress
Less hostility and the chance of depression
Better sleep
More hope, higher self-esteem
Greater spiritual and psychological Wholebeing
Happier relationships

"I Forgive you" are three words that, when heartfully said together, can dry an ocean of grief and fill a chasm with love, turning foes into friends—or, at least put two opposing sides into a healthier place to deal with one another. Besides, who wants the sum of one's life to be that of anger, resentment, and hurt? I certainly do not.

Journaling with Forgiveness: What Does Forgiveness Mean to You?

I encourage you to journal how you can bring more Forgiveness into your life. I have given my answers in italics and left space for you to fill in yours.

How do you define Forgiveness and its benefits?

Forgiveness is my ability to transform anger or hurt by accepting that there is goodness inside the person who hurt me and acknowledging that we are both operating at our level of awareness and emotional maturity. However, it might take me a beat to get there. Nevertheless, being more forgiving moves me out of being stuck in the past, reliving and perpetuating negative emotions that are not serving me so I can live without the claws of resentment. It frees and lifts me emotionally, therefore mentally and physically.

_____

_____

_____

What role does Forgiveness currently play in your life?

The process of forgiveness helps me understand that many of the upsets we have in our daily lives do not matter in the grand scheme of things. Ultimately, it enables me to keep peace within myself.

_____

_____

_____

How easily can you Forgive?

One of my top character strengths is the ability to forgive—something I have had to consciously develop. The practice of being the observer of my thoughts and detachment from them has helped tremendously.

How are you, or will you, be more Forgiving?

My growth area is in noticing and releasing emotionally charged judgment or resentment toward those who hurt me even sooner and resting in knowing that the universe will show me a better way.

Take a photograph of what Forgiveness looks like for you. Give it a caption. Then, journal about your thoughts and feelings.

I did not know how high I could fly until I forgave.

Journal Entry: *I did not realize the albatross around my neck called Unforgiving. Blind to see the other person's side or their humanity, maybe they felt hurt too. However, I was too caught up in my own needs, my hurt to see other possibilities. Yet, what else could be, would be possible if only I forgave more? So, I let go of the debris that was blame. I am now like a bird freeing itself from its cage and happily soaring into the world again.*

Forgiveness Photo Ops and Action Opportunities

Forgiveness is for living, for moving forward again. Use the following Photo Op prompts and Action Opportunities as a guide to open your heart to being more compassionate toward yourself and others.

Forgiveness Snapshot No. 1:
The Past Is Just That

Photo Op. *Free Your Heart, Free Your Mind.* Capture images that reflect what healing or freeing your heart feels like to you. Try this Photo Op along with its Action Opportunity.

Action Opportunity. Give yourself the time to think and consider whom you need to Forgive or ask for Forgiveness. You can begin with the Centering Thought: "Free my spirit." When you have determined who and how you want to practice Forgiveness, take the necessary steps to set up a phone call or video chat, write a letter, or plan a face-to-face meeting. Do it with love in your heart. If the person is no longer living or nearby, consider a ritual such as reading a letter aloud to a close friend or family member. Seal this Forgiveness with the Affirmation: "I release the pain of the past and live to embrace the joyfulness of today." During this process, make sure that you are Forgiving yourself too.

_____

_____

_____

Forgiveness Snapshot No. 2:
Forgiveness Is Another Word for Compassion

Photo Op. *Looking at Both Sides.*

One, choose a situation where you are having difficulty Forgiving. Collect images you find online, in magazines, or that you capture that reflect how you feel and think.

Two, do the same step again, though now find or capture images of what you perceive as the other person's point of view.

Three, use the Action Opportunity to write about how this Photo Op shifts your perspective. What actions does it motivate you to do?

Action Opportunity. Reflect on the images from the Photo Op, both perspectives. Start with the Centering Thought: "Be compassionate." Then, try to see if some shared humanity exists, even remotely, especially in cases that cry out to resolve layers of hurt or unfairness. When it is within you, either give or accept Forgiveness. Bless the moment with the Affirmation: "I understand we are both just humans trying to make the best of our lives." This Action Opportunity could be quite cathartic and may even reveal a profound insight that you had not previously seen.

Forgiveness Snapshot No. 3: Be Kind Instead of Right

Photo Op. *Notice the Hearts Around You.* Wherever you find them, be aware of heart-shaped floral wreaths, the barista creating a heart with the foam for your latte, or a puffy cloud in the shape of a heart. Notice how surrounding yourself with pictures of hearts opens yours toward accepting with kindness that the other person has a different perspective on things and that it is okay to agree to disagree.

    Action Opportunity. When you find yourself at odds with someone you care about, honestly ask yourself, do I want to be right? Or do I want to keep this relationship intact by agreeing to disagree? Use the Centering Thought: "Choose kindness." Then, after thinking through your answer, seal it with the Affirmation: "I choose an open heart that does not always have to be right over a closed heart that only feels right." Now, take the necessary steps that align with your decision.

Forgiveness Snapshot No. 4:
Rejection Is Often a Blessing in Disguise

Photo Op. *Change Rejection to New Possibilities.* The next time you feel rejected, make a vision board of images that reflect the possibilities that are now available to you. This Photo Op is a good one to do along with the Action Opportunity.

    Action Opportunity. When you feel rejected, allow the hurt to go its way while keeping in mind the Centering Thought: "I am blessed." Then, when you are ready, move on to putting your trust and faith into making something even better happen for you. I encourage you to create a list of opportunities now open and the first steps toward achieving one of them. Finally, consider, just maybe, the rejection you feel is the universe protecting you, and seal it with the Affirmation: "I let go of disappointment, knowing that I am so very blessed in other nurturing ways."

Forgiveness Snapshot No. 5:
Kiss and Make Up

Photo Op. *Capture Images That Open Your Heart.* These images are symbolic to you. Seeing and surrounding yourself with meaningful photos will give you the space to open your heart to Forgiveness.

    Action Opportunity. Consider where making up is more important than remaining upset. Use the Centering Thought "I kiss you" to look for answers to some difficult heartfelt questions:

    What wounds can you heal, and is it important to you?

    How would it feel to kiss and make up? Before taking action with someone, say the Affirmation: "I kiss you today so that we can move forward with tomorrow stronger than before."

Conversely, ask where you need to cut your losses, save your heart, and move on. The Affirmation still applies to you to be stronger without this person. Replace the word "we" with "I."

_____

_____

_____

Forgiveness Snapshot No. 6:
Forgive Others, Forgive Yourself

Photo Op. *A Collage of Forgiveness in Action.* Create a collage or series of images of people in every size, shape, color, age, and gender hugging, shaking hands, or giving a compassionate touch.

Action Opportunity. Using the images from the Photo Op, journal how this practice helps you be more Forgiving. See where there is a lack of Forgiveness in your life and seek to change it. Start with the Centering Thought: "I understand." Then, notice what changes happened because of this willingness to Forgive others or yourself. Finally, say out loud or silently the Affirmation: "I Forgive others and myself, accepting in each the loving essence of who we are as spiritual beings having a human experience."

_____

_____

_____

Forgiveness Snapshot No. 7:
Breathe into Forgiveness

Photo Op. *I Forgive You, and I Forgive Myself.* Create an image that includes the words: "I forgive you, and I forgive myself." Send it to the person you want to Forgive.

Action Opportunity. Instead of harboring anger and resentment, take a long, deep breath and say, "I forgive you. I forgive myself." Core to these words is the Centering Thought: "I Forgive." Use it to reflect on the images from the Photo Op. Ask what is now emotionally present for you. If they reject your Forgiveness, try to understand they are entitled to their emotions and opinions. In light of this, can you still Forgive and appreciate yourself for trying to make amends so you can gracefully move onward? Seal this practice with the Affirmation: "Each time I Forgive, I cleanse my heart and mind."

_____

_____

_____

Forgiveness Snapshot No. 8: Forgiveness Gives Back Your Life

Photo Op. *A Reflection on Forgiveness as Freedom.* Create a collage or series of images that reflect the goodness, the freedom that Forgiveness can bring into your life.

Action Opportunity. Our Centering Thought "Forgiving is for living" can be especially helpful here. The moment you consciously choose to Forgive is when your life begins to change. When you choose to Forgive, you let go of the past and step into the present.

First, create a list of where you can make this conscious choice. Then, act on this list one mindful choice at a time and give yourself grace when it is challenging. Remember this with the Affirmation: "I choose to Forgive as an act that gives me life once again."

_____

_____

_____

PICTURING PEACE

Peace

\ˈpēs\

noun

    : a state of tranquility or quiet

    : freedom from disquieting or oppressive
thoughts or emotions

    : harmony in personal relations

*"By taking care of the present moment,
we take good care of the future.
Working for peace in the future is to work
for peace in the present moment."*

—THICH NHAT HANH
Vietnamese Buddhist Monk and Peace Activist

SNAPSHOT OF PEACE

In My Viewfinder

Peace and love are so strongly interconnected, the inward and outward positive connections you share with the universal community. The level of Peace you have within gets sent outward to everyone and everything you encounter. The same goes for love. While it will vary in expression from one person and situation to the next, it will be so with "in," so with "out." I bet you cannot think of one case where this does not hold true. I cannot. The more at Peace I am with someone, the warmer, more loving feelings I have towards them, and this get reflected in how I react when I see them. Inner Peace means being at ease, content, and resolved with your place in the world as you move along in life and in all your relationships: family, friends, neighbors, community, country, world, higher source, and yourself. However, I also do not think you find inner Peace. You create it. You develop it. The good news is that the seeds of it already exist inside you.

Creating inner Peace is about realizing what can trigger a disturbance of it and doing something constructive to resolve it—letting go of the petty things that do not mean anything in the grand scheme of life and only get in the way of being Happy in the present moment. It is setting free your desires and knowing that God, the universe, will engineer things to work out as they should in perfect timing, allowing you to enjoy the journey along the way, clearing out the useless clutter that collects in your mind, body, and environment, letting simplicity rule the day.

You can choose whether to allow some thought, a person, or an event to disturb your Peace of mind. Understanding this is critical. It is when ongoing internal chats come into play—conversations about who you are, your place in the world, how you want to be in it—and being accountable in relationships, including the one with yourself. You have these private dialogues with yourself, so you are clear on what is okay with you or not. This clarity acts as an internal barometer for all decisions, making you the driver of your life versus a passenger. It is your time, your life, not anyone else's. When you feel in control of your life, there is an overriding sense of calm; creating the space for inner Peace to flourish means regularly hitting the pause button so you can just be.

Snapshots on Developing Peace of Mind (and Heart)

Peace Snapshot No. 1:
Own Your I Am

"I am R-rated sexy!"
Emma Stone as Hannah in *Crazy, Stupid, Love*

"I am also just a girl!"
Julia Roberts as Anna Scott in *Notting Hill*

"I am kick ass!"
Aaron Taylor-Johnson as Dave Lizewski in *Kick-Ass*

"I am the dude!"
Jeff Bridges as The Dude in *The Big Lebowski*

"I am a golden god!"
Billy Crudup as Russel Hammond in *Almost Famous*

"Naval Aviator is not what I am. It's who I am."
Tom Cruise as Maverick in *Top Gun: Maverick*

Saying "I am" is a declaration of who you think and feel you are, reflecting a state of being. The question is, is it a state of being you want? Does it feel good inside? Are you at Peace with yourself? If you do not feel good about yourself, you do not feel calm, at ease, or content inside. Likely, you feel uneasy, uncomfortable, and twisted inside your head and heart. You want to uncoil these feelings. So, start by identifying three positive words that define the essence of who and what you are or would like to be in the world. They should be words that reflect the love you have or would like to have toward yourself that nurture the good that genuinely resides inside you.

Happy, open, passionate, loving, energetic, loyal, powerful, connected, honest, compassionate, empathic, curious, adventurous, joyous, boundless, grateful, forgiving.

Choose your top three defining words and put "I am a(n)" in front of them and your gender after.

"I am an open, loving, and powerful woman."

The words "I am" have profound power, for it names God. It calls the universe—this is what "I am" means. If you believe that you were created in the image of God and understand that the universe is embodied in each of us, then saying "I am" is the recognition of your God-essence. The following three descriptive words about you activate the essence of the divine within. To realize and accept your true spirit is one of the most uplifting, loving, and impactful things you can do for yourself. So, be very conscious of how you use "I am." When you say:

"I am broke."

"I am a failure."

"I am unlovable."

You are defining yourself in a way that is not serving you well, as we reflected on negative self-talk in Health Snapshot No.1: Think Healthy Thoughts. You are putting huge limitations on yourself, therefore on God, the universe within. Last time I checked, God and the universe were still limitless, so then are you. Reframe these negative thoughts to activate the power, the good that lies inside you.

"I am abundant."

"I am successful."

"I am lovable."

If you do not believe this about yourself now, you will when you act "as if." Meaning act the way you want to be, and you will become it. The father of American psychology, William James, said, "If you want a certain quality, act as if you already have it." What your body does impacts what you think and feel, and vice-versa. Help your cause by finding proof that you are already abundant, prosperous, and lovable. Look for the evidence. Think about where this is already true in your life, even if it is only a slight bit. If you want to be more lovable, instead of saying, "I am unlovable," look for where you are already loved. If it is your sister, replace "I am unlovable" with "Thank God my sister loves me. I am lovable." Keep looking for other evidence. Using your "I am" this way, bit by bit, synapse by synapse, creates a neural pathway toward positive or constructive thoughts and away from negative ones. You train your mind to believe in itself. Realizing and reminding yourself of where or how what you desire presently exists will support a new belief. Then, you can confidently act *as if*, so it will eventually *become* your reality because you know who you want to be is aligned and genuine.

It may help to meditate using "I am" or "Om," a form of "I am." On the in-breath, quietly say to yourself, "I." On the out-breath, say "am." As you meditate, you may experience radiating light, feel your heart is full, have an epiphany of profound wisdom, or only just a sense of quietness inside you. Everyone is different, and all of it is right. Use the meditative stillness to allow the power of "I am," your I am, to sink into your very being. With time, this insight will stay with you off the meditation cushion.

When I first chose my three descriptive words, open, loving, and powerful, I was not feeling open nor particularly powerful. That was what I wanted to develop for myself. I did feel loving, so at least I had that going for me. Eventually, I stepped into my statement, "I am an open, loving, and powerful woman," which helped me choose my associations.

Owning my "I am" triggered thoughts about the relationships in my life—who was supportive, who not so much—led to editing out the not so much. This reflection is critical because you want the right relationships in your life that are, for me, open and loving. I want transparent and supportive relationships across the board in business and my personal life. So, consider the people in your life. Do they support your "I am"? Then, intentionally create relationships that will lift you.

"The more you know who you are and what you want, the less you let things upset you," says Bill Murray as Bob Harris, an American movie star having a mid-career crisis in Tokyo in *Lost in Translation*. I think the character Bob Harris is right. When you know and own your "I am," you are so much clearer on what matters and what does not.

Centering Thought. I am (fill in this space).

Affirmation. I own, nourish, and love
who I am and the Peace within me.

Peace Snapshot No. 2:
What Others Think of You Is None of Your Business

Looking down, he was silent for what seemed an eternity. "Hmmm." He flipped over several cards on the table that separated us, nodding as if acknowledging someone talking to him. Maybe they were. He was a medium, after all. He stopped flipping and brought his gaze to meet mine. "Lemme give you some advice. What others think of you is none of your business." His words took their own journey in my head.

"What??"

"What does that mean?"

"Hmmm. Maybe."

"Ohhhhh, I get it."

"Huh, that is exactly, and unfortunately, what I do—make it my business to want to know and react to people's opinions of me—and it is emotionally and mentally costing me."

Like many of us, I cared too much about what others think of me, and this section is about the business of your life, minding it, making a few promises to yourself, and never minding what others think you are or should do.

For starters, promise to do what you want to do versus giving in to what family, friends, colleagues, teachers, or bosses want you to do. Respect and believe in yourself. Live your dream. Like owning your "I am," seek to own the life that goes with it. Do this, and you will have greater Peace within. Never mind the opinion and judgments of others. We often know this yet forget to abide by it. Then what happens when you get caught up in other people's thoughts of you? It messes you up in a way that most certainly disturbs your Peace of mind. That is not good. You know yourself better than anyone, so use this knowledge to your advantage to create the life you want.

Minding my own business and not taking on other people's opinions of me was a difficult lesson to learn, spanning many years of my professional life, I worried and tried to please others. I found this to be most notably true when I was in production. I always have a strong vision for how I want something creatively done. However, it most definitely disturbed my Peace when I was at odds with my cameraman, editor, other key people on the production team, or our show's network executive. These moments of creative differences churned me up for too long, taking up creative energy that I could have used. There was no inner peace, whether I won or lost a creative dispute. My stress and anxiety levels were flying high, and eventually, I crashed. I felt I had become an ineffective showrunner, and it was time to step back for a while to regroup. I finally realized that other people's opinions are just that, an opinion—a point of view that is not necessarily based on fact or knowledge. Their judgments did not, do not define me or anyone else. You determine who you are. The message here is to stick to your business and let others stick to theirs.

Miguel Ruiz's book *The Four Agreements* suggests that you make some promises to yourself, which are solely your business and not anyone else's. Promise to be impeccable with your word, not to take things personally, not to assume, and to act with integrity. Each of these promises is a guiding light to follow in your daily life. They will help you navigate any situation, any relationship issue that comes up.

Promise to be impeccable with your word. Say what you mean. Mean what you say. Your word is the gold standard by which people will trust you, the faith they will put into your promise to do something. Of all the agreements, this is the one I most value, the one I apply to myself as well as to those I deal with in every aspect of life. People will show you who they are by how they back up the words they say.

Promise not to take things personally. Most people's actions and agendas have nothing to do with you. Many times, when things go sour, someone breaks up with you, yells at you, blames you, what is really going on has more to do with the one sending the poison darts your way than with you. You just happened to get caught in the crosshairs of their aim, and it does hurt. What softens these blows is to change the focus from that other person to what is relevant to you. Think about the positive lessons you can take from the situation, which can be very challenging, especially when wounds are still raw. Try anyway. It will better serve you. Grow from these experiences instead of getting caught up in them by asking yourself these questions:

What was your role in attracting the situation or inciting the person's reaction?

How could you have handled the situation more diplomatically, more compassionately, more empathetically?

What stories around the situation are you telling yourself that no longer serve you?

Promise not to assume. You know the saying: "When you assume, you make an ass out of you and me." Ask if you do not understand something, what to do, or how a thing works. Do not assume your partner knows you want to do something romantic together, that your best friend knows your feelings are hurt by something they said, or that your boss knows you want to be the next project manager. Most people do not read minds and, as already suggested, are probably pretty caught up in their own world— especially if they are working with you or in a relationship with you. They should be asking you when they do not understand or desire something. This promise is about being a good communicator so people can support you. Make your wishes, desires, and needs known. People generally want to help. They want to accommodate others. However, you need to help them help you by clearly and explicitly saying what you want in a kind tone. Harsh demands fall on deaf ears.

Part two of this promise is to be mindful of your emotions and communicate in a way that serves everyone involved. It will help to take long, deep breaths, a big inhalation and long exhalation, before speaking—this activates your parasympathetic nervous system, which creates soothing sensations in your body when you are overly excited, angry, or flustered. I find this to be both effective and challenging when dealing with family members and annoyingly difficult people.

Promise to act with integrity. Looking in the dictionary for "integrity" synonyms, you will find listed "honesty" and "honor," which define one's character and actions. The root word, *integr*, is Latin, meaning "entire." So, when you act with integrity towards a situation or person, your full character, including your actions, behaves in trustworthy and honorable ways. You make this promise to others as well as yourself. The latter is essential. When screenwriters learn about character development, one of the tips is that true character is revealed by actions when no one is looking. I have always thought this applicable to everyday people as well.

To Ruiz's agreements, I would add another four promises:

Avoid being a gossip.

Resist being petty.

Keep your own counsel.

Withhold judgment.

The underlying reason for these is the same. When you gossip, are petty, get into the mix of things uninvited, when you judge, you are playing small. It is wasteful, limiting the energy that could be better spent on expansive thinking. You are turning your thoughts outward. Turn them inward. Instead of worrying about what someone else is doing or not doing, focus on the dreams you want to manifest, the remarkable life you are creating. Abiding by these eight promises, these agreements will uplift the quality of the Peace within, bringing into focus what is worthy of your time and energy and what it means to mind your business and not worry about what others think. The medium's advice was insightful.

Centering Thought. Mind my business.

Affirmation. I Peacefully mind my
business and never mind others'.

Peace Snapshot No. 3:
Apply the Golden Rule to Yourself First

"Whatever you want someone to do to you, do also to them." However,
when was the last time you consciously considered exactly what makes up
your Golden Rules for living?

It is incredibly worthwhile to explore, realize, and write down the Golden
Rules you want to live by; this is your personal code, your commandments
(in addition to God's if you so believe). The immediate world around you is
of your own doing. Realize it or not, it is. The sooner you take responsibility
for it, the sooner Peace becomes part of how you frame the world you see
and feel. Being present and alert to your thoughts and emotions is essential. We all make hundreds and thousands and millions of decisions every
moment, every day, every week, every year that are motivated by what we
think and how we feel, and these inform our values. Every decision influences the neurocircuitry in the brain, shaping whether or not your inner
compass points towards the positive, your innate goodness. When you follow your true north, it feels good inside, causing you to cease caring so
much about other people's critical opinions and judgments, thus giving you
a greater sense of Peace and control over your own life. Your brain is the hub
for this activity, specifically the prefrontal cortex, which forms your values
and your ability to differentiate between good and bad. At the same time,
the limbic area governs your emotions and motivation. Together, they shape
how you learn, what you remember, and how you act.

Over time I have refined my Golden Rules to fifteen things that I live
and stand by, admittedly, at times more successfully than others. Almost
every rule listed comes as a result of doing its opposite to a not-so-good
outcome. My trials and tribulations and the repeated recognition of what I

value now inform how I move through the world. Knowing the rules I play by makes many decisions obvious and saves me a lot of grief.

Here they are in no particular order, except the first:

One. Be strong in my faith and spirituality.

Two. Be truthful with myself and others, following my heart and mind rather than anyone else's vision for me.

Three. Forgive myself as well as others, showing empathy or compassion.

Four. Every day, give thanks and be grateful, dwelling on what I can do and do have versus what I cannot do and do not have.

Five. Follow through on my promises.

Six. Avoid gossiping, swearing, and pettiness.

Seven. Mind my own business and not others'.

Eight. Leave other women's men alone.

Nine. Phrase things in the positive, in what is constructive, staying on the upside of things.

Ten. Be proactive and solution oriented, always looking for the lesson, especially when times are challenging.

Eleven. Find a bit of quiet time every day to meditate and pray for others as well as myself.

Twelve. Support causes that serve others.

Thirteen. Keep my ego, temper, and impatience in check.

Fourteen. Always consider my Wholebeing and others holistically, in mind, body, and spirit.

Fifteen. Keep life simple and clutter (of any kind) to a minimum, throwing away or giving away things regularly.

So, now think of what you want to do unto yourself first. What are your Golden Rules? Be honest with yourself.

Centering Thought. Golden rules.

Affirmation. I do unto myself as I would unto others.

Peace Snapshot No. 4:
Be a Loving Battery

Harry: "I know, I know. I shouldn't have done it."

Sally: "Harry, you are going to have to try and find a way of not expressing every feeling that you have, every moment that you have them."

Harry: "Oh really?"

Sally: "Yes, there are times and places for things."

Harry: "Well, the next time you are giving a lecture series on social graces, will you let me know because I will sign up."

Sally's comment only added fuel to the fire Harry is feeling inside after running into his ex-wife and taking it out on his recently married best friends in the romantic comedy *When Harry Met Sally*. The conversation explodes into a huge fight between Harry and Sally about how they are handling their respective recent relationship breakups. Clearly, they have romantic feelings for each other they have yet to realize and, in the meantime, need to figure out how to keep Peace in their friendship. Perhaps you have had some version of this in your life, where someone agitates feelings about one issue that triggers other emotional ones, resulting in two angry people who care about each other now in a standoff. This scenario can happen between friends, lovers, family members, or colleagues.

What to do? Try to be a loving battery, a positive charge to someone in distress.

Learn to avoid adding fuel to the fire of a conversation, especially when, or better yet, before it becomes gossip. The more you toss kindling onto an already heated discussion, the more inflamed it will likely grow. Try, when someone comes to you with a problem, complaint, or issue, to allow that person to say their Peace, whether it is about you or someone else. Respond neutrally or as objectively as possible rather than defending, taking sides, or lecturing. The other person often only wants to be heard rather than having their fire ignited more; be an empathic listener. Lean into what they are feeling inside—something Sally could have done for Harry instead of giving him advice he did not ask for. Being a loving battery for your friend, colleague, or partner will actually bring you closer together because they will feel safe and, more importantly, heard. People want to know that their thoughts and feelings matter. You can be a supportive listener without overly engaging and worsening a bad situation.

However, the other part of this is that many people unthinkingly, un-consciously complain. They are caught in their automatic Negative Bias hamster wheel of unproductive thoughts. I have only come across two people who said they like complaining. The others likely complain because that is their unconscious view of the world.

That said, just because you are an empathetic listener does not mean you have to take on someone else's negative charge. Refer to my earlier comment from Health Snapshot No. 2: Mind Your Environment; other people's stuff does not have to be yours. At some point, save your own battery and cut off or redirect the conversation, especially if they repeatedly say the same thing with no movement toward resolving their issue. They just want to complain, to not really do anything about it. That is when my thirteenth Golden Rule, keeping my patience in check, gets challenged. I lose empathy, along with my patience, when someone is just unloading on me without wanting to do anything proactive to change their circumstance. Neuroanatomist Dr. Jill Bolte Taylor talks about a "Ninety-second Rule" that I think can be applied to complainers.

First, the Ninety-second Rule. When there is an emotional reaction to something in your environment, a chemical reaction is released in your brain. This reaction takes about ninety seconds to work through your system and dissipate. Once this time passes, how you continue responding to the situation is your choice. Either you keep complaining, or you do something proactive. If you stay upset, you just reinforce the brain's negative neural pathway. *So, stop it.*

The other necessary thing when being a loving battery is to refrain from being a social worker. Resist trying to fix, to change people into behaving as you want or see fit unless they ask for your help. Register in your head when people show you the views and conditions of their life. Either that works for you or does not. If it does not, resist further engagement in the direction that is not working to keep the Peace within both you and them. Preserve the friendship, the companionship, whatever it is that makes for a more comfortable, more harmonious relationship; this is a genuinely valuable effort. We humans are wired for connection. It gives us a sense of belonging that feels good. Disconnection is its opposite, isolation that leads to hurt, feeling unwanted, not good enough—all things that disturb your Peace. Let go of the situations that cause these latter feelings. Actively develop ones that create the former, a felt sense of connection and belonging.

Harry: "Are you finished now?"

Sally: "Yes."

Harry: "Can I say something?"

Sally: "Yes."

Harry: "I'm sorry." Hugs Sally. "I'm sorry."

Sally hugs him back.

Centering Thought. I am a loving battery.

Affirmation. I am a Peaceful, loving battery
to those who need a positive charge.

Peace Snapshot No. 5:
Protect Your Head

"Paris. 29 December 1386" fades up on the small television screen embedded behind the seat in front of me. The words dissolve into an image of a dueling field. "Ooooh, this is going to be good," I thought, a period piece with fighting knights. Pretty much if an actor puts on a suit of metal plate armor in a film, I am there. This one was a historical drama by one of my favorite directors and actors, Ridley Scott and Matt Damon, *The Last Duel*. I was on only the fourth hour of an eleven-hour flight between London and Johannesburg and had loads of time to watch a film. When I started watching the movie, I did not know that it was based on a true story about the last officially recognized duel in France over one nobleman accused of raping another nobleman's wife. As they got to the rape scene, I switched off the film. I did not want the visuals or the sounds of rape floating around in my head for the next seven hours of my flight or the several days or weeks after, when I often still think about films. As soon as I clicked to exit the television screen, my father came to mind.

As a kid, my father both limited the amount of television I could watch each day and censored the television programs and films I saw. I was always less than happy when I would go to turn on the television, and there would be a lock at the end of the cord. When I was done being mad, my father would explain that at my young age, my mind was impressionable. He wanted to protect me from hearing a lot of harmful use of language and from seeing anything overly violent. I did not appreciate it then, though I certainly do today. I now have my own self-imposed limiters.

Because it is so important, this part reflects a little more on Health Snapshot No. 2: Mind Your Environment. In addition to monitoring the content you take in, focus on maintaining your inner Peace equilibrium. I think along with "you become the focus of your thoughts" and "you are what you eat" goes, "you reflect what you absorb," and keep absorbing and keep absorbing. Unconsciously, you look for what supports your likes and dislikes. Eventually you are reflecting outwardly the content you have been consuming, television, films, news, books, articles, social media. Look at the people around you, especially those with extreme viewpoints: highly politically opinioned, religious zealot, big gun spokesperson, very green conservationist, outspoken advocate for non-violence. Each reflects the content they have taken on board and their associations. These people choose who they hang out with based on whether they are in sync with their point of view. You and I do this too. It is human nature to gravitate to who and what is familiar.

What started as learning eventually became gathering evidence to support their ideas and worldviews. The term for this proof-gathering is "Confirmation Bias," when you look for and find what you already know and believe. You want so much for your idea, for your position to be right, that you keep gathering intel until it eventually becomes true through your lens. You stop seeing, dismissing another point of view, and that is when we get into trouble and prejudices become deep-seated.

For some of us (I am in this category) there comes a time when you consciously block out and minimize what you are exposed to because it disrupts your state of Peace. I absolutely filter the type and amount of negativity I take on board. I no longer have a television in my bedroom. I got rid of it altogether in 2011 when I came home from being on location for three months and did not watch television. I used to fall asleep with it on, and whatever was playing would influence my dreams. Same if I argued with someone not long before putting my head on my pillow. I would still be fighting in my dreams. Many couples make it a policy not to go to bed mad at each other. It is a good policy because your brain continues processing while you sleep. If you are still angry with your partner, you keep duking it out in your sleep.

During the rapid eye movement (REM) stage of sleep, the production of the stress-related hormones cortisol and epinephrine significantly decreases and helps you recover from emotional stress, which is likely why you feel better in the morning after a good night's rest. Going to bed mad makes this process harder. Side note: sleep is when the brain prunes toxic atrophied neurons and resets the nervous system. So, why replace the neuron toxins that have been cleared out with new ones? It is like cleaning out your closet only to fill it again with more junk you do not need.

Thanks for the lesson, Dad. It has served as an invisible suit of metal plate armor, shielding me from much unwanted negativity over the years.

Centering Thought. Protect my head.

Affirmation. I am the guardian of my inner Wholebeing: my mind, my heart, my spirit.

Peace Snapshot No. 6: Release Your "I Am Upset Because"

The last time you were upset with someone, did you stop to consider the real reason why you were angry? So often, it is not what you are saying in the heat of the moment and is something that lies beneath the surface.

When you are upset, it is always linked to a reason, a cause. That reason becomes the catalyst for churning up the calm that would otherwise exist inside you. What is going on inside is an emotional reaction that causes a physiological one based on your perception of a situation, usually informed by past experiences. You see a circumstance, an event, or a person as an obstacle obstructing your Peace and then getting articulated in the form of "I am upset because."

"I am upset because they showed up late."

"I am upset because my partner spends too much money."

"I am upset because my boyfriend broke up with me."

"I am upset because I do not have enough time to do everything."

"I am upset because (fill in the blank)."

Saying "I am upset because" is you calling out grievances and directing them to someone or something outside yourself. How you relate to someone showing up late for an appointment, the number of bills in your wallet, rejection from a romantic date, or demands on your time all point to outward scenarios instead of inward, where you should be looking.

One way of reflecting on what or who is disturbing your Peace is by seeing them as shining light on unresolved internal issues. Realize that much of the time, what you are upset at and blaming the outside world for is really about you. When you blame things outside yourself and hang onto your grievances, you darken the light of the Peace within. It is like keeping the lens cap on your camera, preventing you from seeing through your viewfinder. Holding onto an upset may also cause you to want to fix or change a situation disturbing you that is external and could be impossible to change. Yet, your only absolute control resides within you. You can change how you relate to a situation. How you relate to the issue is the issue.

The invitation is to use these situations of upset as opportunities to heal or learn and grow from them. Use your "I am upset because" to investigate why you are really upset. Get underneath the statement to discover the root cause of your feelings. Ask yourself these questions inspired by Byron Katie's book *Loving What Is*:

One, is your "I am upset because" statement beyond a doubt true?

Two, what irrefutable evidence do you have that statement is true?

Three, where in your life could you be doing the same thing that is upsetting you now?

Four, being completely honest with yourself, is this something you need to clean up with yourself?

Now, reframe your "I am upset because" statement. Make the same statement, relating it to what you need to clean up.

When someone annoys you because they are late, say to yourself, "I am upset because I am often late and need to clean that up with myself."

When someone shows financial irresponsibility, say to yourself, "I am upset because I act irresponsibly with my money and need to clean that up with myself."

When someone backs out of a relationship you want with them, say, "I am upset because I am choosing relationships that are not right for me and need to clean that up with myself."

When someone misuses time, and it affects you, say, "I am upset because I do not set time boundaries well and need to clean that up with myself."

The ideas in this section intertwine with some discussed earlier: taking responsibility for yourself, looking at what is mirrored back to you, and the charge you give a situation. So, when you say "I am upset because" realize that one upset may be impacting not only your inner Peace. It could be one or more other aspects of your Happiness that need some love.

Centering Thought. What is true?

Affirmation. I see the truth of my upset and release it.

Peace Snapshot No. 7:
Be a Human Being Versus a Human Doing

"How beautiful it is to do nothing, and then rest afterward."
—SPANISH PROVERB

Consider the times you have intentionally sat and listened to the sounds around you. Are there any? Have you stopped to feel the breath coming through your nose and lungs, making its way to your belly and traveling back out? Tried gently closing your eyes to be in your environment, discerning the shape of your body occupying its space, letting go of thoughts as they arise, thoughts about yesterday, thoughts about later today, thoughts about tomorrow, just *being* instead of doing? If you do not already have a practice of this, the invitation is to start. If you already do this, then keep doing it. What you are creating is the spaciousness to observe a moment as it is happening. The rise and fall of sounds. The rise and fall of your breath. The rise and fall of a thought. The rise and fall of a sensation. The surge and fall of an emotion. No analysis, no judgment, no defense, no story. It is merely noticing with openness and without attachment. In this being, you come to realize how temporary, how transient many things are in your daily life, and grasping, clinging too tightly onto an idea, thing, or person only needlessly disturbs your Peace.

I bet there are many times where if you suddenly stopped, hit the pause button, and asked yourself what is going on at this very moment, you would say, "Not much, really. I am just sitting. I am safe. I am comfortable." Yet, what could otherwise be a Peaceful moment gets obliterated. A chattering internal conversation overruns it, streaming images from the past and ones to be had in the future. This rumination is set to autopilot, always running as you sit, get dressed, bring the kids to school, attend business meetings, dine with friends, or grocery shop. You continuously add to that to-do list that never gets done. Even though you have your list, you still lose track of things.

"Damn, I forgot to send that email!"

It is all just too much, and you are physically and emotionally exhausted. A lot of harried feelings could be reduced if you merely paused to focus on the present moment, becoming aware of what is going on mindfully versus mindlessly, consciously versus unconsciously. Do this often enough, and you will develop a better relationship with your thoughts, emotions, and body. You learn to tune in to your intuition, allowing its wisdom to guide you through the world with greater ease and Peace. The added benefit is that you will become more open to appreciating that which already flourishes in your life.

So, try doing nothing and resting afterward.

Centering Thought. Just be.

Affirmation. I cease doing to simply,
Peacefully, mindfully *be.*

Peace Snapshot No. 8:
Make Experientialism Greater Than Materialism

> *"Greed, for lack of a better word, is good. Greed is
> right. Greed works. Greed clarifies, cuts through, and
> captures the essence of the evolutionary spirit."*
> —The '80s anthem from the film *Wall Street*

Maybe it worked for the Yuppie lifestyle, maybe not. Whoever coined, "He who dies with the most toys wins" probably had a rude awakening when they came to that point. So, hang it up, Gordon Gekko. I think and hope we have been evolving since those Young, Urban, Professional days.

What truly counts are your experiences in life rather than your possessions. Experientialism trumps materialism. Close your eyes for a moment and reflect on the car you currently own, the home you have, or that great jacket hanging in your closet. Think about how much you wanted each of these items before possessing them. Now do the same with the vacation you took to walk the Camino de Santiago in Spain. Your birthday dinner on the beach with friends. That sunrise balloon ride you did in the Maasai Mara. *Well, these are mine. Think of yours.* Of all these memories, which brings you the most joy to recall? Likely, it is the moments you experienced. A twenty-year research study at Cornell University points to this being the case.

The joy of owning material possessions is likely to wear out. Why? Because of what is known as "Hedonic Adaptation," you adapt to things with time, no matter how you initially felt about them. You get used to them. You can either go back to your feelings as before or create a new emotional, sensory baseline that you now seek to go beyond. This tendency to get used to things is why that beautiful red cashmere jacket hanging in your closet becomes this old thing. The sweet cottage you moved into two years ago now feels small and cramped. Your luxury SUV now drives like a tank, and you want something smaller and sleeker. Your level of satisfaction in owning something new fades into the dissatisfaction of owning something old. It is now stirring up your Peace and motivating you to want the next level or levels up. You keep repeating this, wanting more, getting it, and that new thing eventually not being enough, especially when you compare yourself to others. To compound this, accumulating stuff and too much of it increases stress levels. Greed is not good. It is not all that fun keeping up with the Joneses, peers, or whomever and cleaning or warehousing stuff. Another thing about material possessions: they will always remain outside of you. That jacket, that car, and that home are all external and always will be.

Experiences, on the other hand, become part of the sum of you. They reflect and define your purpose, your passion. You internalize experiences. Your senses absorb them. They help shape who you are and your identity, so their effects last longer.

You experience climbing mountains. You describe yourself as a mountain climber.

You experience tango dancing. You describe yourself as a tango dancer.

You experience volunteering as a firefighter. You describe yourself as a volunteer firefighter.

In each case, you have memories and stories you can call upon. They were likely made even more memorable because of the relationships and the friends they created. Attached to every one of your memories are the emotions, the sensations, that made, and still make, you feel good. That made you feel alive. That make you smile even years later, long after the excitement of a new car has worn off.

Experiences can open new worlds. No Mercedes sitting in my driveway, no Tiffany pendant around my neck, no Michael Kors bag will ever supersede what it was like to see my first elephant, my first lion, my first giraffe in the African bush many years ago. If I had to choose one over the other, it would be, again and again, that maiden voyage to Africa. The time between the day of my first footstep on that continent and the day I left is a profound memory that still exhilarates me. That experience shaped who I am today 100 percent. These kinds of experiences fill my senses, bringing me inner Peace and joy that goes beyond words.

A Mercedes-Benz AMG C 63, valued at $78,250.

An 18K gold Tiffany pendant with diamonds costing $2,810.

A large leather Michael Kors tote bag, $398.

A trip to the African bush, pri$eless.

Centering Thought. Embrace my experiences.

Affirmation. I fully live my life in every way, every day.

♥ ♥ ♥

Peace Meditation Prayer

Peace of mind. Peace of heart.

On calm, gentle white wings, may I take flight with you.

Guide me toward filtering rays of Faith,
Love, Gratitude, and Forgiveness.

Let them be as watchful guardians of
my mind, body, and spirit.

Peace inside. Peace outside.

Peace for all my days.

And so let it be.

DEVELOPING PEACE OF MIND (AND HEART)

*"My salvation comes from me. It cannot
come from anywhere else."*
—A Course in Miracles

True that. Nothing external can create Peace within, no book, including this one, no seminar, no course, no retreat. All of these are great tools and resources. However, like all the other Happiness Essentials, you must choose Peace and develop it.

Feelings and emotions fall into three categories, pleasant, unpleasant, or neutral, and play a significant role in directing your thoughts and action. Naming them without attachment or judgment as they come up—anger, sorrow, joy—helps you more profoundly recognize them. You can face the unpleasant with an objective heart, transforming the constricting negative energy into expanding positive energy. You may even realize a misperception, or two, or many, or a fresh perspective. You can do something more constructive, kind, and loving when you observe and better understand your thoughts and emotions and what causes them.

"Be still and know that I am God."—Psalm 46:10

Having a sense of Peace gives your mind, body, and spirit the time it needs to rejuvenate, helping you look, feel, and be Happier, healthier, and more in control of your emotions. It allows you the space to reflect on what is happening in your life so you can have healthier relationships. It prevents anxieties, worries, and fears and awakens inner strength and confidence. You react with a greater ability to concentrate and to be calm. You can more efficiently handle your daily life with patience, tolerance, and tact because you carry an inner sense of bliss, *ergo*, Happiness.

Journaling with Peace: What Does Peace Mean to You?

I invite you to take time to think about Peace, inner Peace, in your life. As before, my answers are in italics, and there is space for you to fill in yours.

How do you define Peace and its benefits?

Being at peace is a state of contentment, "all is good." My inner being is soft, gentle, and restful. Regrets about the past and worry about the future have no place.

_____

_____

_____

What role does Peace currently play in your life?

It is the recognition that I want to exist peacefully within myself, with others, my community, and the world itself. This desire guides how I act and react. It is part of what enables me to be grateful, forgiving, and less attached to how I think things should be or people should behave.

_____

_____

_____

How easy or difficult is it to have Peace within you?

I have certainly had to work on this one over the years. However, I do feel a sense of peace more often than not, and when I feel unpeaceful, I do not dwell there as I once did. For that, I am thankful.

How are you, or will you, create greater Peace within?

I will continue the daily practice of counting my blessings, not attaching to what people think of me, using mindful awareness to recognize unproductive thoughts and behavior, and reframing them to constructive ones. Above all, keeping my faith that things are as they should be and are part of my spiritual curriculum here on planet earth.

Take a photograph of what Peace looks like for you. Give a caption. Then, journal about your thoughts and feelings.

Emotional peace is like that easy feeling I have when I am on the water at sunset.

Journal Entry: *I have spent most of my life churned up about something or someone. It took a simultaneous fall in my personal and professional life, when I did not get the guy or the job I wanted, to realize that I could do something constructive about my emotional world. I could choose how and for how long I remained "upset because" I could become the observer of my thoughts instead of being my thoughts. When I became the observer of my thoughts, I could see the lessons intended for me. I could choose to reframe my attitude toward my upset. This observational and attitudinal shift was monumental in bringing me inner peace. Yes, be still and know that I am at peace.*

Peace Photo Ops and Action Opportunities

See how you can manifest more of that Peaceful easy feeling in your life by using the following Photo Op prompts and Action Opportunities to guide you in developing more Peace in your daily life.

Peace Snapshot No. 1:
Own Your I Am

Photo Op. *Who Am I and What Do I Really Want?* Do the Action Opportunity first. Then, create a collage or series of images of people who reflect those who support your "I am" statement. Notice how it makes you feel.

Action Opportunity. One, ask yourself the following questions before creating your "I am" statement.

What is the life you desire?

What do you want to experience in your relationships, personally or professionally?

What do you desire to contribute to the world through these connections?

How do you want to be, to act toward yourself and others?

Two, create your "I am" statement by choosing three words that describe you to go after "I am (fill in this space)." This statement will become your Centering Thought.

Three, then use the Affirmation "I own, nourish, and love who I am and the Peace within me" to ponder who in your life supports this statement and edit those who do not.

_____

_____

_____

Peace Snapshot No. 2:
What Others Think of You Is None of Your Business

Photo Op. *Mind Your Business.* Create a series of images that reflect what the eight promises mean to you: to be impeccable with your word, not to take things personally, not to assume, act with integrity, avoid gossiping, resist being petty, keep your own counsel, and withhold judgment.

Action Opportunity. Meditate on the Centering Thought: "Mind my business." Then, use the Affirmation "I Peacefully mind my business and never mind others" to put the above eight promises into action. Consider where you are living these promises and where you are not. What actions do the images from the Photo Op motivate?

_____

_____

_____

Peace Snapshot No. 3:
Apply the Golden Rule to Yourself First

Photo Op. *First Do Unto Yourself.* Do the Action Opportunity first. Then, capture an image of your written Golden Rules, frame it, and hang it somewhere that you will frequently see it.

Action Opportunity. Become present with the Centering Thought: "Golden rules." Then, take some reflective time to create your Golden Rules. As you write, remember the Affirmation: "I do unto myself as I would I unto others."

_____

_____

_____

Peace Snapshot No. 4:
Be a Loving Battery

Photo Op. *Keep Peace in Your Mind and Heart.* Capture an image of what being a loving battery feels like to you.

Action Opportunity. Begin with the Centering Thought: "I am a loving battery." Consider where you can be a Peaceful presence for someone. You are not trying to fix anything or steer things in a particular direction. You are just present as a loving battery, only offering help when asked. Use the Affirmation "I am a Peaceful, loving battery to those who need a positive charge" as a reminder.

_____

_____

_____

Peace Snapshot No. 5:
Protect Your Head

Photo Op. *You Become What You Consume.* Instead of capturing images this time, become conscious of the photos and videos that you usually see. See what it is like to takeaway, delete, or avoid those that disturb your Peace.

Action Opportunity. Meditate using the Centering Thought: "Protect my head." Then invoke the Affirmation, "I am the guardian of my inner Wholebeing: my mind, my heart, my spirit," to consciously be mindful of things that will feed your predisposed Negative Bias. Lean toward the things that help develop a Positive Bias and journal about your thoughts and feelings doing this experience.

_____

_____

_____

Peace Snapshot No. 6:
Release Your "I Am Upset Because"

Photo Op. *Drop Your Emotional Bag of Rocks.* Capture an image of a hand releasing a rock. The rock represents held grievances. Use this image to remind yourself to let go of the things that are weighing you down and disturbing your Peace. Do this along with the Action Opportunity.

Action Opportunity. Use the Centering Thought, "What is true?" to observe where you can let go of "I am upset because." Then, ask yourself these three questions:

Is the grievance you are holding onto worth the Peace that it costs?

Are you willing to let go of your complaint?

If so, when will you let it go? Your answer should be *now*.

The longer you hold on, the longer you will lack the Peace you desire. If it helps, invoke the Affirmation: "I see the truth of my upset and release it."

_____

_____

_____

Peace Snapshot No. 7:
Be a Human Being Versus a Human Doing

Photo Op. *Enter the Stillness.* Create a series of images of you or others in different states of just being. What comes up for you?

Action Opportunity. Look to balance your outer world's busyness with your inner world's quietness by meditating with the Centering Thought: "Just be." Make it your practice every day, if only for a few minutes. It will make a notable difference. You become more aware of your life and life itself by merely *being* instead of always doing. How you handle life's demands and challenges will be more informed and less mindlessly reactive.

To calm yourself, scan your body, focusing on its main parts, noticing areas of tension and relaxing them. Start from the top of your head, working downward; imagine a light similar to that of a photocopying machine. The light goes back and forth across a document, though instead, it is across your body: toes, feet, ankles, shins, knees, thighs, torso, fingers, palms, wrists, forearms, upper arms, shoulders, neck, and head.

This body scan can be done in a matter of moments or as a slower forty-five-minute relaxation. You can be lying down, sitting, or standing.

Seal this practice with the Affirmation: "I cease doing to simply, Peacefully, mindfully *be*."

_____

_____

_____

Peace Snapshot No. 8:
Make Experientialism Greater Than Materialism

Photo Op. *Experiences Trump Stuff.* This Photo Op has two parts.

One, create a vision board with images of all the things you want to do. Keep it where you can frequently see it. Notice how you are being motivated to take action to do the things you desire most.

Two, when you are doing, experiencing what you most want to do, capture an image of this moment. See how energizing it is to experience.

Action Opportunity. It is perfectly okay to want material things. One does not have to be at the exclusion of the other. The suggestion is to balance materialism and experientialism with a strong leaning towards spending your time and money on the latter. Try something new at least once a year. It could be something that you do locally, in your backyard, or bigger and more exotic. It is whatever is meaningful to you. Use your money to buy an experience instead of something that will eventually just collect dust.

Become present with the Centering Thought: "Embrace my experiences." Then list the things you would like to experience. Finally, close this writing session with the Affirmation: "I fully live my life in every way, every day."

_____

_____

_____

PICTURING DETACHMENT

Detachment
\di-ˈtach-mənt, dēs-\

noun

    : the action or process of detaching

*"Anything you want can be acquired through
detachment because detachment is based on the
unquestioning belief in the power of your true Self."*
—Deepak Chopra
Bestselling Author, The Seven Spiritual Laws of Success

SNAPSHOT OF DETACHMENT

In My Viewfinder

This one Happiness Essential has been the hardest for me to put into play in my life. I am very loyal and only choose a few things in life. I am basically a minimalist from the number of possessions I own, the circle of friends I have, even the number of projects I take on. Since I was eleven years old, I have been like this and decided that I wanted quality over quantity in life. So, when I become attached to something or someone, it is often challenging for me to Detach.

I grew up in a slightly upper-middle-class, Midwest suburban community outside Cleveland, Ohio. We lived in one of the more beautiful subdivisions primarily made up of white-collar professionals, doctors, and lawyers. My dad was a scientist. So, nobody was starving around my neighborhood. As a high schooler, I began to notice how much useless stuff everyone around me had, and our family was no exception. It just seemed to me that all that *stuff* was actually getting in the way of living because you had to spend time taking care of it, sorting through it, storing it, and paying visits to it. *What a bother!* One of my more prominent childhood memories of my dad is watching him in a perpetual state of organizing our family's stuff. My dad would spend hours boxing and filing all his long-held, worldly belongings. He would go through one pile of things and then move to the next, going from his office in our home's loft to the stockpile in the basement. The items either had sentimental value, or he felt he would for sure need that box of a thousand rubber bands one day, as well as every leftover can of paint, type of glue, and keys to who knows what. There were endless books on an array of subjects. We could have opened our own library. We had an abundance of VHS tapes, CDs, and DVDs. We certainly could never find things with any sort of ease. All I could think was I sure as heck did not want to be doing this endless sorting through stockpiles later in life and figured the only way that would happen was if I simply had fewer things to look after. That is when I started to envision a life of fewer things.

As the years unfolded, this life of fewer things began to have some not-so-great emotional byproducts. When I did choose, whether it was a possession, a project, or a relationship, and things did not work out the way I wanted, it was brutal and often traumatic for me to get unstuck, not to care as much, to Detach. It took me a very long time to realize how embracing Detachment could actually be my lifesaver, because attachment was killing me.

What I needed to learn, and I think most of us need to learn, is not to have a vice grip on a specific outcome and how things, circumstances, or people should be. Fear and insecurity limit one's field of view, darkening hopes and possibilities and leading to suffering. We can learn how to release our desires into the unknown and trust that things will work out by asking these questions inspired by the Mindfulness RAIN practice: Recognize what is going on, Accept the experience, Investigate what is happening, and No longer identify with it. So:

R. What is happening in your life?

A. Can you be with this circumstance as it is now?

I. Where and how do you feel this situation manifesting in your mind and body?

N. If you desire to change things, can you let go, trusting the universe to guide you? If not, can you continue to be with your situation without identifying with it or being defined by it? Hopefully, you will say "yes" and believe you can.

Detachment is an ongoing practice of surrendering and having the faith that good things will happen when and as they should. Instead of having a churned-up mind, it is a more peaceful mind.

Snapshots on Developing Mindful Detachment

Detachment Snapshot No. 1:
Detachment Is an Emotional State of Balance

"I know what I have to do now, I've got to keep breathing because tomorrow, the sun will rise. Who knows what the tide could bring." For 1,460 days, top international FedEx manager Chuck Noland existed on a deserted island and, eventually, a makeshift raft surrounded by shark-infested waters in the *Cast Away*. His only company is a volleyball named Wilson. That is, until Wilson is lost to the waves. Chuck is completely at the edge of his mind and hope when a rusty tanker finds him and brings him home. There is a lesson for us in this film. It is about using all your inner resources to pull you through the uncertainties in life, letting go of how and when things will work out. As Chuck steps on the tanker's deck, his first words are a deliriously Happy, "Thank you. Oh, thank you."

While extreme circumstances and intense desires can push us to our edge, those who can Detach from a specific outcome and accept *what is* in a situation, the good and the bad, are more likely to be emotionally balanced. They are not grasping for feel-good experiences or avoiding the bad ones. Even when aspects of their lives cannot change, their general state remains relatively constant. These folks know that life moments and circumstances change, ebb and flow, twist and turn. So, they go for the ride. Those who can Detach will reap the benefits of their success and learn from their missteps, then try again and again. The key is to continue Detaching from an outcome, a particular result. Mindfulness and meditation can play a big role in opening your awareness and settling your mind and body, allowing you to focus on solutions or a better idea rather than complaining or blaming. And know that all talented people, including the exceptionally gifted, bump into their share of challenges and make adjustments too. The willingness to face adversities and course-correct when necessary separates the average person from the exceptional one. It is also what it means to be proactive about your life.

One of the greatest lessons I have learned from running television shows is that when things do not go as planned, which will happen, it is not helpful to dwell on blame nor obsessively worry about what I cannot change—to Detach from what just happened and focus on what can happen next. This insight came from years of working with executive producer Mark Burnett, who brought *Survivor* to American viewers. During the early days of producing *Survivor*, I realized that I could not go to Mark with just the problem at hand. That was not helpful to him. He wanted to know how I, as a producer, would resolve the situation.

CUT TO: a few years forward and now producing *Expedition Africa: Stanley & Livingstone* for the History Channel. We had hopes of having modern-day explorers retrace Henry Morton Stanley's nine-hundred-mile journey across Tanzania to find Dr. Livingstone. It is one of the hallmark expeditions of all time. We wanted to do Stanley's nearly eight-month expedition in thirty days because that was the amount of time our budget would cover—an undertaking that was no easy task to pull off as a production team of 120, especially in Tanzania, where the further west you traveled from the east coast, the less infrastructure you had, including communication, food, and medical. Pretty much any modern creature comfort you can think of at the time. The bar to deliver a show and the difficulties that went along with it were set high. In the initial stages of development, we could only afford to look at dated satellite maps. We also talked to local fixers, who arrange logistics, and people we found online about various portions of Stanley's cross-country journey, which was helpful only to a certain point. We were well into planning our show before we could send our first location scouts. When the reports from the field started coming back, it was far from encouraging. As it turns out, Tanzania is one of the most populated African countries, and much of Stanley's route is now overrun by humanity.

So now what?

I still had to deliver a series about a historical expedition with modern-day explorers, highlighting Stanley and his men's hardships. Knowing that I had to go to Mark with solutions, I started Detaching from what I was told I could not do. Instead, I started looking for what I could do. It was within the problem that my team and I found the solution. It began with the following questions. What still does exist? And is this representative of what it was like at the time?

Through those questions, we discovered a patchwork of what we understood to be the original expedition route and areas that remained much as Stanley experienced back in 1871. The solution was that our explorers could retrace and experience just those portions. We Detached from our original concept of what Stanley's route had to be. Because we did, we were able to create our modern-day expedition route similar in spirit and still incredibly hard to pull off. In addition to the harsh remote terrain, we faced weather that would not be in our favor, poisonous snakes and other animals that could bite us, and the genuine threat of malaria.

Letting go of what was originally in my mind's eye enabled us to create a representative route for the explorers to follow. I found this letting go to problem-solve in my professional life to be equally helpful in my personal life. Like a garden, sow the things you can do, what you are good at. Use these to cultivate the seeds of your desires into a flowerbed of intentions. Let the universe be your rain and sunshine. Soon your intentions will sprout up as your will, eventually blossoming into your destiny.

> Mom: "What a journey you've had. It seems more than a person should have to bear."
>
> Chuck Noland: "The tide saved me, Mom. I lived by it. I'm just wondering where it will take me next."
>
> Mom: "Remember the family motto: 'In time. It will come to you, in time.'"

Centering Thought. Let go.

Affirmation. I release attachment
to how things should be.

Detachment Snapshot No. 2:
Check Your Ego at the Door

A Buddhist saying, "not flattered by praise, not hurt by blame," is the practice of Detachment. When you get caught up in praise a bit too much, as in believing your own press, that is your ego puffing up. When you get caught up in judgment, as in feeling you are not good enough, that is your ego beating you down. Either direction will ill-serve you. Over time, I have found that developing one's Happiness also includes three vital components:

Detachment to things, people, opinions, and outcomes

The practice of non-judgment

The lack of inner resistance

The key here is acting from an egoless place of peace, love, gratitude, or forgiveness rather than an ego-filled place of judgment, criticism, ungratefulness, and lack of forgiveness. Let me just say one thing here—*well, two.* I work as a producer in television and live in Los Angeles, an industry and city brimming with ego. Add to that, I am of Greek ethnicity, a very strong-minded culture. So, putting into practice any one of these components is, to say the least, challenging, although with practiced awareness, not insurmountable. Nevertheless, I have found that life flows more effortlessly when I let go of collecting grievances or clinging to righteousness.

Your head is less caught up by worry and anxiety. Sensations in your body are more relaxed. Thinking kind thoughts just feels better than being entangled in angry ones. However, Detaching from attachment is a sticky one at best.

To help get unstuck:

Decide whose business it is. We humans seem to be so drawn to drama, whether our own or someone else's. We slowly creep by that car accident on the freeway, making ourselves a hazard in the process. We take sides in a friend's argument with their partner, forgetting that once they kiss and make up, they will remember the bad things you said about their loved one. So often we get involved in situations that have nothing to do with us and then find ourselves embroiled in the unfolding, escalating the heat of a moment that we, you, cannot so quickly disengage from and find ourselves in the crosshairs of someone else's problem. I love what I once heard Bryon Katie offer at a Wisdom 2.0 mindfulness conference. "If it is their business, leave it to them. If it is genuinely your business, then get involved. If it is God's business, let Him take care of it."

Find the oneness in things. Finally, science is catching up, and scientists are becoming more vocal about what the sages, mystics, and spiritual leaders have known over the millennia: we are all one. No matter what you believe, we all come from the same source and go back to that source—cosmic dust, the stuff stars are made of. We could not be here if stars had not exploded, giving us all the evolutionary elements that formed to create you and me.

While hard to believe, every atom inside us came from a star. As astrophysicist Neil deGrasse Tyson says, "We are part of this universe, we are in this universe, but perhaps more important than both of these facts is that the universe is in us." From this point of view, we are all connected. We are all related to what is going on around us. In this realm, there is no place for one's overinflated ego to reside.

Embrace each new day as a gift. See every day for what it is: the gift of a new beginning, a fresh start. The same is true for each moment of your day. When you continually look to begin anew, you are free from the limiting thoughts of your ego and are open to the limitless possibilities of the egoless.

"Treat every moment as a gift, that is why it is called the present." — Deepak Chopra

Focus on what matters. Dwell on the things you can make happen, where you can affect positive change. Leave the things that are already done in the past. I am Greek Orthodox by baptism, and I go to church, though oddly enough, I would not think of myself as religious. Instead, I see myself spiritually strong in my faith. Perhaps this is splitting hairs, though it is a subtle and meaningful distinction for me. At any rate, one Christian prayer that has come to resonate with me is theologian Reinhold Niebuhr's "Serenity Prayer."

"Lord, give me the courage to change the things that I can, the strength to accept the things I cannot, and the wisdom to know the difference."

This prayer reminds me to leave my ego at the door. It holds in my mind that there are things well beyond my control and that the best I can do, any of us can do, is to control that which you can do. How you react to any situation is up to you and only you.

Centering Thought. Check my ego.

Affirmation. I release yesterday's upsets, disappointments, grievances to stand in the gift of today.

Detachment Snapshot No. 3:
Out of Control Is an Opportunity to Be in Control

"When you're twenty, you care what everyone thinks. When you're forty, you stop caring what everyone thinks. When you're sixty, you realize no one was ever thinking about you in the first place." This is a quote often attributed to Winston Churchill. Maybe he said this, maybe not. The point is what friends, family, neighbors, co-workers, and bosses feel influences us far too much, for far too much of our lives. We are overly attached to what people think of us. I touched on this in our Peace Snapshot, No. 2: What Others Think of You is None of Your Business, instead focus on minding your business and the promises you make to yourself. This Snapshot is the next step, Detaching from how others think of you.

It can be virtually debilitating when you are worried, anxious that someone important to you does not think you are all that, whatever the reason. You can coax, defend, send a dozen roses every day to try to change their perception. Maybe your power of persuasion will work. However, you cannot bank on anything you do to alter someone's opinion of you. Why? Because they must want, desire, to change their mind about you, and that can take a very long time to happen, if ever. You cannot control others' actions, much less their thoughts toward you. What you can control is how you react. So instead of spiraling out of control and being upset that someone does not like you, take control by letting go of how they view you. Believe in yourself, not in what others believe about you.

Something else while we are here, you may be worrying about what someone thinks of you when, in truth, they have long since moved on, consumed by something more immediate in their world. So often, hanging onto what you think someone feels about you only leaves you feeling twisted in a knot you cannot undo.

As the year approaches Easter, there is a "Day of Forgiveness" in the Greek Orthodox faith. On this day, whatever grievances you have with someone are aired, forgiveness is given, and you are done with the issue. It never needs to be addressed again. Several years ago, on that day, I decided to contact every person I either had a problem with or thought had one with me. I reached out to several people. Some did have an issue with me that then got worked out. Some apologized, saying they had wanted to reach out to me and were glad that I did, though the majority said they had long forgotten the event that I was still so churned up over. I believed those who said they had forgotten any offense on my part. The fact that they took the time to respond to an email that could easily have been ignored and how they wrote their replies showed me this. They had moved on; egregious issues and situations were long forgotten.

This Day of Forgiveness writing exercise was incredibly cathartic. It cleared and settled many anxious emotions inside me. I wrote what I needed to say and asked for forgiveness where I felt necessary. It was emotionally cleansing to do, regardless of anybody's response. I felt a sense of relief that I had initiated a dialogue to right any wrongdoing on my part. It also felt good to take responsibility for what I felt and address it. Though the most significant takeaway was that I had spent far too much mental and emotional real estate on what I thought was someone else's opinion of me when they were not thinking of me at all. They were probably obsessing over what someone else was thinking about them. The message is that people are not sitting around thinking about you. They are too busy being focused on themselves. You can feel so out of control, buying into your perception of someone's thoughts toward you, feeling helpless to change the situation. Instead, use this as an opportunity to regain control of yourself by realizing that it is likely not valid. Detach from your attachment to what you believe is another's view of you. Though most importantly, care more about what you think of yourself. If your desires and values align, who really cares what anyone thinks of you?

Centering Thought. Assume control.

Affirmation. What others think of me does not matter; what matters is what I think of me.

Detachment Snapshot No. 4:
Get Out of Your Way

Enough! He was on his way home to burn his manuscript, probably thinking no one would ever buy anything he writes. Twenty-seven publishers had turned down his first book. However, it seems the universe had other plans that day when Theodor Seuss Geisel ran into a Dartmouth classmate who was an editor at Vanguard Press and published the very book the others dismissed, *And to Think I Saw It on Mulberry Street.* Almost a half-century and one Pulitzer Prize later, Dr. Seuss had sold over six hundred million books worldwide by the turn of the twenty-first century. And it all could not have happened had Theodor bought into the belief that he would not sell his book or that no one was interested in his fanciful musing about Mulberry Street, including his disapproving father.

Most of us have some limiting belief, the story we use to cover why we are not aiming for our full potential, hiding the shameful secret about our lack of self-esteem. Saying things like:

"I do not have enough time."

"I need to get more experience."

"I do not have the contacts."

"No one is interested."

These statements are all just excuses. The sooner we let go of these limiting thoughts, the sooner we can become the people we are meant to be.

I had never climbed a mountain, much less even thought I could. Yet I got it into my head that after I finished production in Tanzania on *Expedition Africa: Stanley & Livingstone* for Mark Burnett and the History Channel, I wanted to climb Mount Kilimanjaro. I think all the miles we logged scouting, shooting, and the stories about the early explorers swirling in my imagination inspired me. Except I had no clue about mountain climbing, how I was going to fare at altitude, and, most of all, how I was going to deal with the fact that I am a tad bit afraid of heights. Despite these daunting questions, I went for it.

I was slow, plodding along. Left, right. Left, right. I grew up with my mom telling me the Greek proverb: Φασούλι τὸ φασούλι γεμίζει τὸ σακκούλι, "Bean by bean fills the bag." That is precisely what I was doing, filling the bag, making my ascent one step at a time. I would not even allow myself to look up toward the summit. I did not want to be scared by how far I still had to go nor the height I had to ascend. When I finally reached the top, I burst into tears. I was genuinely amazed that I had just climbed a mountain, the fourth tallest one in the world, having never climbed anything before. It was exhilarating. That victory gave me the confidence to next trek to Everest Base Camp, which eventually led to the marathons I walked on every continent. All because I Detached from a singular belief I had about myself, that I did not know how to climb a mountain.

> You have brains in your head,
>
> You have feet in your shoes.
>
> You can steer yourself any direction you choose.
>
> —*Oh, the Places You'll Go!*

Seven continents and countless passport stamps later, I have found Dr. Suess's wisdom to be true.

Centering Thought. Step aside.

Affirmation. I let go of the limiting thoughts that confine me to welcome in a world of possibilities.

Detachment Snapshot No. 5: Surrender to the Direction You Are Being Led

Dark blue end-of-day clouds form a golden hole to spread a ray of light on a corn field as Iowa farmer Ray Kinsella walks between the aisles of tall green stalks. A voice from nowhere and everywhere whispers, "If you build it, he will come." Ray looks around to see who spoke. No one is there. With a slight smile, he keeps walking; it must have been his imagination. Again, the whispers cause Ray to look around, trying to locate the voice. He yells out to his wife, sitting on their house porch, asking if she heard a voice, no, and she calls him to dinner. As Ray walks toward the house for the third time, the voice whispers, "If you build it, he will come." In *Field of Dreams*, a farmer follows a voice he cannot ignore to do something that does not seem possible: make a baseball diamond in his cornfield for fans from all over to watch the game.

Surrendering or Detaching is a leap of faith, something we discussed in the Faith Snapshot No. 5: Take the Leap of Faith, and this is the next part of it: free-falling into the vast unknown to do something impossible. It can be seemingly scary and inspiring all at the same time, just like it was for Ray Kinsella. When you let go of rigid ideas of how things should be, you move from the vast, scary unknown to the infinite Field of Possibilities, your Field of Dreams. When you are not stuck on one outcome, you become more creative, alert, and aware of how things are unfolding. You can discover that within the challenge lies the solution and ability to create something even better. It enables you to look for and take advantage of opportunities you would have otherwise not seen.

Detaching from an outcome does not mean that you stop caring about your intentions and desires, that you should no longer set goals. However, it does mean you stop fixating on when and how it will all look once fulfilled. Instead, you will find yourself focusing on the exploration, experience, and joy of getting to your endgame. Rather than forcing a path you may not enjoy with likely less than stellar results, allow yourself to tap into the power of your true self. Free the creative and knowing thoughts that have been pushed into the recesses of your mind. Do this, and you will find your real wealth and wisdom. It also will be seen with greater ease and enjoyment; this is when your preparedness meets opportunity that some call "luck."

Ray Kinsella: "I have just created something totally illogical."

Annie Kinsella: "That's what I like about you."

Centering Thought. Surrender and trust.

Affirmation. I trust the universe will lead me
to the perfect answer in perfect timing.

Detachment Snapshot No. 6:
Stop Running Your Mind into Brick Walls

When you drive a motorcycle, wherever your head points will be where you end up, so if your head is pointing toward a brick wall, guess where you will end up. It is called "Target Fixation," a phenomenon that happens when you are so focused on an object that you risk colliding with it. Something similar goes for your thoughts. You know how you have those reoccurring thoughts you get caught up in and wear on you? That is your emotional brick wall. You keep going over and over in your mind the same thought about a person or situation, reliving how things should or could be different. Not only is this emotionally unhealthy and exhausting, it also takes up mental real estate that would otherwise be propelling you forward.

I first noticed how painfully attached I can be to unproductive thoughts when wrapping up that production in London I mentioned in the Happiness Essentials on Faith and Love. This piece is the last and most important part of that story.

A broadcaster brought me in to fix a troubled series and Americanize it for US viewers. However, many on the UK production team hired by the previous producer did not want their show fixed by someone else and certainly not by someone from across the pond. I felt that no matter how much effort I put into being a collaborative team leader, they wanted none of me. I felt completely rejected and found myself cataloging through other emotionally challenging productions and realizing how I dealt with those situations. Each instance I could think of reminded me of how I had invested all of myself, and it was not always appreciated nor reciprocated. *Well, that was my perception.* By the time production would end, I was completely spent. Though this time in London did me in, I wanted help to feel not ever again as I did then.

The first step toward resolving my unhealthy attachment to work projects was talking out my feelings to a couple of trusted colleagues, although mostly the location scout, who thankfully endured me during production. I vented to them until even I was getting tired of listening to myself. Then, I got serious about meditation and discovered my emotions and body followed my mind when it settled. Eventually, I became aware of the profound art of Detachment, learning to care more objectively and be less stuck on people or events going a certain way. It is the freeing practice of not engaging in unproductive thoughts.

After I had this insight around Detachment, I started to have more fun during production. I started feeling emotionally lighter. I laughed more. I let things roll off my back. I slept better. This took serious work to find ways to quiet the overwhelming negative chatter in my head. The secret was unlocking the mental and emotional prison I was in by consciously looking to change the relationship I had with my thoughts. Of course, the same thoughts could still come up, though I saw I could view them from a more helpful and compassionate perspective. Then one day, upsetting thoughts about that London show experience stopped coming up. Why? Because I was no longer feeding it by feeding into it. Since then, the overall quality of the content of my thoughts and the emotions they incite has become notably upgraded from where I began. Ultimately, I feel more effective and Happier moving through life, which I consider a true blessing.

Learning to Detach from unconstructive thoughts and behaviors to nurture constructive ones that create a more stable state of being requires constant intention and attention. It may seem daunting to be so attentive to your thoughts and emotions in the early going, maybe even like a chore; although, as you start seeing the positive shifts and changes in your life, choosing, developing, and ultimately rewiring your tendency toward Happiness will become a sincere desire. A Mindfulness practice will support you in this endeavor. Eventually, you will want to put effort into it because you feel so much better. Acting from a positive place that is anything else will feel foreign and off.

Now aware of the benefits of Detaching from negative thoughts, I take a lot of deep breaths and try to look at things objectively while taking inspired guidance from Bishop Tutu's Four Steps to Forgiveness to Detach through the act of forgiving myself—a practice I learned after I wrapped the show in the UK and spent time emotionally healing.

One, I allow all my feelings.

Two, I forgive myself when I behave in ways I do not want.

Three, I call to mind that I and the others are doing our best within our respective abilities, while...

Four, witnessing our shared humanity. I also call to mind the saying, "Why do you look at the speck in your brother's eye but do not consider the plank in your own eye?" —Matthew 7:3 (NKJV)

I am not always emotionally tidy when carrying all this out. However, I genuinely try to deal with challenging work and personal situations sanely and kindly. The most significant benefit of developing a constructive point of view is that you now have the emotional tools to navigate rough times. You do not stay upset as long, take things as personally, feel so victimized, or as unworthy. Instead, you get through the hard stuff still emotionally intact.

As you learned in the Faith Snapshot No. 5: Take the Leap of Faith, when you have an unhappy thought, try connecting it with a Happy one— to a time when your current unhappy thought was a Happy one—to create a neural pathway toward the constructive, a positive bias versus negative.

Try your version of this thought:

"Working with this series' production team is so frustrating." Unhappy thought.

"I loved shooting with the team on my last series. Working together was fantastic." Happy thought.

Appreciate this Happy thought over the unhappy one for twenty to thirty seconds, allowing it to sink into your brain, nourishing and easing the negativity you are currently feeling. It takes a bit of practice, though the more you do this, the more natural it will become. You are encouraging the release of negative thoughts in a way that is constructive, thoughtful, and without judgment; this is where realizing people are doing the best they can comes in handy. Processing negative thoughts this way is more likely to last because of the positive neural pathway you are nurturing. It will become your habit not to get so churned up by unproductive thoughts. You will continue to expand into a much kinder, healthier way of being. These Happy thought steps have pulled me into the light many times when I could have easily sat in darkness.

Centering Thought. Nurture productive thoughts.

Affirmation. My Happy thoughts nurture a Happier me.

Detachment Snapshot No. 7:
Get Rid of the Clutter

Remember the monumental task I took of clearing out my father's possessions during the Covid pandemic? My father and sister passed away the same year, three months to the day, in 2012. Before the world shut down, I only returned to see my mother in Ohio for long weekends. She always wanted to spend our limited time visiting, not cleaning out my father's and sister's belongings. This desire was a seemingly understandable cover for the thing neither of us wanted to face doing. Over the years, I did go through my sister's things. However, with my dad, it was just too much for my mom or me to face until I came home for two weeks, intending to finally tackle my father's lifelong collection of the items that defined his life. After nine years, I was emotionally ready. I knew I had to do it and wanted to do it while my mother was still around. I wanted her to have a say in what was kept, what was important to her in honoring my dad's memory.

It was emotionally hard to get going and start the process. I felt stuck and daunted because I knew it would be an exhausting job. However, once I did, I became possessed, surgically going through decades' worth of my dad's methodic collecting, gathering, and storing of things. The goal was to go room by room, closet by closet, drawer by drawer, starting with what felt the easiest and the most obvious to get rid of. I sat my mother down in each room and held up items for her to say "yes" or "no," keep or discard. The "no" pile became so big that I lost count of the number of trips I made to Goodwill, and I thought for sure the garbage collector would not take the mountain of bags piled at the end of our driveway. It was a lifetime of once-coveted stuff now in a big heap waiting to be hauled away.

Going through my father's things was a mixture of emotions. I loved seeing photos of my dad as a budding scientist and my parents when they were first married. I was touched that he saved all the cards our family ever gave him, amazed that he still had his first passport. Then I got into his writings, his voluminous writings. On top of being prolific, my dad saved everything he ever wrote in triplicates, stored in different places. It was maddening to consolidate. I would think I had the definitive collection of his work, only to find another version of it in a filing cabinet or storage box. If he wrote it, he saved it. Fun memories turned into a major annoyance to go through. I resented being left with all his things to sort and organize. I became irritable at his vanity to save every scrap of his work.

Then something inside turned, and I realized how hard he genuinely tried in life to be seen and heard. I finally got it. He had a brilliant analytical mind that never received the recognition for which he had longed. I felt sad compassion for my dad that I had not felt before because I was too caught up in judging the size of his ego. It was humbling to feel, if that makes sense. Not only was I Detaching from my father's belongings, I was also Detaching from my resentment toward him. I felt a softening inside and around the rigid judgment I had levied on my dad. My scowl turned into a smile, allowing the warmth of a daughter who loved and missed her father to wash over me. I felt a sense of closure, no longer held by my past anger, frustration, and disappointment.

Years ago, my dad gave me an article written by an unknown author titled "What Matters." It was a riff on all the things we spend time trying to achieve, the things we collect, and in the end, does it really matter? Judging by the number of trips I made to Goodwill and the heap of years of accumulated stuff at the end of our driveway, *no*, most of it does not matter. I learned that much of what we think is important truly is not, and we can save ourselves a lot of time grasping and suffering if we let go of that which does not matter. When you let go of the bad stuff, you then have the space to let in the good stuff.

Clearing out my father's possessions made me more resolved to keep stripping away what I do not need, both physically and emotionally. The process of going through my father's belongings reminded me not to get so caught up in myself and my achievements, to just live each day as it feels fulfilling to me and not anyone else.

If you are attempting to tackle your physical clutter or to declutter the items of a dear loved one, begin with what is emotionally comfortable to get rid of and gradually work your way toward the more challenging things to let go of, to release, to give up. Go through your closets, drawers, desk, medicine cabinet, spice rack, refrigerator, garage, car trunk, glove box, computer hard drive, purses, wallets, and room corners. If it has a surface or storage space, clear it out. Get rid of that which is of no use or sentimental value. Some folks suggest throwing out, giving away, or selling anything they have not used in the last twelve months. Others have a twenty-four/seven practice. For seven days straight, you get rid of twenty-four things each day. If you bring something new into the house, send something old out. It is psychologically liberating when you eliminate the clutter in your life. You feel much lighter, more expansive because you are not being weighed down by things you do not use nor need. Also, make yourself right for wanting and desiring positive change versus wrong for having negative behavior that needs to be changed. This self-compassion piece is the key to being kind to yourself when caught up judging yourself.

The other area to clear out is the clutter of toxic people in your life. We touched on an aspect of this in the Peace Snapshot No. 5: Protect Your Head, paying attention to the conversations, film, television, books, and news media you consume. Letting go of those who are negative in your life is challenging—no question about that—especially if they are a family member, someone who has been in your life a long time, or you have to work with a lot. Even limiting your exposure to anyone who is bad news, a constant downer, hypercritical can make a significant difference in your life. Think about the five people who are around you the most. Are they the ones who are not supporting you, uplifting you? If so, set yourself free of them. Noxious people can be damaging in ways you cannot even imagine. They can set you off course in life without you even realizing it. It happens in small incremental ways that will lead you to an unwanted place. Those you spend time with influence how you act and think, the decisions, the life choices you make. What kind of people do you want to influence you every day? Hopefully, the answer is uplifting people who are out doing good in the world and making a difference.

So, keep who and what matters in your life and discard the rest.

Centering Thought. Release.

Affirmation. I Happily release that which
does not serve me or the greater good.

Detachment Snapshot No. 8:
Worry and Regrets Are Useless Emotions

Rafiki: "Ah! Change is good."

Simba: "Yeah, but it's not easy. I know what I have to do,
but going back means I'll have to face my past. I've been
running from it for so long."

Rafiki in *The Lion King* whacks Simba on his head with
his walking stick.

Simba: "Ouch, aww, jeez, what was that for?

Rafiki: "It doesn't matter. It's the past!"

Simba: "Yeah, but it still hurts."

Rafiki: "Oh yes, the past can hurt. But the way I see it, you
can either run from it or learn from it. Ah, you, see? So,
what are you going to do?"

Worry and regret are two incredibly sticky emotions I try to keep a handle
on and release. It is a constant practice to let go of the predisposition to
worry about things, people, events or have regrets over what I should have
or could have done. Worry and regret should maybe be redefined as the
obsessive compulsion to ruminate about things you often have no control
over, like the past or the future—this is where leaning into your faith can
help. You believe that things have a way of working out when and as they
should in perfect cosmic timing. Faith in life working this way has helped
me navigate my most challenging times as an adult career woman—breakups with guys I deeply cared about, shows I did not get to produce, or things
I wanted taking far longer than I initially anticipated.

Recall from the Peace Snapshot No. 4, Be a Loving Battery, that any event in and of itself is neutral, and the chemical reaction of a specific emotion lasts only ninety seconds. Your unwillingness to let go of an event's emotional charge is what messes you and me up. I think this is why people say time heals. With time, you can disengage your negative thoughts toward someone who hurt you and reframe the experience into something more constructive, a life lesson that makes you a better person.

I started this section by talking about how challenging it has been for me to learn Detachment. Personal and professional heartbreaks triggered a turn to take a difficult and uncomfortable look at my feelings and reactions. I did not want to be bitter about the people and situations that hurt me, and I made up my mind to figure out how to turn my disappointments and defeats into lessons and victories. That choice propelled me onto a path that has transformed me in ways I did not know I needed to be changed. It took a lot of effort, and I genuinely believe I am a more hopeful, more thoughtful, more concerned human.

When I look at my life, I feel whole, and I realize if one of those events in my past had not happened, good or bad, I would be writing a different life story. Regretting the past is useless, not because I cannot change it, because I like myself. I needed all that life experience to form the sum of who I am, even and especially the parts that are hard to admit doing. I am not excusing any past wayward behavior; however, instead of beating myself up over something I cannot undo, I can take the tough lesson learned to be a better person today and tomorrow.

Worrying about the future is equally futile. There is no certainty other than our eventual life transforming into another energetic form. The more significant takeaway is that where despair once reigned can now be a kingdom of Happy possibilities.

Centering Thought. Worry and regret are useless.

Affirmation. I release my mind from worry and regret.

♥ ♥ ♥

Detachment Meditation Prayer

*I let go, and the world opens up in unexpected
ways. What was unpleasant becomes pleasant.*

*The ordinary becomes extraordinary. Where
there were boundaries, now there are none.*

*So, may I Detach from any thoughts or
feelings that no longer serve me.*

May I Detach from what is harmful and seek what is good.

*Instead, may I attach to words, thoughts,
feelings, and people who lift me.*

*I let go of regret, fear, and worry, knowing that a loving
universe is always there to guide and support me.*

And so let it be.

DEVELOPING MINDFUL DETACHMENT

While hard to put into practice, Detachment from sticky, unproductive thoughts or a specific result of a situation will bring you freedom and control. When you give up forcing, resisting, struggling with what you want in the future, you can be present to create possibilities out of uncertainty. You let go of past thoughts, habits, and attitudes that do not serve you for ones that do. A daily meditation practice will support you. When preparedness meets opportunity, without grasping, exciting things happen.

You can stand in your power and release any stories or attachments to how you think or want things to be. Giving up your obsession with a specific outcome enables you to see a broader picture. It helps you focus on the true essence of *what is*—no longer getting caught in the minutia of what does not matter in the grand scheme. You are also leaving yourself available to other possibilities that could fulfill your dreams, perhaps in far more significant ways than you ever thought possible. So, keep your desire to do and create things, just not the attachment to them, and get rid of what is holding you down.

Ask:

Do I need this circumstance, item, or person in my life?

What purpose does it or they serve?

Ultimately, you are developing the ability to remain Detached in a way that keeps you emotionally centered with an open heart in the face of adversity. As a result, you worry less and accept more, creating greater peace of mind, opening you to experiencing more love, joy, and contentment on every level.

Now, without attachment, release your dreams to the universe and let it conspire to support you.

Journaling with Detachment: What Does Detachment Mean to You?

Time to journal about creating a Detachment mindset. I have offered additional thoughts in italics to the questions posed with space for you to fill in yours.

How do you define Detachment and its benefits?

I see detachment as the shedding of thoughts and ideas that no longer serve me, my growth, or the highest good. It is letting go of my stories, judgments, and perceptions of how I think the world should be or how I want people to act. Detachment releases attachment from the suffering that keeps me stuck in the past and from grasping for wants in the future so that I can be present and relish today. I feel less anxious, more open, and joyful to life unfolding in miraculous and supportive ways.

_____

_____

_____

What role does Detachment currently play in your life?

The continued refinement of being able to detach from a specific result or unwanted thoughts has changed the quality of my experiences in every aspect of life. Obsessive comparing, judging, and shaming of myself and others has significantly reduced and most assuredly helped increase my state of happiness.

_____

_____

_____

What is your ability to Detach from a specific result or way of being?

Pulling back far enough to take a ten-thousand-foot view of a situation helps me understand what is most important in the grand scheme, what is truly relevant now, and ask how I want to be in this moment. However, this ability is still a work-in-progress for me. Sometimes, I get an A. Other times, a big red F. The point is that I stay aware and keep trying to show up as my best self in any situation.

_____

_____

_____

How are you, or will you, develop Detachment to achieve greater Happiness and Wholebeing?

I will continue having serious chats about detaching myself from people, places, and things that no longer serve me. At least once a day, I will pause to take a temperature read on how I feel. Is there anything or anyone that I need to release attachment from for my overall Happiness and Wholebeing? As I do this release, I will say this affirmation: "Thank you _____ for being with me. However, I no longer need you, and you are free to go. I release you now and forevermore."

_____

_____

_____

Take a photograph of what Detachment looks for you. Give it a caption. Then, journal about your thoughts and feelings.

When I separate from how it should be, I see the beauty of what is.

Journal Entry: *When I let go, I feel myself floating above, able to see a reflection that is not contrived nor forced. Instead, I see things as the universe intends them to be. When I detach, life seems to fall into place. I feel a sense of calm, a sense of knowing that all will be well and as it should be. So, I detach, no longer feeling I need to control the reactions of my mom, brother, friends, colleagues, or anyone else around me; I feel relieved. I can simply be me, and they them. I set the boundaries I need for my wellbeing, and they set theirs. Detachment is one of the most critical Happiness Essentials in my life. I am a far better, saner human for it.*

Detachment Photo Ops and Action Opportunities

Using the following Photo Op prompts, create or find photographs reflecting how Detachment can activate greater Happiness and Wholebeing within you. The Action Opportunities will help you see where to let go of what is not serving you well.

Detachment Snapshot No. 1:
Detachment Is an Emotional State of Balance

Photo Op. *Come Back to Center.* Do this Photo Op along with the Action Opportunity. Capture images of the things you want to release, be it literally or metaphorically. This assignment could take a while to complete. Honestly, this could become a practice you do for the rest of your life as you grow and change and life ebbs and flows.

Action Opportunity. Focus on the Centering Thought, "Let go," to release attachment to a specific result or way a situation should be and allow things to unfold freely. Journal about the things, people, and situations weighing you down. What do you need to Detach from to make life better, more joyful, and more fulfilling? They can be literal or metaphoric.

Then, focus on one thing to let go of in your life. Using the above Photo Op prompt, put an X on the appropriate image when you have done so.

Move on to the next item to release. As you work your way through your list, notice and journal about the shifts inside you. How are you becoming a better version of yourself? Remember to be loving and forgiving with yourself. It will help to lean into the Affirmation: "I release attachment to how things should be."

Keep track of how it feels to allow things to go their way naturally. Note your progress and prize yourself for it. It is healthy and well-deserved to celebrate your personal growth.

_____

_____

_____

Detachment Snapshot No. 2:
Check Your Ego at the Door

Photo Op. *No Ego.* What is a saying, a passage, or a prayer that reminds you to check your ego at the door? Create an image of these words and put it somewhere to see as a reminder.

Action Opportunity. In a challenging situation, pause to say the Centering Thought: "Check my ego." Do this while slowly breathing in and out of your nose for as long as needed. This way of breathing activates your parasympathetic nervous system, bringing a sense of calm. Next, ask yourself whether your mind or your heart is reacting. Is your ego or egoless self in charge? Then, respond to the situation at hand. Chances are, you will act with more grace and clarity. Acknowledge that you have moved on with the Affirmation: "I release yesterday's upsets, disappointments, grievances to stand in the gift of today."

_____

_____

_____

Detachment Snapshot No. 3:
Out of Control Is an Opportunity to Be in Control

Photo Op. *Your Day of Forgiveness.* Ask for forgiveness and forgive others. Begin by doing the Action Opportunity. Afterward, you can create an album of the responses you receive from people. Use it to remind yourself that most people are not sitting around harboring ill thoughts of you. So, let go of your worries and move on.

Action Opportunity. Take time out to create a Day of Forgiveness for yourself. Spend thoughtful time considering who you want to ask for forgiveness from and who you are ready to forgive. Use your Centering Thought: "Assume control."

Then, reach out to each person on your list. You can call, write, or see them in person—journal about what happens and how you feel. When you are done, remember that the issue is resolved forever once forgiveness is given. You do not need to discuss it again. After each forgiveness encounter, seal it with the Affirmation: "What others think of me does not matter; what matters is what I think of me."

———————————————————————

———————————————————————

———————————————————————

Detachment Snapshot No. 4:
Get Out of Your Way

Photo Op. *Stand Aside.* Capture or find an image of something that scares you to do and stick it on your bathroom mirror. Every day, look at this image and yourself, and say, "I got this one." Then, actively take steps towards being victorious over your fear. If you fear speaking, give a talk to a small group of friends and record it. Fear of heights? Climb something tall, even if it is a ladder, to reach a ceiling where you live. Whatever you do, document it with images or video.

Action Opportunity. Using the Centering Thought, "Step aside," think of what could happen if you let go of just one limiting belief about yourself.

What is the one thing that scares you yet you really want to do? Muster the courage to do it. You can start with micro-steps if that feels more comfortable.

What obstacle is blocking your way? What can you do to remove it or get around it?

Put what you wrote into action. As you do, remember your Affirmation: "I let go of the limiting thoughts that confine me to welcome in a world of possibilities." When you conquer a limiting belief, pick another one. Keep a running list of these beliefs, how you overcame them, and how each empowered you when you let go of them.

———————————————————————

———————————————————————

———————————————————————

Detachment Snapshot No. 5:
Surrender to the Direction You Are Being Led

Photo Op. *Trust Within Yourself.* Create a side-by-side image of you and the universe. Place it somewhere you will frequently see as a reminder that you already have infinite possibilities. Then, pick a bold possibility and go for it without attachment to a timeline or an overly specific outcome. Instead, leave room for unseen opportunities to come your way that can make your dream even more fantastic.

 Action Opportunity. This Action Opportunity is two-fold.

 One, start with the Centering Thought: "Surrender and trust." Then, take some time to dream without limits, without being fixated on how it should look, a particular result.

 Two, practice patience and awareness. Let go of both the result and timeline. Have faith that things will work out when they should, as long as you stay alert to opportunities when they arise. Use the Affirmation: "I trust the universe will lead me to the perfect answer in perfect timing." Keep track of what shows up to support your dreams in the space below.

_____

_____

_____

Detachment Snapshot No. 6:
Stop Running Your Mind into Brick Walls

Photo Op. *Make a Doorway.* Create or find an image of a mind that is unlocked. Use it as a reminder that this is the mental state you want.

 Action Opportunity. Using inspiration from Bishop Tutu's Four Steps to Forgiveness to Detach by forgiving yourself, do the following. First, settle yourself with the Centering Thought: "Nurture productive thoughts." Then, start journaling.

 One, what are all my feelings about (fill in the blank) situation with (fill in the blank)?

Two, reflect on and forgive any behavior you are ashamed of doing.

Three, acknowledge that you and the other person are doing your best.

Four, choose a constructive way forward that will keep you emotionally intact

This process is an inquiry and reflection of *what is* in a situation. Use it to reveal perceptions about a circumstance or person. You could find it is a mirror into yourself. End this inquiry with the Affirmation: "My Happy thoughts nurture a Happier me."

Detachment Snapshot No. 7: Get Rid of the Clutter

Photo Op. *If You Do Not Love It, Get Rid of It.* Capture before and after images of the areas in your life that you want to declutter. Share this experience with our *Take a Shot at Happiness* community as well. Comparing notes could be very insightful.

Action Opportunity. First, go through the clutter in your physical space, clear out what you are not using, and organize what you are using. You may even try treating this step as a meditation using the Centering Thought: "Release."

Then, take the more daunting step of looking at your relationships and either minimizing your time with emotionally unhealthy people or cutting the ties altogether. Understand that this second step can be very challenging and painful, so give yourself time and grace to work through the relationships you need to let go of to protect your Wholebeing. The Affirmation, "I Happily release that which does not serve me or the greater good," will help you.

Journal before how you feel about the clutter, and then how you feel after it is gone. Do you feel more liberated? Clearer with your thoughts? Less stressed?

_____

_____

_____

Detachment Snapshot No. 8:
Worry and Regrets Are Useless Emotions

Photo Op. *Create Productive Emotions.* Capture a photo of you smiling and holding up a giant pink heart. Look at it when you start to feel worried or regretful about things you have no control over or cannot change, and remember the Centering Thought, "Worry and regret are useless." You are freeing your mind from unconstructive thoughts and protecting your heart from unnecessary pain.

Action Opportunity. Reflect on the Centering Thought: "Worry and regret are useless." Look at how you can reframe a hurtful or challenging situation instead of regretting it.

What can you learn about yourself?

How does that painful situation help you grow as a person?

Once you have answered these questions, say the Affirmation, "I release my mind from worry and regret," and begin anew.

_____

_____

_____

PICTURING ABUNDANCE

Abundance

\ə-ˈbən-dən(t)s\

noun

: a large amount of something

: an ample quantity

: profusion

: affluence, wealth

: relative degree of plentifulness

"Whatever the mind of man can conceive
and believe, it can achieve."

—NAPOLEON HILL
Bestselling Author, Think and Grow Rich

SNAPSHOT OF ABUNDANCE

In My Viewfinder

Faith plus Love plus Health plus Peace plus Gratitude plus Forgiveness plus Detachment equals Abundance. All these essentials together equal Happiness as one's state of being, *ergo*, Wholebeing. More directly, Faith equals Abundance. The road between the two is Love, Health, Peace, Gratitude, Forgiveness, and Detachment. These are the foundational Happiness Essentials we have been creating and developing. When you put them all together, you create a Happier, more fulfilling life for yourself and those around you. True Abundance lies far beyond your bank account. If you notice in this Happiness equation, nowhere does it mention money, though financial wealth is often a byproduct.

My eleven-year-old self, realizing Happiness is not defined by financial wealth, has been my lens of choice for most of my professional decisions. The other is the belief that money would flow by doing what I loved, professionally as well as personally. Throughout my television career, the shows and stories I loved most were about people who would be doing what they were doing, whether there was a camera or not. One such person was Sue Aikens, best known as a cast member in National Geographic's *Life Below Zero*. I met Sue before this series was on-air when I was doing a show about Alaska that included an episode at her wilderness camp on the Kavik River, just a few miles from the Arctic National Wildlife Refuge. So, here was a woman who loved living in the great outdoors, and somehow cameras and success found her even though she lived almost five hundred miles away from the nearest big city, Fairbanks. That remote river camp and Sue's lifestyle already existed before we came along and did after we left, and this is my point. Even when it seems so far-fetched that you will ever be able to create the life and livelihood you want, think again and back it up with Faith and Love.

So, back to me at eleven. Even at that early age, somehow, I understood that I needed to pursue what I loved. I needed to be Happy first inside my skin and head, and the money would come out of that. If I did what I loved, I would be good at it and thus paid well. Then as life went on, I came to understand that being paid well is not necessarily, exclusively, about money, nor should it be. When you make money your definition of Abundance and your singular goal, you end up with a very one-dimensional life.

"For what does a man profit if he shall gain the whole world and lose his soul?" —Mark 8:36 (NKJV). That is why you see people who seem to have it all yet are depressed and lonely. Life overwhelms and stresses them, and in turn, they reach out for external things that will never offer lasting Happiness, a sense of purpose, or benefit their Wholebeing. Expensive clothes, jewelry, nail and body enhancements, hair extensions, another expensive car, a bigger house with more rooms to fill with things you do not need, endless partying, and casual friendships. Some of this is fine and even a lot of fun; however, it becomes not fine when they are just covers for an emptiness inside at the soul level. Somehow, they lost their way, despite fame and fortune, and it is rising to the surface in unhealthy, unproductive behavior patterns. These people are enacting a type of karma that only gives them more of the same. What they need to do is step out of themselves, even for just a minute, to look at things as they are and ask themselves if this is what they truly want. The fortunate ones will bump into that startling question, is that all there is? Then likely realize they have so much on the material level yet lack on the soul level. That is the starting point to changing life as they know it, and they choose to develop from a one-dimensional life to a three-dimensional one.

So, this part is not about making money. It is about so much more. It is about creating a world where you can have more, more in a fulfilling way that is healthier all the way around, a life that points you in the direction of "I want more because I genuinely feel Happy and want to share it with others" versus wanting more to dull the pain as a diversion to dealing with what is not making you Happy.

It is also not to imply that fame and fortune lead to unhappiness; that would be a false statement. On the contrary, I think many who have succeeded in achieving great financial wealth and notoriety are Happy because these people have a deep sense of purpose and use their status for good in the world. Virgin Group founder Richard Branson is an excellent example, feeling that success, wealth, and connection have come to him because he is Happy. Warren Buffett is one of the top ten wealthiest men, with a net worth is $88.8 billion. Yet, he has given away almost half that amount over his lifetime to alleviate poverty and solve health issues. An *Inc.* magazine article attributes the billionaire's success to his relentless optimism.

Snapshots on Developing True Abundance

Abundance Snapshot No. 1:
Harness the Power of Intention

Emerging from the *Chamber of Secrets*, alarm flickers in Harry Potter's eyes. Maybe, he, too, is like Tom Riddle and will one day turn into a dark wizard like Voldemort, who uses his power to manipulate and murder. Quickly, he makes his way to Headmaster Albus Dumbledore's office to warn of what he saw in the chamber and voice his alarm about what he is afraid he will become. Dumbledore sizes up the youth with wise, fatherly eyes. "It is our choices, Harry, that show what we truly are, far more than our abilities." Our intentions guide our choices based on perceived skills and desires. Two people can share similar capabilities; however, one uses them for good and the other for the very thing Harry Potter fears, evil. Being clear on your core values, coupled with patience, can serve you well in the intentions you set.

For about a year after choosing to refocus my life in a more positive and constructive direction, I had these words pinned to the bulletin board at my desk: God, Love, Peace, Abundance, Detachment, Forgiveness, and Gratitude. On the fifth anniversary of this decision, I put these words back up on my board as a reminder that they were still relevant to me, though now being in a far better place emotionally than when I wrote those words in a state of heartache and needing to heal. The only word change was replacing God with Faith, adding Health in mind, body, and spirit, and reordering the words to be Faith, Love, Health, Gratitude, Forgiveness, Peace, Detachment, Abundance—one virtue or quality begetting and supporting the other, altogether the greater sum of its parts became the virtues and qualities that guide me today and created this very book.

The list was partially influenced by Wayne Dyer's book *The Power of Intention*. A concept that he referred to which profoundly struck me came from *A Course in Miracles*, "infinite patience yields immediate results." Things happen for a reason and at the right time.

When you have an intention coming from a good place, those things meant to be will stick, while the other stuff that does not matter goes by you. Having infinite patience is the mindful pathway to raising your awareness of the many ways your intentions are already being supported. As a result, you are more available to possibilities and realize there is no need to be anxious or jealous of others. Your desires will come to be if you have the Faith to stay the course.

So, keep taking action toward your desires while patiently keeping alert to what shows up in your life. Do this with Love, Openness, and Detachment. Be like the stream of fast-running water. The water rushes by, around, and over the rocks. The solid rocks stay firmly seated into the earth, while the loose ones get swept away. When you are not clinging to a result or timeline, what is meant to stay will take hold.

For the times you feel that you need to redirect yourself, first of all, it is okay. You may come across information or realize a level of awareness you did not have when you initially set your intention that now impacts your way forward.

Just pause, breathe.

Look at your current situation. What works for you? What does not?

Consider where you want to go. What do you truly want? How do you want to act and be?

Then choose a course of action that will take you from your present self to become your future self.

When you find thoughts framed around "I can't," or, "I shouldn't," remember this self-talk keeps you stuck in all the ways you lack, what you do not have, what you do not want, constricting your mind, body, and spirit. Instead, focus on what you do have and want to create. "Yes, I can" multiplies into infinite possibilities, being more aware, seeing life clearer and further into the future, beyond your current intellectual and emotional horizon. Nothing transforms in your world until you perceive it consciously, believe it as possible subconsciously, and see it as already here. Now you are in an expanded state that motivates you to be proactive and solution oriented. Your clarity focuses on what needs to be done, exciting you to get busy.

"You will also find that help will always be given at Hogwarts to those who ask for it," says Albus Dumbledore.

The spiritual version of this is,
"If you ask Me anything in My name, I will do it."
—John 14:14 (BSB).

Centering Thought. Power my intentions.

Affirmation. I consciously set the intention to be Abundant in all meaningful aspects of my life.

Abundance Snapshot No. 2:
See What You Already Have

I once heard this story about Oprah Winfrey. A guest showed up at her home with flowers. Oprah graciously thanked them, then put the flowers into an elegant vase and found a prominent place to display them, all the while admiring the beauty of its petals. The amount of appreciation that Oprah gave for the flowers so took her guest. Finally, she asked why all the fuss. Oprah looked around the room with a broadening smile, then replied, "How do you think I was able to have all of this?"

Appreciating what you already have and are being given brings more of the same, along with feelings of Abundance. Even when times are lean, you have more than you think, and I do not mean the vase of flowers on your coffee table, the make of your car, or the season of your clothes. So often, we default to living in what we do not have, causing us to exist in a place of scarcity and unhappiness. Instead of seeing your life's cup as half-full, you see it as half-empty—time to reframe that picture in your mind. You already know that what you put your attention on expands. It also often consumes you. This focused attention is fundamental to the Law of Attraction. You can either use this focus to your advantage or be used by it to your disadvantage. So, take a moment to reflect on what is filling your cup:

What is important to you?

What is going right in your life?

What do you now have and want more of?

What gives your life meaning and purpose?

Focus on what is already positive in your life, what already is working, no matter how seemingly small and insignificant. It will grow when you pay more attention to it. Acknowledging what you already have offers hope for more in the coming days. As you feel confident about an area you once felt lacking, you will naturally want to manifest more in other parts of your life.

When you feel things are hard, scarce, and will never happen, recall when it was easier and more plentiful. You may have to reach into the darkness to shine a light on these memories. Trust that they are there. Remember what you learned in the Happiness Essentials Faith and Gratitude about Taking in the Good. Notice and savor an experience for twenty to thirty seconds and use positive memories to override the current negative ones. Use them as light to expand your mind's aperture to behold even more Abundance. Learn to see what fills your cup and take a bit of inspiration from Oprah: "Be thankful for what you have; you'll end up having more. If you concentrate on what you don't have, you will never, ever have enough."

Centering Thought. My cup overflows.

Affirmation. I appreciate the great abundance that already fills me, surrounds me, and supports me.

Abundance Snapshot No. 3:
Know Your Endgame Means

Male Passenger (rudely): "Hey man, how long before we get there?"

An eighty-something-year-old English taxi driver looks into his rearview mirror. Three young American professionals, two males and a female, sit in the back of a cab with open windows fanning themselves with pieces of paper as the full-day sun streams across them.

Taxi Driver: "Not too much further."

Male Passenger (continues sarcastically): "First class, so far."

The two males laugh while the female giggles uneasily as she tries to calculate their remaining drive time out loud. Their test had already begun, and they did not even realize it, and hidden cameras were rolling. The three were contestants on a new reality competition show. Each would be vying for a job that would ignite their careers.

The driver kept a discreet and pleasant demeanor as they made their way along the forty-four miles from Heathrow airport to Oxford on a very hot day. Not so for the two guys. However, the woman was sweet and even tried helping the driver with some of the heavy bags at the airport before they went on the road to an unknown destination.

Finally, they arrived at a beautiful countryside home. The driver got out of the cab and followed the group inside. Once there, the driver peeled off his older man's mask, revealing that he was Sir Richard Branson. The two guys who had been in the back were now returning to America for being cheeky and unkind to an older man who was just trying to do his job. They failed their first test.

In 2004, the FOX network launched *The Rebel Billionaire: Branson's Quest for the Best*. The famous daredevil billionaire wanted to find someone to take over as president of Virgin—though he wished for someone good with people, who cared about others, and was not just wrapped up in themselves and only focused on the prize without much consideration of how they were behaving getting there. The woman who paid attention to the older driver in the cab was the show's winning runner-up, Sara Blakely, who went on to start the intimate apparel company Spanx. Eventually, making it on *Time* magazine's "Time 100" annual list of the most influential people in the world for her business success and philanthropy. This story displays Blakely and Branson's attention to how they created their net worth and what they would do with it. Being kind and giving were non-negotiables.

As you think about Abundance in different areas of your life, finances in particular, what will you use it for? All that effort and time spent accumulating will be to what end? How will you get there? Hopefully, not the same way as the two rude guys who never got to unpack and compete in *The Rebel Billionaire*. Think about it because how you plan to acquire—your *means*—and use your Abundance—your *endgame*—will impact almost every choice you make, including the relationships you nurture. The way you treat others. The activities you pursue. The way you take care of your mind and body. The way you view success. The way you see the means of getting to your success. It all matters, and it all matters a lot.

I admire Branson, who turned his intense desire to be an innovative entrepreneur, controlling over four hundred companies, who uses his success, resources, and wealth to champion a host of social causes. I have heard him say he did not plan for Virgin's exponential growth. Though what he did was made businesses in areas that interested him. He hired those aligned with his values, who had the know-how in specific industries, and then let them do their jobs. He got his means and endgame into healthy alignment, making the conscious choice to use his wealth and resources philanthropically.

When you choose how to be in the world and start thinking and acting in that direction, you will attract more good stuff. You attract more positive things happening to you that will increase your Abundance in terms of overall quality of life. I think the Law of Attraction also has an attribute that helps you become alert to your thoughts and actions and guides them in the direction you want. Instead of people and opportunities seeming to just show up, you become tuned into, selectively attentive to, seeing what will support your vision.

It is like after I bought my Chrysler Crossfire, which they made a limited number of and now no longer sell. Suddenly, I saw Crossfires everywhere, and I often do many years later. My frequent car sighting is known as the "Baader-Meinhof phenomenon," also called the "Frequency Illusion." It happens after you learn something new, or in this case, make a unique purchase and then see it everywhere. It is because I am unconsciously alert to seeing Crossfires.

So, frequently spotting Crossfires, Branson, knowing your endgame and its means—how do they connect?

You set an intention, one that is heart-based. Your mind becomes watchful of seeing and acting on supportive opportunities as they present themselves. You build and accumulate your resources around your desire in a conscious way. Then, use your Abundance to do good in the world. What you do with what you have and how you get there counts. You want your journey and arrival to feel like your soul remained intact. Your journey had meaning, value, a purpose. Know that the good guys can and do win. If you are reading this book, you likely want this for yourself and to be with others of a similar mindset. So, be kind, respectful, and alert to the Baader-Meinhof phenomenon supporting you.

"Too many people measure how successful they are by how much money they make or the people that they associate with. In my opinion, true success should be measured by how happy you are." Full stop. Richard Branson.

Centering Thought. Get in alignment.

Affirmation. I see my endgame and consciously
make choices that are in alignment.

Abundance Snapshot No. 4:
Your Past or Present Does Not Have to Define Your Future

Shortly before we lost one of our national treasures, I had the honor of going to Dr. Maya Angelou's home to interview her for a *Women of the Bible* special for the Lifetime cable channel. After our interview, she asked the entire crew to have lunch with her. As we ate, Dr. Angelou went around the table, asking each of us what we wanted to do in life and how she could help. I was floored by this gesture. She then closed our time together with a thought-provoking riff on what it is to be a human. The essence of her words was that if you are thinking it, it is because you can do it, especially if someone has done something similar before you. If there was ever a human with the extraordinarily varied life experience to deliver a message like this, it was Dr. Angelou. So, if you want to learn six languages as she did, you can. If you desire to climb the highest peak on every continent, like the American rancher Richard Bass, who was the first to do this in 1985, you can. If you wish to go into space like the Russian engineer Valentina Tereshkova, who in 1963 was the first woman in space, you can. "If you can dream it, you can do it." Just look at what Walt Disney, who coined this phrase, created.

"You are today where your thoughts have brought you; you will be tomorrow where your thoughts take you." These words were written by British philosopher James Allen, best known for authoring *As a Man Thinketh* in 1903 and point to an illusory world we each create through the lens of our perception, formed by thoughts linked to our emotions and the results of past actions.

We, as individuals, give our world, our lives, their meaning. Your views and emotions define your world. That said, are there things beyond your control? Do death, destruction, and disease happen? Yes, yes, and yes. However, what is essential is finding personal meaning even in the face of indescribable pain and adversity. That is what Dr. Angelou did throughout her highly accomplished life, despite being raped at the age of seven by her mother's boyfriend, surviving the depression in the south, and working both as a pimp and prostitute. None of these life circumstances stopped Dr. Angelou from rising to her celebrated stature as a memoirist, poet, journalist, playwright, actor, singer, and civil rights activist loved and respected by millions. Why? Because she rose above thoughts of despair or shame that could easily have obstructed her from what she needed or felt compelled to do. Those with a sense of meaning in life can push through hardship and find joy and Happiness more so than those who only sense the meaninglessness.

How you frame your perception of the story of your life and what you think will happen in the future informs the amount and type of Abundance that will come to you. What you believe about yourself will probably manifest, and just because something happened in the past or is happening now will not make it so in the future. Likewise, believing that you control what you achieve will create that reality.

In setting a higher, brighter vision for yourself that goes beyond material and financial accumulation, you will realize Abundance as a fulfilled human. There is so much to live for when you widen your spectrum to see it. My only addition to Dr. Angelou's riff is a reminder that what you want to do or have may come in a slightly different form than envisioned. So, be open, be curious, be attentive, be intentional, and be grateful. See life not as freedom *from*, but instead as freedom *to* do and create the world you want.

Centering Thought. Today is what matters.

Affirmation. My past does not define today or tomorrow.

Abundance Snapshot No. 5: Mind the Gap

One of the world's greatest classical composers started losing his hearing around his mid-twenties yet continued writing music until his death at fifty-six: Ludwig van Beethoven, the father of the Romantic era in music, widely recognized as one of the greatest composers of Western European music.

Standing five feet three inches, he played fourteen seasons as a point guard on four teams: Muggsy Bogues, the shortest NBA player ever.

A drag queen receives twelve Primetime Emmy Awards, three GLAAD Media Awards, a Critics' Choice Television Award, two Billboard Music Awards, and a Tony Award: RuPaul Andre Charles, the "Queen of Drag."

These three people share a dedication to not letting loss, deficiency, or social stigma prevent them from attaining Abundantly successful careers. Whether they consciously acknowledged it or not, their mindset to succeed was more significant than any obstacle that someone else may have perceived, including themselves. Beethoven, Muggsy, and RuPaul must have each innately understood that there is no limit on the amount of Abundance you are entitled to, no invisible line that selects who can and cannot have, no matter who you are or your circumstance. You just have to find access to your unique talent (we each find it in different ways with varying outcomes), and the ability to take on an exponential life is uncovered.

However, it is worthy of note that some may create wealth and power early, then crash and burn because they are not ready to handle it, and have to start over. Others' paths may be like slow-burning embers that suddenly burst into a magnificent bonfire. Then, some achieve a lot of notoriety and the privileges that go with it and sustain it—or do they? Maybe because they were so focused on the result, sacrificing their physical and emotional health at all costs, these seemingly successful people ended up tragically empty, often turning to drugs to dull their pain. Think about Elvis Presley, Jim Morrison, Marilyn Monroe, Howard Hughes, Michael Jackson, John Belushi, Philip Seymour Hoffman. Each seemed to have everything yet felt so profoundly, painfully lacking that all their outward Abundance was of little value. My dad used to say, "Never judge a man until you know their end."

So never mind what your neighbor is doing. Just pay attention to what you are doing. It is easy to look at someone else's success, tragic or not, and think you will never be able to attain their heights or at least the level of success you want, and you will be correct. There is a gap between what you do not have and desire, and the obstacle between these two points is you. Closing this gap will likely start when you realize your gifts and connect to the excitement that creates enthusiasm, curiosity, and Abundance. Engaging your gifts fuels the intentions you set to reach your desires.

When you set intentions, activate them by doing two things. One, ask to receive them. Two, take action toward attaining them. Many inspirational speakers and spiritual traditions suggest that one should ask to receive. "Ask, and it will be given to you; seek and you will find; knock, and the door will be opened." —Matthew 7:7. Then, believe with all your heart that what you want is coming your way.

Ask, Believe, Receive.

Then, there is one more vital step, *accept*. You may think receiving and accepting are the same thing. However, the two are not. You need the mental and emotional depth and the ability to accept what you ask for in life. The accountability to deal with financial wealth. The self-love to take care of yourself. The responsibility to serve social causes. This depth and ability to *accept* will support the belief that you are worthy and deserving of what you ask for.

We can ask for things, yet deep inside we do not feel worthy of receiving them. An often-cited reason for people not going after their dreams, or self-sabotaging, is that they do not feel worthy—worried that if someone pulled back the curtain, they would see that the Wizard is just an ordinary, insufficient human. If you think this way, you are far from being alone. My invitation is to use one or all of the following affirmations:

I am receiving and accepting financial and professional prosperity. It is in my life now, and I am worthy.

I am receiving and accepting a healthy mind, body, and spirit. It is in my life now, and I am enough.

I am receiving and accepting a happy, sensual, loving relationship. It is in my life now, and I am deserving.

Nurture the possibilities rather than the limitations. When you are tough on yourself, remember moments when you were in sync with life, then say one of the relevant above affirmations. This will activate your brain to rewire around what you want. If you remain focused and consistent, the results will come. Your early wins and opportunities may seem small and unnoteworthy, yet they are hugely significant. These small victories, bit by bit, become bigger and bigger, as does your awareness of what is happening around you. As you accomplish one thing, reach for the next. Keep doing this, and you will eventually see that your seemingly insignificant achievements will accumulate into something noteworthy.

There is a Japanese word for this concept of small actions adding up over time, which was developed into a philosophical approach to improving the manufacturing process in that country. It is based on the idea that continuous, incremental improvement over time yields notable changes without the radical upheaval of dramatic, disruptive change. It is called "Kaizen," translated as *Kai* for change and *Zen* for good, and can apply to every aspect of life where you seek improvement. I have used it to clear piles of dusty paperwork covering my living room floor, train to walk the distance of a marathon, and write my PhD dissertation. I was applying the Kaizen philosophy before I even knew it existed. I thought I was just using my mother's simple Greek wisdom of filling a bean bag one bean at a time.

So, the next time you think you cannot do something, think about Beethoven, Muggsy, and RuPaul and know that you are worthy of whatever you desire.

Centering Thought. I accept.

Affirmation. I am gratefully receiving and accepting
the Abundance of all good things in my life.

Abundance Snapshot No. 6:
Be the Writer, Director, and Producer of Your World

"Our education was a dress rehearsal for a life we never lived," Oscar-nominated filmmaker Nora Ephron recounts a former classmate's summation of their time at Wellesley College in 1962. Thirty-four years later, Nora stands before the next group of female Wellesley graduates urging them not to do the same as many in the classes before them, the ones who had lives not lived because of personal circumstances, societal norms, cultural values, glass ceilings, all the ways they were prevented from creating an Abundantly fulfilling life.

"Be the heroine of your life, not the victim. Because you don't have the alibi my class had—this is one of the great achievements and mixed blessings you inherit."

No excuses for not living your best life today. You are the writer, director, and producer of your world. Unfortunately, those who play the victim role will always be victims until they take responsibility for how they react to adversities, deal with the people and events that block them, and view the world at large. Victims look from the outside in, blaming others or their circumstances for what is scarce, unfair, or impossible in their lives. Victors look from the inside out. When you see from the inside out, you are taking control of how you move through this world, which directly affects the Abundance you create. Indeed, like the other virtues and qualities we have been discussing, Abundance is an inside job.

I had a close colleague who was always involved in some high-level drama. A senior team leader was blocking them from advancing at work. Someone else was bullying them on social media. Their romantic partner left them after ransacking their house. Their drama continued and expanded because they were not seeing how they were responsible for the maelstrom that swirled around them. They would helplessly retreat into the "I can't do anything about this." They could not fathom that if they simply said, "Stop!" no longer further engaging in victim-felt situations and changing their lens of perception, most of their distress would do just that, end. Why would you want to stay in a work environment that does not offer the opportunity to advance? Try blocking mean people on social media, and good riddance to a destructive partner. You do not ever need that in your life.

I think we all know one person who constantly asks for advice yet takes none of it, preferring to complain rather than actually do something about an unhappy situation. Because they continually play the victim, they perpetuate more of the same, often leading to some kind of lack: lack of having the people they want in their lives, lack of having the career they want, lack of financial resources. That is because they leave control to outside influences, either limiting or forgoing any kind of Abundance in their lives except pain and suffering. When you assume control of your life you receive a huge confidence boost, which supports overall life satisfaction, enabling you to feel more positive and resilient.

Your life is not a dress rehearsal. No one is going to care about your life more than you. Seriously, ask yourself, do you want to be the auteur of your life, making life happen, or do you want to merely be an on-set assistant, letting another dictate what you do? The choice is yours and will result in the amount and kind of Abundance you create.

Centering Thought. I am the auteur.

Affirmation. I choose to be the writer, director, and producer of a happy, fulfilling, and Abundant life.

Abundance Snapshot No. 7: Choose Right Thoughts, Right Action

It was his first sermon after being entirely still for forty-nine days under a generously leafed Ficus religiosa, a species of fig tree imbued with sacredness, this one in Bihar, India. Maybe he had soft, smooth skin, a lion-shaped jaw, deep blue eyes with eyelashes like a royal bull, and a voice deep and resonant, though we will never know for sure. Yet we do know his message, the Buddha's, his guidance for living a good life lasted for the ages to come: right understanding, right intent, right speech, right action, right livelihood, right effort, right mindfulness, and right concentration.

Drawing inspiration from the Buddha's Eightfold Path, you want to make healthy choices in caring for yourself, your thoughts, and your behavior. Mind your word choice. Mind your thought choice. Think about the consequences of your asks and your deeds.

Right understanding is experiencing reality and its problems as they are, not as you want them to be.

Right intent comes from the heart, compassionately seeing the equality in all life, including yourself. Then, set and commit to a meaningful path in life.

Right speech recognizes the truth and kindly communicates, avoiding harsh words and gossip.

Right action considers those in the world and the world itself, honoring your word and behavior, not taking what is not yours, and being stewards of the planet and each other.

Right livelihood is doing work that respects all life.

Right effort is having a steady positive attitude that avoids extremes, not too intense, not too slack, and embraces focused action.

Right mindfulness is being aware, undistracted, and focused on the present moment.

Right concentration selects worthy objects or concepts to focus the mind on seeing things as they really are in the present moment.

A Buddha nature or Christ mind is within reach for all of us. Like everything in the pages before, it is a choice of how you want to live. When I remember that I am created in the image of God and Christ resides inside, it helps me to be a little kinder, a little gentler, a little more open, and a little more compassionate, just a little bit better of a human that day, and people generally respond in kind. You teach people how to treat you by how you treat them. Use thoughts and actions constructively by consciously framing them as ones that encourage Abundance.

Try:

Be kind, be helpful.

Have a plan, yet be flexible.

Pursue your dreams every day.

Good Health leads to a good life.

Smile! A lot!! It makes a difference.

Own your position, own your dreams.

Resolve and let go of your anger quickly.

You want to be first-class, then act first-class.

Resist harboring negative thoughts and emotions.

Take *it* seriously, have fun doing *it, have serious fun.*

Come from a good heart and act with good intentions.

Stay focused on your dreams, even after seeing significant
success, avoiding complacency.

When you feel *right*, you feel good. When you feel good, you do good.
When you do good, you do well. When you do well, you feel
Abundant.

Centering Thought. Choose healthy Abundance.

Affirmation. I choose right thoughts,
right action, get the right results.

Abundance Snapshot No. 8: Float Downstream

"Hold on to that fundamental quality of faith, that on the other side of your pain is something good."
—DWAYNE "THE ROCK" JOHNSON

Sometimes we go through patches in life where nothing seems to work—not in our professional life, not our personal life. Every day you feel like you go left then right, each way bumping into an invisible closed door. You try jumping up yet hit a glass ceiling. It is like you are bouncing around a room with no way out. What you may consider doing is course-correcting instead of trying to make lateral moves or trying to go up. Go down, as in downstream. Get into a better flow with life by looking at your core values and intentions. See if they are aligned. Things work much better all the way around when your values support what you want to achieve. You tend to hit obstacles when your values are not aligned with your current direction.

If you are not getting that job or that relationship you want, it may very well be because of one of two reasons: a limiting belief that you do not deserve to have what you want, or your core values are not in sync with your desires. Neither of which is a great place to be. Both will restrict the flow of Abundance, like stepping on a garden hose to stop the water from coming out. You are blocking the flow of what you can have and do. Until you take your foot off that Abundance hose, you will continue feeling some kind of lack, some sort of limitation.

Even if you have life circumstance obligations, you can still take the small deliberate Kaizen steps we discussed in Abundance Snapshot No. 5, Mind the Gap, toward your dreams. If you are in a position you are not loving and wish you were traveling, performing, starting a business, or whatever your vision is, honestly ask yourself, if not now, when? Is it scary to throw off the shackles of limitation? Yes. However, it is even more terrifying if you do not and end up with a life of regret.

Consider whether you are afraid because you think you lack talent, know-how, or ability, then get busy practicing and learning what you feel you need to get better at doing. Most people are not naturally gifted speakers, ballplayers, writers, photographers, filmmakers. They have to practice becoming good. Those who continuously practice eventually succeed.

Michael Jordan, one of our basketball legends, did not start off being good. He did not even make his high school's varsity team. So how did Jordan do it? First, he practiced longer and harder than anyone else every day until he became the best at playing the game. Then, he did not stop once he reached that status. Throughout his career, Jordan was the first to hit the gym and the last to leave.

Jerry Seinfeld applied a similar concept to becoming a great comic, except his involved a calendar and a big red marker. Every day, he spent time creating new jokes and made a big X across that day on his calendar. It motivated him to do it again the next day and the next. He liked seeing the long chain of red Xs that accumulated after weeks and months and the results that came with it.

Dwayne "The Rock" Johnson was down to his last seven dollars. He never made it to the NFL, was cut by the CFL, and was living with his parents when he chose to turn around his life and pursue his dreams of being a wrestler. His father thought The Rock was throwing away his life. Not so. He went on to become one of the greatest professional wrestlers of all time and then proved himself equally in films. To this day he gets up every morning at 4 a.m. to train and get his game face on because The Rock remembers what it was like to have only seven dollars in his pocket. He knows the competition is always waiting to take his place. Warren Sapp did. He played defensive line at Miami University back in his college days and snatched the NFL dream that The Rock missed. Now Dwayne Johnson keeps his edge by abiding by the motto, "No one will outwork me."

These stories about Michael Jordan, Jerry Seinfeld, and Dwayne "The Rock" Johnson are of them finding their way downstream when life was not working. The three of them, Dr. Maya Angelou, Muggsy, RuPaul, and so many other famous people mentioned in this book turned their defeats and obstacles into victories, and so can each of us, regardless of circumstance. So, find and nurture something you love and can become good at doing and do it, and have faith that opportunities, Abundance, and a significant boost in Happiness and Wholebeing are coming your way.

Centering Thought. In the flow.

Affirmation. I move through my life
with clarity, direction, and ease.

Abundance Meditation Prayer

Abundance has no bounds.

It is I that set that which binds me.

It is I that can set myself free.

I ask for clarity and strength to set a course toward freedom.

*Oh, bountiful universe, please guide me in following
a heartful path aligned with a meaningful end.*

May I feel worthy.

May I feel enough.

May I feel deserving.

*May my cup be overflowing with goodness
to be shared with others.*

And so let it be.

DEVELOPING TRUE ABUNDANCE

Abundance is the continued realization of worthy intentions that magnify your Happiness, and if you are Happy, you set honorable intentions. The two intertwine and become the perception of your life. Your perception is your reality.

Deepak Chopra describes three components that make up your reality, whether you see a world of Abundance or lack. Spirit, or whatever name works for you, is the source of all creation—the *observer*. The mind is creation in motion—the *process of observing*. The body is creation as an object in the physical universe—the *observed*. All three components come out of nothing into something. Remember our earlier conversation about the quantum realm? The unmanifest in the Field of Possibilities manifests when you observe and believe you are the conscious creator of your dreams and ultimate Happiness. Abundance, as your perception and desires define it, is sent into the universe and put into action driven by your mindset that becomes your reality. To affect an Abundance mindset, consciously set worthy intentions. These intentions become the energetic charge that awakens you to see who and what is already available. It is how we see, expect, judge, believe, and give a situation, thing, or person its meaning.

If your world is not working for you, it is likely because of limiting thoughts, beliefs, and behavior that you are still operating from and need to change. Be still and ask what you need to let go of to realize your full and true Abundance.

Where can you let go of fear or indifference to be more loving?

Where can you let go of judgment or criticism to be more appreciative?

Where can you let go of blame or victimization to let in forgiveness?

Abundance goes way beyond what is in your bank account. It is being rich in your relationships, experiences, purpose, health, spirituality—feeling full in every aspect of life that is important to you. It comes from seeing the unbounded possibilities in the world that fill your golden goblet and are active in shaping the blessings around you. Your work tends to be your play, and your play is your work. You make healthy, productive lifestyle choices. You are willing to try and keep trying, knowing that you are supported, ethereally, materially, or both, and that things will work out as they should in perfect timing.

Journaling with Abundance: What Does Abundance Mean to You?

Now that you have read my ideas about Abundance, time to journal about creating more Abundance in your life. I have some additional thoughts in italics and space for you to fill in your responses.

How do you define Abundance and its benefits?

Abundance is when I feel I have so much. Even when there is an apparent lack in some areas of my life, I genuinely still feel happy. I count my blessings for the many good things that already exist. Feeling abundant gives me a sense of security and confidence to either set the intention for something else I desire to do or enjoy what I have now. It reduces the need to always strive for something because I already feel I have enough.

_____

_____

_____

What role does Abundance, or perceived lack of, currently play in your life?

When I note what I already have, the areas I feel lacking seem less acute and give me hope that if I created abundance in one place of my life, I will be able to do the same elsewhere, which makes the future less daunting.

How do you perceive your ability to create or attract Abundance in your life?

On balance, I feel good about my ability to create or attract abundance on the big-ticket items in life: healthy in mind and body, having positive relationships, a purpose in life, a lovely home, and freedom to travel.

How are you, or will you develop Abundance to achieve greater Happiness and Wholebeing?

I will continue acknowledging and counting my blessings every day, focusing on what I do have rather than what I do not. The areas where I perceive a lack of abundance: one, I will not shame myself; two, I will make a micro-step plan for how to turn lack into fullness; three, say my centering thought and daily affirmation.

_____

_____

_____

Take a photograph of what Abundance looks like for you. Give it a caption. Then, journal about your thoughts and feelings.

Abundance uplifts and opens me to infinite possibilities.

Journal Entry: *When I am in an abundance mindset, I feel like I can do anything. The field of infinite possibilities is open to me (abundance). The boundaries of limiting beliefs dissolve. My mind and body release the churning angst in me (detachment). A sense of ease and contentment wash over me (peace). I feel kind and benevolent toward others and myself (forgiveness). My heart bursts with thankfulness and openness (gratitude). Every cell, every ounce of my being, feels vibrant* *(health). I feel nurtured and nurturing (love). And my belief that a source greater than I is guiding me is comforting, encouraging, and unshakable (faith).*

Abundance Photo Ops and Action Opportunities

Your last series of Photo Ops and Action Opportunities in this book—you have come a long way. Congratulate yourself by looking back at all the images of Happiness and Wholebeing you created. What have you learned? How have you grown? I now invite you to capture photos reflective of how you perceive Abundance in your world. The Action Opportunities will guide you in seeing how you can manifest even more Abundance in key areas of your life.

Abundance Snapshot No. 1: Harness the Power of Intention

Photo Op. *Step into Your Power.* Create an image that reflects your intention(s) and the type of Abundance you believe it will yield. Keep this somewhere you will frequently see as motivation to stay the course.

Action Opportunity. Start with the Centering Thought: "Power my intentions." Then set your intention(s). Afterward, get busy being proactive and take action. This Action Opportunity to grow is about picking and focusing on those few things you believe will create Abundance in your life on your terms. The key? Decide on your intention as best you can with what you know at this moment in time and pursue it with all your heart. Use the Affirmation: "I consciously set the intention to be Abundant in all meaningful aspects of my life." You can always readjust your aim as you gain more experience and insight.

This Action Opportunity can also be done with Abundance Action Opportunity No. 5: Mind the Gap.

_____

_____

_____

Abundance Snapshot No. 2: See What You Already Have

Photo Op. *You Have More Than You Already Realize.* Create a collage or series of images that show the things in your life that are significant to you.

Action Opportunity. Get settled into this writing prompt with the Centering Thought: "My cup overflows." Then, thoughtfully observe where you are already Abundant in your life. Recall Oprah's story.

Do you have a renewed appreciation for what is already present in your life? By naming what you have, do you feel more Abundant and Happier for it?

Close your journaling with the Affirmation: "I appreciate the great Abundance that already fills me, surrounds me, and supports me."

_____

_____

_____

Abundance Snapshot No. 3: Know Your Endgame Means

Photo Op. *The Real Happiness Journey Is Your Means, Not Your Endgame.* Create a photo series that reflects the answers to the questions in the following Action Opportunity. So, start there, then do this Photo Op.

Image one, your endgame.

Image two, your means.

Image three, the words that state your core values over a meaningful background. Note: you may want to first look at Abundance Photo Op and Action Opportunity No. 8, which asks you to identify your core values and create an image of them.

Action Opportunity. Recall the Centering Thought: "Get in alignment." Then, answer these questions:

What do I want to achieve, endgame?

What are the means to fulfilling my desires?

What are my core values, and are they in alignment with my means and endgame?

If it serves you, use the Affirmation: "I see my endgame and consciously make choices that are in alignment."

_____

_____

_____

Abundance Snapshot No. 4:
Your Past or Present Does Not Have to Define Your Future

Photo Op. *If You Can Dream It, You Can Do It.* Capture or find an image of a bright star. Use it to celebrate your progress. Each time you complete a step toward your dream, date a copy of the star and give it a caption that notes your accomplishment. Use this as motivation to keep going.

Action Opportunity. Begin with the Centering Thought: "Today is what matters." Reflect on what matters most to you today and in the future. Seal this writing session with the Affirmation: "My past does not define today or tomorrow."

_____

_____

_____

Abundance Snapshot No. 5:
Mind the Gap

Photo Op. *The Gap Between Two Points Is You.* Capture an image or two of you in a position of receiving and accepting. Put this on a mirror you often use. Look at your photo, then at your reflection, and into your eyes, saying one or more of these Abundance Snapshot affirmations.

"I am receiving and accepting financial and professional prosperity. It is in my life now, and I am worthy."

"I am receiving and accepting a healthy mind, body, and spirit. It is in my life now, and I am enough."

"I am receiving and accepting a happy, sensual, loving relationship. It is in my life now, and I am deserving."

Action Opportunity. Refer to the intention(s) you set in Abundance Action Opportunity No. 1. Sit quietly and ask to receive them. Consciously accept that you are worthy of receiving. Believe this to be true. Use the Centering Thought, "I accept," to open a positive neural pathway to acceptance. Next, acknowledge the Abundance already exists, using the Affirmation: "I am gratefully receiving and accepting the Abundance of all good things in my life." Do this every day, and you will eventually become as you desire.

_____

_____

_____

Abundance Snapshot No. 6:
Be the Writer, Director, and Producer of Your World

Photo Op. *Be the Auteur of Your Life.* Capture several images of yourself in victorious poses. Create a series if you want. Use it as motivation to imagine, see, and feel yourself standing firm in the role of writer, director, and producer of your life. You can look at these images to help recall how you feel being in control whenever you need a boost.

Action Opportunity. Look at the areas of your life where you feel like a victim, not in control. Start with the Centering Thought: "I am the auteur." Then spend time thinking about how you can consciously take control of a challenging situation. It could be that you need to reframe how you perceive things. Use the Affirmation, "I choose to be the writer, director, and producer of a happy, fulfilling, and Abundant life," to guide you in seeing lessons that will help you develop instead of the misfortune that will trample you down.

_____

_____

_____

Abundance Snapshot No. 7:
Choose Right Thoughts, Right Action

Photo Op. *Be the Change.* Capture or find an image of someone whose way of living inspires you. It could be Gandhi, Buddha, Christ, your parent, or a coach. Whoever it is, look at their image when you are challenged. Ask yourself, what would they do if they were in my position? Ideally, do this in stillness and notice the answers that come up.

Action Opportunity. Meditate on this Centering Thought: "Choose healthy Abundance." Off the meditation cushion, consciously pay attention to your thoughts, words, and actions. Write your reflections on this Action Opportunity to grow. It may also be helpful to use the Affirmation: "I choose right thoughts, right action, get the right results" periodically throughout the day.

_____

_____

_____

Abundance Snapshot No. 8:
Float Downstream

Photo Op. *Align with Your Core Values.* This Photo Op is done in conjunction with its Action Opportunity, identifying your core values. Once you have identified your core values, create an image of the words. Put this image somewhere you can frequently see it. Use it as a reminder for the bases of your major life decisions.

Action Opportunity. Time to reflect on the alignment of your values with your life. Settle into the Centering Thought: "In the flow."

If you are unsure that your values and current life circumstances are aligned, try a thought exercise inspired by success mentor Darren Hardy.

First, list your top twenty values, like Faith, Love, Health, Gratitude, Forgiveness, Peace, Detachment, Abundance, and so on. Does this look like a familiar list? It should. As I mentioned at the start of this chapter, these Happiness Essentials—virtues and qualities—guide my life.

Two, after you have your list of twenty values, circle your top ten.

Three, circle your top five.

Finally, your top three.

While your top twenty values underscore all your decisions, the top three are the real drivers, whether you realize this or not. The top three are your core values. Mine are Faith, Love, and Health because they give rise to the following five virtues and qualities I appreciate most. Now, look at your life. Do your core values support the life you are living? More importantly, the life you want? If not, it is time to make some serious changes. The person you are to become, the life you want to lead, is waiting for you. Use the Affirmation, "I move through my life with clarity, direction, and ease," for this journal Action Opportunity.

_____

_____

_____

THE END IS JUST THE BEGINNING

The more I continue to study and write about the art and science of Happiness and Wholebeing, the more I believe that Faith, Love, Health, Gratitude, Forgiveness, Peace, Detachment, and Abundance are inextricably intertwined. Each of these virtues and qualities needs the other to be present within us. However, it is not one size fits all. In your journey through these pages, you may have discovered a different set of Happiness Essentials that you value. That is okay. The beauty of this inner work is that it is unique to what serves you. Hopefully, this book has been a foundation, springboard, or reawakening of your inner journey. You may now want to go back and retake the Happiness Survey at the beginning of this book. Find out what shifted for you and where more inner work is still needed. Remember your Happiness Set Point is at least 40 percent within your control, through intentional activities to raise your wellbeing.

As you notice and feel yourself becoming Happier, you will be motivated to keep on your journey. You will want to choose Happiness continually and consciously as your state of being, your homeostasis for Wholebeing. You can help this choice by making it a habit to revisit the chapter Snapshots, Photo Ops, and Action Opportunities. Also, keep engaged with the *Take a Shot at Happiness* community through our social media and app. Continuing to develop while engaging our community will support your Happiness and Wholebeing journey.

Sometimes you may find that one or two of these Happiness Essentials may need more attention. Someone profoundly hurts you, and you are not feeling particularly forgiving or grateful toward them. So, you need to make an extra effort in those two areas, Forgiveness and Gratitude, though you might find that your Peace is also being disturbed. Why? Because you have attached to how someone should or should not have behaved instead of just seeing *what is* in a situation. Now, you realize that you must also work on your feelings around Detachment.

In this scenario, Forgiveness, Gratitude, Peace, and Detachment are intertwined. You can start to see that when you are out of alignment with one or two Happiness Essentials, there is a downstream effect in other areas as well. Awareness of this happening is critical. The work is to settle back into alignment and a positive state where you feel Forgiving, Grateful, Peaceful, and Detached once again.

Think of Happiness and Wholebeing as an endeavor you consciously take on for a lifetime. It is a practice like mindfulness, meditation, going to the gym, or eating well. All are necessary for one's wellbeing and must be consistently attended to and nurtured. You do it because it genuinely matters in the big picture, within the grand scheme of life, and there are many compelling reasons.

You become more friendly, energetic, charitable, cooperative, and better liked.

Happier people have stronger relationships, a more vibrant network of friends, more social support.

They are more flexible, better creative problem-solvers, more productive in their work.

They are better leaders, more effective negotiators, and tend to earn more money throughout their careers.

They are more resilient, have more robust immune systems, and are physically healthier.

Research studies concluded that, currently, Happier people are more likely to live until eight-five, if not longer. That is heartening news when you consider that in 2022, the average lifespan worldwide was 72.98 years; this is just the tip of the iceberg when it comes to the reasons why you choose Happiness and taking care of your Wholebeing each and every day. Many good things happen when you feel uplifted in a natural state. It gets reflected toward those around you and closest to you. Learning to consciously reframe your thoughts into constructive thinking and acting is the best investment you can make in yourself. Mindfulness and meditation can support opening and deepening awareness of the world around you and your path to wisdom and insight. Use these as mind-training tools to refine your understanding of how things are and what you would like them to be; put this refined understanding to constructive use.

I now end with my final Action Opportunity to develop and grow. Start by making one critical and consistent choice—the *choice to be Happy*. In truth, Happiness is more than a choice and is far more significant. It is a vow you take every day, every moment. The benefits will only enhance every single worthwhile aspect of your life. So, *take a shot*. Be the conscious creator of the best life ever.

May you be Happy, *now and always*.

♥ ♥ ♥

"This choice to enjoy life will lead you
through a spiritual journey.
In truth, it is itself a spiritual teacher."
—Michael Singer

New York Times Bestselling Author, The Untethered Soul

CHAPTER SOURCES OF INSPIRATION

The references listed to support my thoughts throughout this book are neither definitive nor exhaustive. I intentionally drew a lot from books, courses, films, and events that inspired me early in my journey and helped form how I live today. I tried to be accurate with my numbers and science notations; however, information varies from source to source. Researchers do not always agree. Even going back to a source, the content will get updated online. Ultimately, I went with what embodied the spirit of what I wanted to convey, understanding that some may know of other findings, or our interpretations of the same material may differ. I hope you will give me the grace of appreciating my intention to substantiate the insights I believe will help one live a more conscious and Happier life.

As We Begin

Articles/Websites

Canva Staff. "Photography as therapy: Why taking photos can actually improve your mental health." Canva. Accessed March 19, 2021. https://www.canva.com/learn/photography-as-therapy/.

Gottlieb, Jared. "The Art of Mindful Photography." National Geographic. June 6, 2014. Accessed November 25, 2022. https://www.nationalgeographic.com/travel/article/mindful-photography-jonathan-foust.

Saita, Emanuela and Martina Tramontano. "Navigating the complexity of the therapeutic and clinical use of photography in psychosocial settings:

a review of literature." National Library of Medicine. April 12, 2018. Accessed November 25, 2022. https://www.ncbi.nlm.nih.gov/pmc/articles/ PMC7451378/.

Stuckey, Heather L., and Jeremy Nobel. "The Connection Between Art, Healing, and Public Health: A Review of Current Literature." American Journal of Public Health. February, 2010. Accessed March 19, 2021. https:// ajph.aphapublications.org/doi/full/10.2105/AJPH.2008.156497.

Sutton, Jeremy. "Mindful Photography: 11 Therapeutic Ways to use your Camera." Positive Psychology Today. February 1, 2021. Accessed November 26, 2022. https://positivepsychology.com/mindful-photography/.

Quote

Abdelnour, Ziad. K. *Economic Warfare: Secrets of Wealth Creation in the Age of Welfare Politics.* Hoboken, New Jersey: Wiley, 2012. *"Life is like a camera. Focus on what's important. Capture the good times. And if things don't work out, just take another shot."*

A State of Wholebeing: Picturing Happiness

Books

Lyubomirsky, Sonja. *The How of Happiness: A New Approach to Getting the Life You Want.* New York: Penguin Books, 2007.

Singer, Michael A. *The Untethered Soul: The Journey Beyond Yourself.* Oakland: New Harbinger Publications, 2007.

Happiness Essential One: Picturing Faith

Articles/Websites

Basso, Julia C., Victoria Ende, Alexandra McHale, Douglas J. Oberlin, and Wendy A. Suzuki. "Brief, daily meditation enhances attention, memory, mood, and emotional regulation in non-experienced meditators." ScienceDirect. *Behavioral Brain Research*, no. 356. January 1, 2019. Accessed October 21, 2022.

https://www.sciencedirect.com/science/article/abs/pii/S016643281
830322X.

Borowski, Susan. "Quantum mechanics and the consciousness connection." AAAS. July 16, 2012. Accessed November 27, 2022. https://www.aaas.org/quantum-mechanics-and-consciousness-connection.

CERN Staff. "CERN and the Higgs boson." CERN. Accessed November 27, 2022. https://home.cern/resources/faqs/cern-and-higgs-boson.

Feder, Sandra. "Religious faith can lead to positive mental benefits, writes Stanford anthropologist." Stanford News. November 13, 2020. Accessed June 18, 2022. https://news.stanford.edu/2020/11/13/deep-faith-beneficial-health/.

Gilbert, Jonathan. "Can You Meditate With Your Eyes Open?" *Men's Yoga Journal*. December 13, 2021. Accessed November 26, 2022. https://www.mensyogajournal.com/blog/can-you-meditate-with-your-eyes-open.

Health Information. "Brain Basics: The Life and Death of a Neuron." National Institute of Neurological Disorders and Stroke. Accessed September 27, 2022. https://www.ninds.nih.gov/health-nformation/public-education/brain-basics/brain-basics-life-and-death-neuron.

Lea, Robert. "Higgs boson: The 'God Particle' explained." Space.com. August 24, 2022. Accessed November 27, 2022. https://www.space.com/higgs-boson-god-particle-explained.

Pulla, Priyanka. "Why do humans grow up so slowly? Blame the brain." Science.org. August 25, 2014. Accessed June 28, 2018. http://www.sciencemag.org/news/2014/08/why-do-humans-grow-so-slowly-blame-brain.

Books

Chopra, Deepak, and Menas Kafatos. *You Are the Universe: Discovering Your Cosmic Self and Why It Matters*. New York: Harmony Books, 2017.

Coelho, Paulo. *The Zahir*. New York: HarperCollins, 2005.

Dispenza, Joe. *Breaking the Habit of You: How to Lose Your Mind and Create a New One*. Carlsbad, CA: Hay House, Inc., 2012.

Hanson, Rick and Richard Mendius. *Buddha's Brain: The Practical Neuroscience of Happiness, Love & Wisdom*. Oakland, CA: New Harbinger Publications, 2009.

Kabat-Zinn, Jon. *Wherever You Go There You Are: Mindfulness Meditation in Everyday Life*. New York: Hyperion, 1994.

Lyubomirsky, Sonja. *The How of Happiness: A New Approach to Getting the Life You Want*. New York: Penguin Books, 2007.

Schucman, Helen and William Thetford. *A Course in Miracles: Combined Volume*. Mill Valley, CA: Foundation for Inner Peace, 2007.

Shimoff, Marci and Carol Kline. *Happy for No Reason: 7 Steps to Being Happy from the Inside Out*. New York: Free Press, 2008.

Williamson, Marianne. *A Return to Love: Reflections on the Principles of "A Course in Miracles."* New York: Harper Collins, 1992.

Film/Videos

MasterClass. "Aaron Sorkin Teaches Screenwriting." 2016. 35 sessions. https://www.masterclass.com/classes/aaron-sorkin-teaches-screenwriting.

Fleming, Victor, director. *The Wizard of Oz*. Metro-Goldwyn-Mayer, 1939.

Spielberg, Steven, director. *Indiana Jones and the Last Crusade*. Paramount Pictures, 1989.

Quotes from the Bible

"*This too shall pass.*" 2 Corinthians 4:17–18. This quote is associated with 2 Corinthians; however, it is not a direct Bible quote. The closest version of the passage is found in the King James version, "this, too, shall pass."

"*God will not let you be tried beyond what you can bear. But when you are tried, He will also provide a way out so that you can endure it.*" 1 Corinthians 10:13 (NIV)

"*Seek, and you will find.*" Matthew 7:7 (NIV)

Happiness Essential Two: Picturing Love

Articles/Websites

Cuncic, Arlin. "What Happens to Your Body When You're Thinking?" VeryWell Mind. July 17, 2019. Accessed November 14, 2022. https://www.verywellmind.com/what-happens-when-you-think-4688619.

Heath, Chris. "The Epic Life of Carlos Santana." *Rolling Stone*. March 16, 2000. Accessed June 18, 2022. https://www.rollingstone.com/music/music-news/the-epic-life-of-carlos-santana-89485/.

Lawson, Karen. "What Are Thoughts & Emotions." University of Minnesota, Earl E. Bakken Center for Spirituality & Healing. Accessed November 14, 2022. https://www.takingcharge.csh.umn.edu/what-are-thoughts-emotions.

Selig, Meg. "10 Powerful Benefits of Living with Purpose." *Psychology Today*. August 23, 2021. Accessed November 13, 2022. https://www.psychologytoday.com/us/blog/changepower/202108/10-powerful-benefits-living-purpose.

Books

Gilbert, Elizabeth. *Eat. Pray. Love: One Woman's Search for Everything Across Italy, India and Indonesia*. New York: Penguin Group, 2006.

Holden, Robert. *Loveability: Knowing How to Love and Be Loved*. Carlsbad, CA: Hay House, Inc., 2013.

Kornfield, Jack. *The Art of Forgiveness, Lovingkindness, and Peace*. New York: Bantam, 2002.

Lyubomirsky, Sonja. *The How of Happiness: A New Approach to Getting the Life You Want*. New York: Penguin Books, 2007.

Nhat Hanh, Thich. *Peace Is Every Step: The Path of Mindfulness in Everyday Living*. New York: Bantam Books, 1992.

Shimoff, Marci. *Love for No Reason: 7 Steps to Creating a Life of Unconditional Love*. London: Simon & Schuster, 2010.

Williamson, Marianne. *A Return to Love: Reflections on the Principles of "A Course in Miracles"*. New York: Harper Collins, 1992.

Coursework

Hulnick, Ron and Mary Hulnick. "Soul-Centered Living." University of Santa Monica, Programs in Spiritual Psychology. https://www.universityofsantamonica.edu/.

Film/Videos

Crowe, Cameron, director. *Jerry Maguire*. TriStar Pictures, 1996.

Hand, David, supervising director. *Snow White and the Seven Dwarfs*. Walt Disney Productions, 1937.

Verbinski, Gore, director. *Pirates of the Caribbean: Dead Man's Chest*. Walt Disney Productions, 2006.

Happiness Essential Three: Picturing Health (Mind, Body, and Spirit)

Articles/Websites

Anderson, Jen. "Reduce eyestrain with Bates' method of palming the eyes." Batesvisioneducation.org. November 9, 2018. Accessed June 23, 2022. https://batesvisioneducation.org/reduce-eyestrain-with-bates-method-of-palming-the-eyes/.

Becker, William J., Liuba Belkin, and Sarah Tuskey. "Killing me softly: Electronic communications monitoring and employee and spouse well-being." Academy of Management. July 9, 2018. Accessed June 26, 2022. https://journals.aom.org/doi/10.5465/AMBPP.2018.121.

Comaford, Christine. "Got Inner Peace? 5 Ways To Get It NOW." *Forbes*. April 4, 2012. Accessed November 14, 2022. https://www.forbes.com/sites/christinecomaford/2012/04/04/got-inner-peace-5-ways-to-get-it-now/?sh=3abd95386672.

Craig, Anne. "Discovery of 'thought worm' opens window to the mind." *Queen's Gazette*. July 13, 2020. Accessed November 14, 2022. https://www.queensu.ca/gazette/stories/discovery-thought-worms-opens-window-mind.

Ding, Ding, Kenny D. Lawson, Tracy L. Kolbe-Alexander, Eric A. Finkelstein, Peter T. Katzmarzyk, Willem van Mechelen, Michael Pratt, and Lancet Physical Activity Series 2 Executive Committee. "The economic burden of physical inactivity: a global analysis of major non-communicable diseases." National Library of Medicine. July 28, 2016. Accessed June 23, 2022. https://pubmed.ncbi.nlm.nih.gov/27475266/.

Dixon, S. "Daily time spent on social networking by internet users worldwide from 2012 to 2022." Statista. August 22, 2022. Accessed November 14, 2022. https://www.statista.com/statistics/433871/daily-social-media-usage-worldwide/.

Forbes. "How to Survive a Workaholic Spouse." *Forbes*. December 9, 2008. Accessed June 26, 2022. https://www.forbes.com/2008/12/09/workaholic-marriage-divorce-ent-hr-cx_ml_1209workaholicspouse.html?sh=467190b22225.

Frothingham, Scott. "Benefits of Ujjayi Breathing and How to Do It." Healthline. December 18, 2019. Accessed November 14, 2022. https://www.healthline.com/health/fitness-exercise/ujjayi-breathing.

Gavin, Mary L. "Why Exercise is Wise." Nemours. TeensHealth. Accessed August 9, 2018. https://kidsHealth.org/en/teens/exercise-wise.html.

Gunnars, Kris. "How Much Water Should You Drink Per Day?" Healthline Nutrition. November 5, 2020. Accessed June 23, 2022. https://www.healthline.com/nutrition/how-much-water-should-you-drink-per-day.

Harvard Health Publishing. "Foods that fight inflammation." Harvard Health Publishing. November 16, 2021. Accessed June 21, 2022. https://www.health.harvard.edu/staying-healthy/foods-that-fight-inflammation.

Harvard Health Publishing. "How much water you should drink?" Harvard Health Publishing. May 15, 2022. Accessed June 23, 2022. https://www.health.harvard.edu/staying-healthy/how-much-water-should-you-drink.

Haynes, Allana. "Physician Melissa Freeman, 95, Has Been on the Frontline of the Fight Against Addiction for Decades." *Oprah Daily*. June 19, 2021. Accessed June 26, 2022. https://www.oprahdaily.com/life/a36673119/melissa-freeman-doctor-interview/.

Healthline. "Can a Glass of Wine Benefit Your Health?" Healthline Nutrition. Accessed December 24, 2022. https://www.healthline.com/nutrition/benefits-of-wine#healthiest-type.

Healthwise Staff. "Stop Negative Thoughts: Getting Started." University of Michigan Health Michigan Medicine. February 9, 2022. Accessed November 14, 2022. http://www.uofmHealth.org/Health-library/uf9938.

Kaeberlein, Matt. "How healthy is the healthspan concept?" National Library of Medicine. August, 6, 2018. Accessed June 26, 2022. https://www.ncbi.nlm.nih.gov/pmc/articles/PMC6136295/.

Khatri, Minesh. "7 Wonders of Water." WebMD Nourish. Accessed August 8, 2018. http://www.webmd.com/diet/ss/slideshow-water-Health.

Kirk-Sanchez, Neva J. and Ellen L. McGough. "Physical exercise and cognitive performance in the elderly: current perspectives." National Library of Medicine. December 18, 2013. Accessed June 23, 2022. https://www.ncbi.nlm.nih.gov/pmc/articles/PMC3872007/.

Kohl 3rd, Harold W., Cora Lynn Craig, Estelle Victoria Lambert, Shigeru Inoue, Jasem Ramadan Alkandari, Grit Leetongin, Sonja Kahlmeier, and Lancet Physical Activity Series Working Group. "The pandemic of physical inactivity: global action for public health." National Library of Medicine. July 21, 2012. Accessed November 16, 2022. https://pubmed.ncbi.nlm.nih.gov/22818941/.

Laskowski, Edward R. "How Much Should the Average Adult Exercise?" Mayo Clinic. September 22, 2021. https://www.mayoclinic.org/Healthy-lifestyle/fitness/expert-answers/exercise/faq-20057916.

Laskowski, Edward R. "What are the risks of sitting too much?" Mayo Clinic. July 13, 2022. https://www.mayoclinic.org/healthy-lifestyle/adult-health/expert-answers/sitting/faq-20058005.

Lipton, Bruce. "Bruce Lipton, PhD: The Jump From Cell Culture to Consciousness." National Library of Medicine. December 16, 2017. Accessed June 23, 2022. https://www.ncbi.nlm.nih.gov/pmc/articles/PMC6438088/.

Mayo Clinic Staff. "Mediterranean Diet: A Heart-Healthy Eating Plan." Mayo Clinic. Accessed August 10, 2018. http://www.mayoclinic.org/Healthy-lifestyle/nutrition-and-Healthy-eating/in-depth/mediterranean-diet/art-20047801?pg=1.

Mead, Elaine. "What is Positive Self-Talk? (Incl. Examples)." Positive Psychology.com, September 26, 2019. Accessed November 14, 2022. https://positivepsychology.com/positive-self-talk/.

Medina, Lauren, Shannon Sabo, and Jonathan. "Living Longer: Historical and Projected Life Expectancy in the United States, 1960 to 2060." U.S. Census Bureau. February 2020. Accessed December 23, 2022. https://www.census.gov/content/dam/Census/library/publications/2020/demo/p25-1145.pdf.

Nall, Rachel; Frye. "Does the 20-20-20 rule prevent eye strain?" MedicalNewsToday. Read June 23, 2022. https://www.medicalnewstoday.com/articles/321536.

National Institute on Aging. "Real-Life Benefits of Exercise and Physical Activity." National Institute on Aging. Accessed June 23, 2022. https://www.nia.nih.gov/health/real-life-benefits-exercise-and-physical-activity.

Petre, Alina. "What is Refined Sugar?" Healthline Nutrition. Accessed June 21, 2022. https://www.healthline.com/nutrition/refined-sugar.

Rabin, Roni Caryn. "U.S. Life Expectancy Falls Again in 'Historic' Setback." *New York Times*. August 31, 2022. Accessed December 23, 2022. https://www.nytimes.com/2022/08/31/health/life-expectancy-covid-pandemic.html.

Saunders, Elizabeth Grace. "What To Do When Your Crazy-Long Hours Are Ruining Your Relationship." *Fast Company*. September 25, 2016. Read June 26, 2022. https://www.fastcompany.com/3063885/what-to-do-when-your-crazy-long-hours-are-ruining-your-relationship.

Schwartz, Tony. "A 90-Minute Plan for Personal Effectiveness." *Harvard Business Review*. January 24, 2011. Accessed August 11, 2018. https://hbr.org/2011/01/the-most-important-practice-i.

Schwartz, Tony. "The Productivity Myth." *Harvard Business Review*. May 5, 2010. Accessed August 10, 2018. https://hbr.org/2010/05/the-productivity-myth-2.

Sifferlin, Alexandra. "When to Eat Breakfast, Lunch and Dinner." *Time*. July 15, 2016. Accessed August 8, 2018. http://time.com/4408772/best-times-breakfast-lunch-dinner/.

Sports Health & Fitness. "What Does Moderate Exercise Mean, Anyway?" Cleveland Clinic, Health Essentials. October 23, 2020. Accessed June 2, 2022. https://health.clevelandclinic.org/what-does-moderate-exercise-mean-anyway/.

Stanford Medicine. "Obesity and Overweight." Health Care. Accessed June 21, 2022. https://stanfordhealthcare.org/medical-conditions/healthy-living/obesity.html.

Statista Research Department. "Number of internet and social media users worldwide as of July 2022." Statista. September 20, 2022. Accessed November 14, 2022. https://www.statista.com/statistics/617136/digital-population-worldwide/.

Tracy, Brian. "Subconscious Mind Power Explained." Brian Tracy International. Accessed November 14, 2022. https://www.briantracy.com/blog/personal-success/understanding-your-subconscious-mind/.

United States Census Bureau. "65 and Older Population Grows Rapidly as Baby Boomers Age." United States Census Bureau. June 25, 2020. Accessed June 26, 2022. https://www.census.gov/newsroom/press-releases/2020/65-older-population-grows.html.

Vallance, Jeff K., Paul A. Gardiner, Brigid M. Lynch, Adrijana D'Silva, Terry Boyle, Lorian M. Taylor, Steven T. Johnson, Matthew P. Buman, and Neville Owen. "Evaluating the Evidence on Sitting, Smoking, and Health: Is Sitting Really the New Smoking?" National Library of Medicine. November 2018. Accessed June 23, 2022. https://www.ncbi.nlm.nih.gov/pmc/articles/PMC6187798/.

WebMD Editorial Contributors. "Eye Exercises." WebMD.com. Accessed July 29, 2022. https://www.webmd.com/eye-health/eye-exercises.

Weil, Andrew. "Dr. Weil's Anti-Inflammatory Food Pyramid." Weil. Accessed November 16, 2022. https://www.drweil.com/diet-nutrition/anti-inflammatory-diet-pyramid/dr-weils-anti-inflammatory-food-pyramid/.

Wilkins, Alex. "Human life limit is between 120 and 150 according to a new study." Metro. May 26, 2021. Accessed June 26, 2022. https://metro. co.uk/2021/05/26/human-life-limit-is-between-120-and-150-according-to-new-study-14647315/.

Willingham, Emily. "Humans Could Live up to 150 Years, New Research Suggest." *Scientific American.* May 25, 2021. Accessed June 26, 2022. https://www.scientificamerican.com/article/humans-could-live-up-to-150-years-new-research-suggests/.

World Cancer Research Fund International. "Meat, fish, dairy, and cancer risk." Cancer risk factors. Accessed June 21, 2022. https://www.wcrf.org/diet-activity-and-cancer/risk-factors/meat-fish-dairy-and-cancer-risk/.

World Population Review. "Obesity Rates by Country 2022." Accessed November 15, 2022. https://worldpopulationreview.com/country-rankings/obesity-rates-by-country.

Books

Hanson, Rick and Richard Mendius. *Buddha's Brain: The Practical Neuroscience of Happiness, Love & Wisdom.* Oakland, CA: New Harbinger Publications, 2009.

Hay, Louise L. *You Can Heal Your Life.* Carlsbad, CA: Hay House, Inc, 2008.

Lyubomirsky, Sonja. *The How of Happiness: A New Approach to Getting the Life You Want.* New York: Penguin Books, 2007.

Murphy, Joseph. *The Power of Your Subconscious Mind.* New York: Penguin Group, 2008.

Shimoff, Marci and Carol Kline. *Happy for No Reason: 7 Steps to Being Happy from the Inside Out.* New York: Free Press, 2008.

Coursework

Hardy, Darren. "Insane Productivity, Module 9." www.DarrenHardy.com.

Hulnick, Ron and Mary Hulnick. "Soul-Centered Living." University of Santa Monica, Programs in Spiritual Psychology. https://www.university ofsantamonica.edu.

Film/Videos

Burnett, Mark, executive producer. *Survivor*. CBS, 2000–present.

Huston, John, director. *The Treasure of Sierra Madre*. Warner Bros. Pictures, 1948.

Personal Permission

Pascucci, Christina, American Television Journalist. Instagram Post, June 17, 2022. Permission granted, October 17, 2022.

Quote from the Bible

"*For as he thinks in his heart, so is he.*" Proverbs 23:7 (NKJV)

Happiness Essential Four: Picturing Gratitude

Articles/Websites

Baer, Marlene. "The Power of Gratitude: Expressing gratitude by saying "thank you" is a profound and simple act, but has it become a forgotten art?" LifeWay. November 17, 2015. Accessed September 10, 2018. https://www.lifeway.com/en/articles/the-power-of-Gratitude-thanks.

Baraz, James and Shoshana Alexander. "The Helper's High." *Greater Good Magazine: Science-Based Insights for a Meaningful Life*. February 1, 2010. Accessed September 8, 2018. http://greatergood.berkeley.edu/article/item/the_helpers_high.

Chapman, Gary. "5 Languages of Gratitude." LifeWay. November 13, 2015. Accessed September 10, 2018. https://www.lifeway.com/en/articles/thanksgiving-languages-of-gratitude.

Emmons, Robert A. and Michael E. McCullough. "Counting Blessings Versus Burdens: An Experimental Investigation of Gratitude and Subjective Well-Being in Daily Life." *Journal of Personality and Social Psychology* 2003, Vol. 84, No. 2. Accessed September 8, 2018. https://greatergood.berkeley.edu/pdfs/GratitudePDFs/6Emmons-BlessingsBurdens.pdf.

Grimm, Robert, Jr., Kimberly Spring, and Nathan Dietz. "The Health Benefits of Volunteering 2007." Corporation for National & Community Service. Accessed September 8, 2018. https://americorps.gov/sites/default/files/evidenceexchange/FR_2007_TheHealthBenefitsofVolunteering_1.pdf.

Mejia, Zameena. "How Arianna Huffington, Tony Robbins and Oprah Winfrey use gratitude as a strategy for success." CNBC. February 16, 2018. Accessed December 4, 2022. https://www.cnbc.com/2018/02/16/how-arianna-huffington-tony-robbins-and-oprah-use-gratitude-to-succeed.html.

Ramsey, Dave. "Tithing and Giving: Your 5 Questions Answered." Accessed September 8, 2018. https://www.daveramsey.com/blog/daves-advice-on-tithing-and-giving.

Vulpo, Mike. "10 Unforgettable Oscar Acceptance Speeches That Still Deserve a Standing Ovation." E! News. March 2, 2018. Accessed September 11, 2018. https://www.eonline.com/news/915833/10-unforgettable-oscar-acceptance-speeches-that-still-%20deserve-a-standing-ovation.

Books

Emmons, Robert A. *Gratitude Works! A 21-Day Program for Creating Emotional Prosperity.* San Francisco: Jossey-Bass, 2013.

Hanson, Rick and Richard Mendius. *Buddha's Brain: The Practical Neuroscience of Happiness, Love & Wisdom.* Oakland, CA: New Harbinger Publications, 2009.

Lyubomirsky, Sonja. *The How of Happiness: A New Approach to Getting the Life You Want.* New York: Penguin Books, 2007.

Film/Videos

Burnett, Mark, executive producer. *Survivor: Australian Outback.* CBS, 2001.

Burnett, Mark, executive producer. *Survivor: Africa.* CBS, 2001.

Garfinkle, David and Jay Renfroe, executive producers. *Naked and Afraid.* Discovery Channel, 2013–present.

Mitchell, Mike, director. *Trolls.* DreamWorks Animation, 2016.

Raimi, Sam, director. *Doctor Strange in the Multiverse of Madness*. Marvel Studios, 2022.

Soderbergh, Steven, director. *The Laundromat*. Netflix, 1919.

Zemeckis, Robert, director. *Forrest Gump*. Paramount Pictures, 1994.

Happiness Essential Five: Picturing Forgiveness

Articles/Websites

Hill, Angela. "The secret to happiness? Stanford professor says it's forgiveness." *The Mercury News*. June 21, 2020. Accessed June 21, 2022. https://www.mercurynews.com/2020/06/21/qa-fred-luskin/#.

Mayo Clinic Staff. "Forgiveness: Letting go of grudges and bitterness." Mayo Clinic Adult Health. November 22, 2022. https://www.mayoclinic.org/healthy-lifestyle/adult-health/in-depth/forgiveness/art-20047692.

Weir, Kirsten. "Forgiveness can improve mental and physical Health: Research shows how to get there." American Psychological Association. January 2017, Vol 48, No. 1. Accessed September 26, 2018. https://www.apa.org/monitor/2017/01/ce-corner.

Winfrey, Oprah. "Oprah Talks to Maya Angelou." *O Magazine*. May 2013. Accessed June 21, 2022. https://www.oprah.com/omagazine/maya-angelou-interviewed-by-oprah-in-2013/all.

Books

Frankl, Viktor. *Man's Search for Meaning*. Boston: Beacon Press Books, 1959.

Hay, Louise L. *You Can Heal Your Life*. Carlsbad, CA: Hay House, Inc., 2008.

Lyubomirsky, Sonja. *The How of Happiness: A New Approach to Getting the Life You Want*. New York: Penguin Books, 2007.

Tutu, Desmond and Mpho Tutu. *The Book of Forgiving: The Fourfold Path for Healing Ourselves and Our World*. New York: Harper One, 2014.

Film/Videos

Burnett, Mark, executive producer. *Survivor*. CBS, 2000–present.

Heller, Marielle, director. *A Beautiful Day in the Neighborhood*. TriStar Pictures. 2019.

Quotes from the Bible

"*But for the grace of God there go I*" paraphrases "*But by the grace of God I am what I am*." 1 Corinthians 15:10 (NIV)

"*(You) reap what you sow*." Galatians 6:7 (NIV)

Happiness Essential Six: Picturing Peace

Articles/Websites

Heshmat, Shahram. "What Is Confirmation Bias?" *Psychology Today*. April 23, 2015. Accessed October 5, 2018. https://www.psychologytoday.com/us/blog/science-choice/201504/what-is-confirmation-bias.

Pegg, Mike. "B is for Jill Bolte Taylor: Her Stroke of Insight." The Positive Encourager. Accessed October 5, 2018. https://www.thepositiveencourager.global/jill-bolte-taylors-stroke-of-insight-video-2/.

Rampton, John. "7 Reasons Why Spending Money on Experiences Makes Us Happier Than Buying Stuff." *Entrepreneur*. May 15, 2017. Accessed October 6, 2018. https://www.entrepreneur.com/article/294163.

Science of Psychotherapy Staff. "Prefrontal Cortex." SoP. January 4, 2017. Accessed June 18, 2022. https://www.thescienceofpsychotherapy.com/prefrontal-cortex/.

Books

Hanson, Rick and Richard Mendius. *Buddha's Brain: The Practical Neuroscience of Happiness, Love & Wisdom*. Oakland, CA: New Harbinger Publications, 2009.

Hulnick, Ron and Mary Hulnick. *Loyalty to Your Soul: The Heart of Spiritual Psychology*. Carlsbad, CA: Hay House, 2010.

Katie, Byron. *Loving What Is*. New York: Harmony, 2002. https://thework.com.

Nhat Hanh, Thich. *Peace Is Every Step: The Path of Mindfulness in Everyday Living*. New York: Bantam Books, 1992.

Ruiz, Miguel. *The Four Agreements: A Practical Guide to Personal Freedom*. San Rafael, CA: Amber-Allen Publishing, 1997.

Schucman, Helen and William Thetford. *A Course in Miracles: Combined Volume*. Mill Valley, CA: Foundation for Inner Peace, 2007.

Coursework

Hulnick, Ron and Mary Hulnick. "Soul-Centered Living." University of Santa Monica, Programs in Spiritual Psychology. https://www.universityof santamonica.edu.

Kornfield, Jack and Tara Brach. "Mindfulness Meditation Teacher Certification Program." https://www.soundstrue.com/products/mindfulness-meditation-teacher-certification-program.

Film/Videos

Burnett, Mark and Maria Baltazzi, executive producers. *Expedition Africa: Stanley & Livingstone*. History, 2009.

Coen, Joel, director. *The Big Lebowski*. Gramercy Pictures (USA) and PolyGram Filmed Entertainment (International), 1998.

Coppola, Sofia, director. *Lost in Translation*. American Zoetrope and Elemental Films, 2003.

Crowe, Cameron, director. *Almost Famous*. DreamWorks Picture (USA) and Columbia TriStar Film, 2000.

Ficarra, Glenn and John Requa, directors. *Crazy, Stupid, Love*. Warner Bros. Pictures, 2011.

Kosinski, Joseph, director. *Top Gun: Maverick*. Paramount Pictures 2022.

Michell, Roger, director. *Notting Hill*. Universal Pictures (USA) and PolyGram Filmed Entertainment (International), 1999.

Reiner, Rob, director. *When Harry Met Sally*. Columbia Pictures, 1989.

Ridley, Scott, director. *The Last Duel.* 20th Century Studios, 2021.

Stone, Oliver, director. *Wall Street.* 20th Century Fox, 1987.

Vaughn, Matthew, director. *Kick-Ass.* Lionsgate (USA) and Focus Features (International), 2010.

Quotes from the Bible

"*Whatever you want men to do to you, do also to them.*" paraphrases Matthew 7:12 (NKJV)

"*Be still and know that I am God.*" Psalm 46:10 (NIV)

Happiness Essential Seven: Picturing Detachment

Articles/Websites

Wikipedia. "Target Fixation." Wikipedia. Accessed February 19, 2023. https://en.wikipedia.org/wiki/Target_fixation.

Books

Chopra, Deepak. *The Seven Spiritual Laws of Success: A Practical Guide to the Fulfilment of Your Dreams.* San Rafael, CA: Amber-Allen Publishing and New World Library, 1994.

Dr. Seuss. *And to Think I Saw It on Mulberry Street.* New York: Random House for Young Readers, 1989.

Dr. Seuss. *Oh, the Places You'll Go!* New York: Random House for Young Readers, 1990.

Hanson, Rick and Richard Mendius. *Buddha's Brain: The Practical Neuroscience of Happiness, Love & Wisdom.* Oakland, CA: New Harbinger Publications, 2009.

Kabat-Zinn, Jon. *Wherever You Go There You Are: Mindfulness Meditation in Everyday Life.* New York: Hyperion, 1994.

Tutu, Desmond and Mpho Tutu. *The Book of Forgiving: The Fourfold Path for Healing Ourselves and Our World.* New York: Harper One, 2014.

Film/Videos

Allers, Roger and Rob Minkoff, directors. *The Lion King.* Buena Vista Pictures, 1994.

Krauss, Lawrence, Neil DeGrasse Tyson, and Carl Sagan. *We are stardust harvesting starlight.* NASA: EtherealExposition. April 24, 2013. https://www.youtube.com/watch?v=OEbeRES6D-M.

Robinson, Phil Alden, director. *Field of Dreams.* Universal Pictures (USA) and Carcolco Picture (International), 1989.

Zemeckis, Robert, director. *Cast Away.* 20th Century Fox and DreamWorks Pictures, 2000.

Quote from the Bible

"Why do you look at the speck…in your brother's eye (but do not consider) the plank in your own eye?" Matthew 7:3 (NIV)

Happiness Essential Eight: Picturing Abundance

Articles/Websites

Clear, James. "How to Stop Procrastinating on Your Goals by Using the "Seinfeld Strategy." Jamesclear.com. Accessed June 26, 2022. https://jamesclear.com/stop-procrastinating-seinfeld-strategy.

Kershner, Kate. "What's the Baader-Meinhof phenomenon?" HowStuffWorks. August 10,2021. Accessed June 9, 2018. https://science.howstuffworks.com/life/inside-the-mind/human-brain/baader-meinhof-phenomenon.htm.

Leadership Biography. "The living legend & Basketball Sensation – Michael Jordon Success Story." Accessed June 26, 2022. https://www.leaderbiography.com/michael-jordan-success-story/.

Lopez, Donald S. "Eightfold Path." Encyclopedia Britannica. Accessed June 26, 2022. https://www.britannica.com/print/article/181242.

Mather, Ashish. "Michael Jordon Had Someone Count How Many Steps He Took in Every Game for an Obsessive Craft." Sportscasting. April 7, 2021. Accessed June 26, 2022. https://www.sportscasting.com/michael-jordan-someone-count-steps-game-obsessive-craft/.

Schwantes, Marcel. "Warren Buffet Says Your Overall Happiness and Success May Be Tied to This 1 Mental Habit." *Inc.* October 26, 2021. Accessed December 4, 2022. https://www.inc.com/marcel-schwantes/warren-buffett-says-youroverall-happiness-success-may-be-tied-to-this-1-mental-habit.html.

Wikipedia. "Physical characteristics of the Buddha." Accessed June 26, 2022. https://en.wikipedia.org/wiki/Physical_characteristics_of_the_Buddha.

Books

Chopra, Deepak. *The Seven Spiritual Laws of Success: A Practical Guide to the Fulfilment of Your Dreams.* San Rafael, CA: Amber-Allen Publishing and New World Library, 1994.

Clear, James. *Atomic Habits.* New York: Penguin Random House, 2018.

Dyer, Wayne W. *The Power of Intention: Learning to Co-Create Your World Your Way.* Carlsbad, CA: Hay House, Inc., 2004.

Hanson, Rick and Richard Mendius. *Buddha's Brain: The Practical Neuroscience of Happiness, Love & Wisdom.* Oakland, CA: New Harbinger Publications, 2009.

Maurer, Robert. *One Small Step Can Change Your Life: The Kaizen Way.* New York: Workman Publishing, 2004.

Film/Videos

Columbus, Chris, director. *Harry Potter and the Chamber of Secrets.* Warner Bros. Pictures, 2022.

Downey, Roma, Mark Burnett, and Maria Baltazzi executive producers. *Women of the Bible.* Lifetime, 2014.

Ephron, Nora. "'Be The Heroine of Your Life', Wellesley College." Speakola.com. May 25, 1996. https://speakola.com/grad/nora-ephron-wellesley-1996.

Garvin, Leslie and Sean Travis, directors. *The Rebel Billionaire: Branson's Quest for the Best, Premiere.* Fox, 2004.

Johnson, Dwayne. *The Hardest Worker in the Room.* Chispa Motivation, 2020. https://www.youtube.com/watch?v=gMcRDeA27j4.

Litzinger, Joseph, Kevin Tao Mohs, and Travis Shakespeare, executive producers. *Life Below Zero.* National Geographic and BBC Studios, May 19, 2013–present.

Quotes from the Bible

"If you ask Me anything in My name, I will do it." John 14:14 (BSB)

"For what (does a man) profit, if he shall gain the whole world, and lose his soul?" Mark 8:36 (NKJV)

"Ask and it will be given to you; seek and you will find; knock and the door will be opened to you." Matthew 7:7 (NIV)

The End Is Just the Beginning

Articles/Websites

Lee, Lewina O., Peter James, Emily S. Zevon, Eric S. Kim, Claudia Trudel-Fitzgerald, Avron Spiro III, Francine Grodstein, and Laura D. Kubzansky. "Optimism is associated with exceptional longevity in 2 epidemiologic cohorts of men and women." National Library of Medicine, September 10, 2019. Accessed November 25, 2022. https://pubmed.ncbi.nlm.nih.gov/31451635/.

Macrotrends. "World Life Expectancy 1950–2022." Accessed December 23, 2022. https://www.macrotrends.net/countries/WLD/world/life-expectancy.

Topor, David R. "If you are happy and you know is…you may live longer." Harvard Health Publishing. October 16, 2019. Accessed November 25, 2022. https://www.health.harvard.edu/blog/if-you-are-happy-and-you-know-it-you-may-live-longer-2019101618020.

United Nations Population Division. *Life Expectance of the World Population.* Accessed November 25, 2022. https://www.worldometers.info/demographics/life-expectancy/.

Books

Lyubormirsky, Sonja. *The How of Happiness: A New Approach to Getting the Life You Want.* New York: Penguin Books, 2007.

Word Definitions

Google Dictionary, licensed from Oxford University Press, Oxford Dictionaries.com, 2009.

Merriam-Webster, Incorporated. All rights reserved. Merriam-Webster Online, 2021. www.Merriam-Webster.com.

ACKNOWLEDGMENTS

FADE UP:

I was blessed to have several wise and supportive people around me during my writing journey.

My first thank you goes to *New York Times* bestselling author and friend Martin (Marty) Dugard, who often gave me insightful writing guidance. His best advice was to use my first draft as a blueprint, read my pages out loud, and be ruthless with rewrites. Marty also was the one who suggested asking my longtime friends, executive producer Mark Burnett and his wife, actress Roma Downey, to introduce me to a well-respected literary agent out of Dallas, Jan Miller, at Dupree Miller & Associates.

Roma Downey was kind enough to write a letter of recommendation to Jan, who immediately set a phone meeting with me.

Next, my thanks go to literary agents Jan Miller and Ali Kominsky for taking on a first-time writer and rolling up their sleeves to find a publisher. In one of our early calls, I told Jan that my mom saw *Take a Shot at Happiness* being published through her. Jan got God-bumps and promised to find a home for my book. Many thanks to Consulting Editor Debra Englander at Post Hill Press for seeing something in my book proposal she felt would appeal to their readers. She is a savvy woman of few, however meaningful, words. So, when she spoke, I listened.

Managing Editors Ashlyn Inman, Heather King, and Caitlyn Limbaugh at Post Hill Press were always so positive. I could feel their sunny dispositions coming through their correspondence. I am sure they both have high Happiness Set Points. Thank you Lydia Hall for proofreading my manuscript.

Writer Leah Lakins helped shape my book proposal, asking thoughtful questions about how and when I first realized the power of the images I saw in my mind's eye. She also asked me questions about my father, which gave me pause and ended up as stories in this book.

Then there is Emmy-winning television producer and trusted colleague Michael J. Miller, who read my pages while I was completing the final draft for my agents and Post Hill Press. He offered valuable clarity suggestions and picked up several typos that were overlooked, no matter how many times I ran my manuscript through spell check or read it out loud.

Television producer and beloved friend Mack Anderson also offered several insights and another set of eyes to read through my pages.

Photographer, author, and ArtCenter College of Design classmate Thomas Werner read my first draft. He offered great suggestions on how to frame (no pun intended) the photo assignments in this book.

Charles Nordlander, one of the best network development executives I have ever worked with in television, was the first to appreciate the focused calm I experienced when taking photos with my phone camera. He also saved my book, literally. My computer was stolen while I was doing a show on location. Thankfully, I had sent him my early chapter musings, and he had kept them.

Award-winning writer, producer, and director Brenda Lau, a longtime friend and Covid bubble buddy, has been my constant cheerleader.

Of course, I must thank my mom. At five foot two, she is a force and the one who opened my mind to the power of one's thoughts.

Finally, thank you, the reader, for choosing this book to be part of your inner journey.

FADE OUT.

Author Photo by Jay Farbman

ABOUT THE AUTHOR

Maria Baltazzi is a Happiness Explorer. Her calling is to help you become happier and live more consciously. Maria's experience as an Emmy-winning TV producer, wellbeing teacher, world traveler, and luxury travel designer specializing in transformative adventures has given her a unique lens into conscious living.

Like all of us, Maria has faced challenges personally and professionally. Instead of letting life setbacks defeat her, Maria was inspired to embark on a life-changing journey where she realized eight Happiness Essentials that create a happier, more fulfilling life. Now, Maria helps you discover your path to happiness in a fun, creative way that combines journaling and phone photography.

Maria holds an MFA in film from ArtCenter College of Design and a PhD in Conscious-Centered Living from the University of Sedona. Additional studies include Mindfulness Meditation Teaching Training with Jack Kornfield and Tara Brach, Primordial Sound Meditation Teacher

Training from The Chopra Center, Happiness Studies with Tal Ben-Shahar, Positive Neuroplasticity Training with Rick Hanson, Spiritual Psychology with Ron and Mary Hulnick at the University of Santa Monica, Positive Psychology at the University of Pennsylvania, the Science of Happiness at the University of Berkley, and an Inner MBA from MindfulNYU.

In her own happiness journey, Maria finds joy in giving back. She has walked over 7500 miles to raise funds for charity, including marathons on all seven continents, and is still going. Maria's adventurous life has also involved climbing the 15,000-foot trail to Machu Picchu, leading African safaris, making pilgrimages along the Camino de Santiago, summiting Mt. Kilimanjaro twice, and trekking to Everest Base Camp.

Maria has developed and produced shows throughout the world. She was one of the original supervising producers of the TV mega hit, *Survivor.* She is a member of both the Producers and Directors Guilds of America, a Fellow National Member of The Explorers Club, and an Advisor for the Transformational Travel Council. Given her diverse experiences, expertise, and infectious enthusiasm, Maria is a genuine inspiration for those seeking to live their best lives.

Join Our Private Facebook Community: @takeashotathappiness
Download Our App: takeashotathappiness.app

Website: mariabaltazzi.com
Instagram: @mariabaltazzi
LinkedIn: @mariabaltazzi
Insight Timer: @mariabaltazzi